European Street Gangs and Troublesome Youth Groups

VIOLENCE PREVENTION AND POLICY SERIES

This AltaMira series publishes new books in the multidisciplinary study of violence. Books are designed to support scientifically based violence prevention programs and widely applicable violence prevention policy. Key topics are juvenile and/or adult community re-entry programs, community-based addiction and violence programs, prison violence reduction programs with application in community settings, and school culture and climate studies with recommendations for organizational approaches to school-violence reduction. Studies may combine quantitative and qualitative methods, may be multidisciplinary, or may feature European research if it has a multinational application. The series publishes highly accessible books that offer violence prevention policy as the outcome of scientifically based research, designed for college undergraduates and graduates, community agency leaders, school and community decision makers, and senior government policy makers.

SERIES EDITOR:
Mark S. Fleisher, Director, The Dr. Semi J. and Ruth W. Begun Center for Violence Research Prevention and Education, Case Western Reserve University, 10900 Euclid Avenue, Cleveland, OH 44106-7164 USA, 216-368-2329 or msf10@po.cwru.edu

BOOKS IN THE SERIES:

European Street Gangs and Troublesome Youth Groups

EDITED BY
SCOTT H. DECKER
AND FRANK M. WEERMAN

ALTAMIRA
PRESS

A Division of
ROWMAN & LITTLEFIELD PUBLISHERS, INC.
Lanham • New York • Oxford

ALTAMIRA PRESS

A Division of Rowman & Littlefield Publishers, Inc.
A wholly owned subsidiary of The Rowman & Littlefield Publishing Group, Inc.
4501 Forbes Boulevard, Suite 200
Lanham, MD 20706
www.altamirapress.com

PO Box 317, Oxford, OX2 9RU, UK

British Library Cataloguing in Publication Information Available

Library of Congress Cataloging-in-Publication Data

European street gangs and troublesome youth groups / edited by Scott H. Decker and
Frank M. Weerman.
    p. cm. — (Violence prevention and policy series)
  Includes bibliographical references and index.
  ISBN 0-7591-0792-0 (cloth : alk. paper) — ISBN 0-7591-0793-9 (pbk. : alk. paper)
  1. Gangs—Europe. 2. Juvenile delinquency—Europe. I. Decker, Scott H. II. Weerman,
Frank M., 1968- III. Series.

  HV6439.E8E865 2005
  364.106'6094--dc22

                         2005026516

Printed in the United States of America

Contents

Preface

This book contains a collection of papers about a subject that received little attention in the European context for a long time: gangs and troublesome youth groups. The chapters are written by a variety of European and American researchers who are part of the so-called Eurogang Program of Research, an international network of collaborating researchers devoted to the study of gangs and troublesome youth groups and to the development of common research instruments and protocols. The term *gang* (or *street gang*) is commonly used in the Americas but may be confusing elsewhere. Scholars from these countries often prefer the term *troublesome youth group* to indicate groups that appear to be the same type of collectivities that are investigated as gangs in other countries. Therefore, both terms are used throughout this book to indicate the kind of youth groups that the contributors study.

The main part of the book is organized by method of research. We start with an introduction by Malcolm W. Klein, which is followed by five chapters that are based on qualitative or ethnographic research methods. These chapters provide rich and in-depth images of some interesting European examples of groups that can be called street gangs. The next part of the book contains five chapters that are based on quantitative methods. These contributions provide a more superficial, but also more generalizable and comparable, picture of larger quantities of gangs and troublesome youth groups in several countries. The last part of the book is integrative. It contains a chapter about gang policies and interventions in different countries and a concluding chapter that summarizes the main results of this book, organized around several key themes and subjects.

This book is the result of nearly a decade of work by more than fifty international scholars and more than a dozen governments; it also is the product of the dedication of a large group of support people. Simply put, while we are the editors, we owe a debt of gratitude to a multitude of people and institutions. We should start with acknowledging Malcolm W. Klein, the instigator of the Eurogang program. Under his direction, a group of European and American scholars began meeting annually in the late 1990s. That the group continues to meet and has produced several methodological tools (www.umsl.edu/~ccj/eurogang/euroganghome.htm [May 19, 2005]), and an earlier book comparing U.S. and European gangs (Klein et al. 2001) is largely the result of his vision and efforts. The steering committee of the Eurogang Working Group also played an instrumental role in insuring the commitment and focus of the group. This committee included Finn-Aage Esbensen (University of Missouri, St. Louis, United States), Inger-Liese Lien (Norwegian Institute for Urban and Regional Research, Norway), Hans-Jürgen Kerner (University of Tubingen, Germany), Cheryl L. Maxson (University of California, Irvine, United States), Elmar G. M. Weitekamp (University of Leuven, Belgium), Frank van Gemert (Free University, Netherlands), and Frank Weerman (Netherlands Institute for the Study of Crime and Law Enforcement, Netherlands).

We also wish to acknowledge the contributions of the authors in this volume. They were timely, responsive, and considerate in their treatment of the editors. For that, we are grateful.

This project received support from a variety of institutions. The editors wish specifically to identify and thank their host institutions. The first editor, Scott H. Decker, wishes to acknowledge a variety of means of support from the University of Missouri, St. Louis. The Department of Criminology and Criminal Justice has been supportive of involvement in the Eurogang Project generally and of this book specifically. The Center for International Studies provided travel support for attendance at several Eurogang conferences and for international travel that led to important support for the completion of this book. The second editor, Frank M. Weerman, wishes to thank the NSCR, the Netherlands Institute for the Study of Crime and Law Enforcement, for the opportunity to work on this volume and for travel support to visit Euro-gang meetings and other international conferences.

We also wish to acknowledge the outstanding support of several students who assisted in the preparation of this manuscript. Regan Gustafson read and edited each of the chapters. This was a task of substantial magnitude, given that the majority of chapters were written by individuals for whom English is not their first language. The chapters represent eight different European countries and include a variety of terms and phrases specific to those countries. Ms. Gustafson, a Ph.D. student in the Department of Criminology and Criminal Justice at the University of Missouri, St. Louis, did a marvelous job helping to smooth over language issues. Lindsey Green, also a student in the Ph.D. program in the Department of Criminology and Criminal Justice at the University of Missouri, St. Louis, was instrumental in bringing the chapters into a finished stage and constructing the index, and we wish to acknowledge her contributions in this regard. Both of these students provided important assistance in the preparation of the manuscript.

We also wish to acknowledge the support and guidance of Rosalie Robertson, editor at AltaMira Press, throughout the process of preparing the manuscript, and the support in the publication process of Mark Fleisher, Begun Professor at the Mandel School of Social Work at Case Western Reserve University (United States). The anonymous reviewers of the proposed manuscript provided very helpful reviews that made this book better and more focused.

Over the past decade, the vision for this book emerged from discussions about the status of gangs in Europe. Since the time we solicited chapters and crafted this book, several additional works about gangs outside the United States have emerged. The work of Trevor Bennett and Katy Holloway (2004) underscores the importance of understanding gangs in the United Kingdom and throughout Europe. Herbert Covey's (2003) review of gangs on five different continents reinforces the conclusion that while gangs may have been influenced by the American setting, they also reflect local culture and social institutions. Our book remains the only book to examine specifically the status and nature of gangs in Europe. It is our hope that this book will lay the foundation for more work that can expand on the important theoretical, descriptive, and policy foundations provided in the chapters to follow.

REFERENCES

Bennett, Trevor, and Katy Holloway. 2004. Gang membership, drugs and crime in the U.K. *British Journal of Criminology* 44: 305–23.

Covey, Herbert C. 2003. *Street gangs throughout the world.* Springfield, IL: Charles C. Thomas.

Klein, Malcolm W., Hans-Jürgen Kerner, Cheryl L. Maxson, and Elmar G. M. Weitekamp. 2001. *The Eurogang paradox: Street gangs and youth groups in the U.S. and Europe.* Dordrecht, Netherlands: Kluwer.

Introduction

MALCOLM W. KLEIN

This is a book about street gangs in Europe. It is also about an intellectual development that has come to be known as the Eurogang program. The character of European street gangs and the methods developed to study them will be developed chapter by chapter. A summary chapter by editors Frank Weerman and Scott Decker will provide an overview of the themes that wind through the various chapters describing gang studies in many cities in six nations.

I have been tasked by the editors to provide the context for all of this, to set the stage in terms of the history of the Eurogang program. And so I will, but I will also indulge myself just a bit in highlighting issues of particular importance to me; after all, I must take some pride as well as blame for my role in initiating the program. I appreciate the generosity of the editors in seeking my comments.

I will cover, rather briefly, four questions. First, how has the history of American gang research and policy affected the directions of the newer European gang research? Second, what has been the short history of the Eurogang program? Third, what have been the accomplishments of the program to date? Finally, I will address several points of particular interest to me as an active participant in the program.

American Lessons for Europe. Over the past five decades or so, a very substantial literature on street gangs has led to the accumulation of a great store of gang data. Very competent summaries of these data are now available (Spergel 1995; Klein 1995; Covey, Menard, and Franzese 1997). However, for the most part, the studies producing these data have been uncoordinated and rarely comparative (for exceptions, see Fagan 1989; Huff 1998; Sanchez-Jankowski 1991). Rather commonly, these studies have been based on disparate definitions of gangs and gang crime (and often have not bothered with definitions). Further, the studies have used a variety of methods—ethnographic, observational, survey, archival—with too little attention to the implications of the variations within each method and to the different kinds of results each method tends to produce.

Similarly, American approaches to gang policy, at both the local and federal levels, have been largely idiosyncratic and based on the (many) conventional wisdoms of the policymakers. Prevention, intervention, law enforcement, and suppression programs have been driven by different goals as well as different assumptions and value systems and are seldom adequately evaluated to assess their weaker and stronger points.

The Eurogang program, at least in its most ideal form, has been formulated to reduce these problems as research is undertaken about European gangs. By adopting a single, workable definition of street gangs (see the common definition used or referred to in each chapter of this book) and working toward common operations to determine which groups are street gangs, comparability across studies is being achieved. Further, by developing and using common versions of methods, both ethnographic guidelines and survey formats, the studies are pretesting and applying measures that are common across countries (within the limits required by language differences).

Since comparable definitions and methods will yield directly comparable data, we can expect that it will be easier to involve policymakers and practitioners in more coordinated approaches to gang prevention and control. This result is surely pretty far down the line, but even at this point, we have seen justice and police officials from Belgium, Holland, Norway, Denmark, and England involved in the seven Eurogang workshops held between 1998 and 2004. It's a start.

Clearly, underlying the American research experience has been the effect of political trends on the nature of the studies undertaken. A generally liberal approach characterized the research up to the 1980s, with funding supporting ethnographic and observational studies. Political stances were supportive of intervention programs based on labeling theory and opportunity-structure theory, while social services were mobilized in the pursuit of prevention, treatment, and reintegration of gang members into prosocial life styles. Community organization and mobilization, too, were actively engaged in, recognizing that gangs are spawned by communities with weakened social controls.

Starting with the Reagan era and continuing through the George H. W. Bush, Clinton, and George W. Bush presidencies, the underpinning of gang research and policy changed, sometimes dramatically. Public policy became less oriented by social theory and more by values and ideology (both approaches, however, being articulated as conventional wisdom). Research related more to gang control than to gang prevention was funded. The emphasis on ethnography and observation gave way to archival research, especially of data available from the police or corrections. This shift to a more socially and politically conservative base quite properly adjusted the preceding liberal focus, but it also produced an increased reliance on ideology and a decreased respect for the intellectual base of gang research.

The Eurogang program, at least to date, has neither favored notably nor been favored by proponents of either a strongly liberal or strongly conservative ideology. The many countries involved—more than a dozen at this point—are politically arrayed over a wide range of social service and justice models (Klein 1984). Further, because much of the program's activity has been in the technical development of a broad assortment of instruments, there has been relatively little opportunity for the intrusion of social or political bias. My hope and trust is that these cross-national and multimethod emphases will serve to reduce the more trend-driven approach seen in the American experience.

The final, and perhaps most disturbing, aspect of the American experience is the failure to locate demonstrably useful strategies and programs to deal with street-gang problems. The history of this failure is too complex to cover here (see Klein and Maxson 2005), but there are three components of immediate importance. First, those major gang projects that have been independently and adequately evaluated have proven to be either ineffective or even harmful. Second, most programs have not been subjected to any evaluations, to say nothing of competent ones. Thus, we have learned little to guide policy. Third, there has, in most cases, been a major disjuncture between accumulated, reliable gang knowledge and the design of gang programs. If we do not apply what we know and do not evaluate what we apply, then clearly we cannot make much progress in dealing with street-gang situations. The Eurogang program has only begun to consider these issues, but it has a major advantage compared to the situations in the United States: it is not too late to engage in data-based policymaking, and there is a substantial group of researchers available to undertake the task.

Program Development. The Eurogang program was first conceived in 1997, following my two sabbatical leaves in Stockholm, with a small travel grant from my university. This allowed me to visit cities in a number of countries to check out uncoordinated reports of street-gang activity. The results were shared and discussed with a small group of American and European scholars at informal gatherings in Leuven, Belgium, and San Diego, California. Interest was so high that these informal discussions took off into a self-propelling process that became the Eurogang program (Klein 2001).

With major initiatives by Peter van der Laan of the Dutch Ministry of Justice,[1] the first of seven workshops was held in Schmitten, Germany, in 1998 under the leadership of Elmar Weitekamp and Hans-Jürgen Kerner. American and European researchers and policy officials prepared papers and entered into detailed discussions of gang issues. These, in turn, led to the first coordinated publication describing both American and European street-gang situations, *The Eurogang Paradox* (Klein et al. 2001).

The second, equally pivotal workshop was held the next year in Oslo, arranged largely by Tore Bjørgo of the Norwegian Institute of International Affairs. Here, an expanding group of researchers developed a series of working groups whose efforts would largely shape the future of the program. The working groups included assignments to develop (1) common definitions, (2) youth survey methods, (3) adult expert survey methods, (4) structured ethnography guidelines, (5) assessments of city descriptors, and (6) a survey of intervention programs.

Successive workshops in Holland, Belgium, Germany, and the United States were arranged by various Eurogang participants with funding from diverse sources. These featured the expansion of the program's participants and interested individuals (more than one hundred fifty at this point), discovery of more than fifty gang-involved cities in Europe, a greater willingness to acknowledge the existence of gangs despite earlier denials (e.g., in England, Italy, Belgium, Sweden), a slow takeover of program leadership by the Europeans from the Americans, and the development of a large cadre of congenial colleagues willing and anxious to initiate serious research undertakings. All this, in turn, has led to the creation of the present volume of strictly European research reports[2] and the completion of the tasks of the various working groups. A comprehensive copyrighted protocol for multimethod research is now available by application to the program's steering committee.

Eurogang Program Accomplishments. As noted above, several major products of the program are available. These include this volume and its predecessor, *The Eurogang Paradox.* There now exist a pretested and reviewed youth survey, experts survey, and ethnographic guidelines, all coordinated around the consensus street-gang definition cited in the chapters in this book. These items have been translated into several European languages, and that process is continuing. A procedure has been developed for making the instruments available to serious researchers through a website maintained at www.umsl .edu/%7Eccj/eurogang/euroganghome.htm (May 19, 2005). Finally, an assessment of the location of European street gangs now exists and undoubtedly will be expanded over time.

In sum, it is now possible for interested parties, researchers in coordination with policymakers, to launch multimethod, comparative, multisite studies of European (and American or other) street gangs. For researchers, the knowledge-building potential is obvious. For policymakers, such research presents an opportunity to establish data-based program options in a fashion never attained in the United States until that nation was overwhelmed by a gang problem in more than thirty-five hundred jurisdictions (National Youth Gang Center 2000).

Personal Points of Satisfaction. While I agree that the editors should summarize the main points to be derived from this volume, I will list a few of particular interest to me. I hope I will not be alone in seeing their importance.

Most crucial, perhaps, is the use in each chapter and in each study of a common definition of the term *street gang.* Such a consensus on definitions has never before been achieved or attempted by a consortium of gang researchers. The consensus Eurogang definition allows one to include most groups called street gangs (*bande* in several languages), while also excluding crime cartels, terrorist groups, prison gangs, and motorcycle gangs, as well as a whole host of youthful groups (to which many of us belonged) that help one transition to adulthood without causing the authorities much trouble.

Along with this consensus definition as developed by one of the Eurogang program's working groups are several operational definitions commonly shared and available within the youth surveys, experts surveys, and ethnographic guidelines; that is, there are research operations that refer back to the consensus definitions yet provide several options for determining which groups are street gangs and which are not. And, of course, this allows one to distinguish gang members from those who do not belong to such groups. As the science of criminology goes, I see this as a major conceptual and research accomplishment.

A second point of interest is that this definitional advance, along with a better understanding of the varieties of street groups in both Europe and the United States, has reduced denial of the existence of gangs in some European settings. One of the gang studies included in this volume was produced by a former gang denier. Other locations can and do now acknowledge the existence of one or more forms of street gangs without the risk of creating a moral panic about it.

A third source of satisfaction for me, and an advance for the field, is the ability of many of this volume's authors to describe their gangs structurally. By commonly referring to gang size, duration, subgrouping, and behavior patterns, they provide comparability to build our knowledge base about types of street gangs. This is, in turn, a useful step toward more focused concern for available options in gang intervention and control.

Fourth, some chapters combine two or more methodological approaches. This is not new, but neither is it common. Most gang studies are either observational- *or* ethnographic- *or* interview-based *or* archival-based. Each method has its faults and advantages, and each can provide a somewhat different perspective on the nature of street gangs and their members. Thus, it seems, there is an art to understanding gangs based on melding the views provided by different approaches. The expert gang scholar, it seems to me, is one who accepts his or her place in this art, practices it, and then portrays his or her subject more broadly, transcending a particular methodology.

In sum, what I want to see in the gang world is multimethod, multisite, comparative research capable of yielding general principles that are testable and verifiable across nations. The use of common definitional stances and common techniques makes such a goal possible. This volume, for which the editors should be congratulated along with their contributors, demonstrates that achieving that goal is realistic. All it takes is the will, the willingness to collaborate across borders, and favored approaches and support from public and private agencies. I believe many such agencies can appreciate basing policy on valid research more than on untested conventional wisdoms.

NOTES

1. Now at the Netherlands Institute for the Study of Crime and Law Enforcement.

2. The reader may also wish to examine a complete, worldwide review of street-gang descriptions recently provided by Covey (2004).

REFERENCES

Covey, Herbert C. 2004. *Street gangs throughout the world.* Springfield, IL: Charles C. Thomas.

Covey, Herbert, Scott Menard, and Robert Franzese. 1997. *Juvenile gangs.* Springfield, IL: Charles C. Thomas.

Fagan, Jeff. 1989. The social organization of drug use and drug dealing among urban gangs. *Criminology* 27 (4): 633–69.

Huff, Ronald C. 1998. *Comparing the criminal behavior of youth gangs and at-risk youths.* Research in brief. Washington, D.C.: National Institute of Justice.

Klein, Malcolm. 1984.

———. 1995. *The American street gang.* New York: Oxford.

———. 2001. Resolving the eurogang paradox. In *The eurogang paradox: Street gangs and youth groups in the U.S. and Europe,* ed. M. W. Klein, H.-J. Kerner, C. L. Maxson and E. G. M. Weitekamp, 3–7. Dordrecht, Netherlands: Kluwer.

Klein, M. W., H.-J. Kerner, C. L. Maxson, and E. G. M. Weitekamp. 2001. *The eurogang paradox: Street gangs and youth groups in the U.S. and Europe.* Dordrecht, Netherlands: Kluwer.

Klein, M., and C. Maxson. 2005. *Streetgang Patterns and Policies.* New York: Oxford.

National Youth Gang Center. 2000. *1998 National Youth Gang Survey, summary.* Washington, D.C.: U.S. Department of Justice, Office of Juvenile Justice and Delinquency Prevention.

Sanchez-Jankowski, Martin. 1991. *Islands in the street: Gangs and American urban society.* Berkeley: University of California Press.

Spergel, Irving. 1995. *The youth gang problem: A community approach.* New York: Oxford.

I

QUALITATIVE APPROACHES

1

In the Grip of the Group

FRANK VAN GEMERT AND MARK S. FLEISHER

In the Netherlands, Moroccan boys have a bad reputation when it comes to crime. Since the end of the 1980s, Moroccan juveniles have been overrepresented in Dutch police statistics. Other youngsters (e.g., those of Surinamese or Turkish origin) do not come into contact with the police as often. Several explanations have been offered for this phenomenon, focusing on migration history, social control, socioeconomic factors, and ethnic culture (Junger and Zeilstra 1989; Van Gelder and Sijtsma 1988; van Gemert 1998; Werdmölder 1986, 1990). During the last few years, attention has been centering more and more on Moroccan youth groups. This chapter is about one of those groups, the Windmill Square group. The boys from this group hang out in certain places in their neighborhood in Amsterdam-West. Police reports assert that this group is responsible for a lot of criminal activity. Some of its members are known to commit street robberies and stickups.

In the Dutch media, Moroccan youth groups are regularly called *jeugdbendes* ("gangs"). Among scientists and policymakers, however, there is no consensus regarding the true nature of these groups. The appropriateness of comparing Moroccan jeugdbendes to American gangs has been the subject of considerable debate. In one ethnographic study by H. Werdmölder (1986, 1990), the word *jeugdbende* was used. Conversely, in other ethnographic literature about Moroccan criminal youth, there is little or no support for the use of this label (Kaufman and Verbraeck 1986; Van der Torre 1996; Van Gelder and Sijtsma 1988; Viskil 1999). The existing literature on drug users and dealers suggests that they form small crews that easily change in composition rather than more stable gangs. Research, based on several years of participant observation in Rotterdam, further supports this view (van Gemert 1998). In the Rotterdam study, the Moroccan boys formed a loosely knit group. Because their relations were imbued with fundamental distrust, cohesion was poor. These boys rejected being called a gang, saying that they were very different from American gangs.

This raises the question What is a gang? As M. Klein (2001) argues, studying gangs requires and fosters the abandonment of preconceived, false images. In America, stereotypes of gangs with hierarchical ranks and rules for membership, initiation, and so on, have become a point of reference. However, most gangs in America do not actually share these characteristics. Thus, the prevalence of stereotypes frequently obscures the true nature of the gang phenomenon. In order to facilitate gang research across borders, Eurogang needed a single definition of the term *gang* that is close to reality. Many intense discussions have resulted in the following definition: "A street gang is any durable, street-oriented youth group whose involvement in illegal activity is part of its group identity."

The Eurogang definition guides our description in this chapter of the Windmill Square group. In addition to contributing to the overall mission of Eurogang, this chapter is meant to shed new light on the Dutch debate over Moroccan youth groups. Before we present our findings, we must first discuss the methodology of the research. Given the importance of physical, demographic, and socioeconomic context in the study of gangs, we then describe Amsterdam-West, paying special attention to the migration background of this area and its inhabitants. Finally, we examine the group and the individuals and elaborate on the culture of the group. The structure of this chapter and the research itself are shaped by the guidelines of the ethnography protocol agreed upon by Eurogang researchers.

METHODS

Eurogang researchers aim for internationally comparative research. One way of achieving this is to compare results. Another possibility lies in actually working together. In this research, a Dutch and an American researcher did fieldwork together. The authors set out "hand in hand" to gather data in Amsterdam. Although we were ultimately unable to collaborate on this research as completely as planned, working together brought about interesting insights. While doing fieldwork, anthropologists are themselves the research instruments. This makes doing fieldwork with an experienced colleague interesting because personal styles and orientations come to the forefront. Doing fieldwork with someone whose experience and training are rooted in a different context makes this even more interesting. When on the street, the researchers could not take their own observations and sometimes-implicit interpretations for granted but rather were forced into immediate reflection to spell out what they had heard and observed and what they thought this could mean. The benefits of this "double observation" are discussed in a separate publication (van Gemert 2004).

For our research purposes, the Moroccan group was studied using data collected in Amsterdam between August 2001 and September 2002. The fieldwork was divided into two phases. The first phase involved the examination of four youth groups located in different sites in Amsterdam. The objective was to select one group to be studied in greater detail in the second phase. These four groups were assessed through interviews with police officers, youth workers, teachers, shopkeepers, and youth. Selection was based on three criteria: Is the group problematic? Is it possible to get in contact with the group? Are there other data available on the group?

The group selected for the second phase is identified as the Windmill Square group, located in Amsterdam-West. As in the first phase, half-open interviews were used to gather general information on the group. In the end, forty-one informants were interviewed, but no group members were among them. The boys were reluctant to talk in a formal interview setting, and it took a long time before they would participate even in a simple conversation. Police officers and youth workers were key informants. A second source of information was archival data, mainly consisting of police registrations. Since the selected group was known to the police and was considered to be a serious problem, a special police unit had been watching this group (among others) for years. The third way to learn about the group was by participant observation. Working with Jan Dirk de Jong, who was also involved in research on Moroccan groups, was especially helpful during this phase of the fieldwork.

Visiting hangouts, particularly a community center where the youths meet three nights a week, was a fruitful way to get in contact with the boys casually. Yet, here too, cooperation was not forthcoming. Although we clearly stated our reasons for approaching them and that we would not use their names or give information on illegal activities to the police, simple conversations were the best direct contacts we could get. Distrust of outsiders appears to be common among Moroccan boys, who often averred, "You are going to write bad things about Moroccans, aren't you?" (van Gemert 2002). Participation in their daily routine was limited, and we were not present when criminal activities took place. Nevertheless, we were able to observe how they interacted as a group and how they opposed nonmembers in conflict situations. The group dynamics that we were able to witness were both interesting and relevant for understanding their behavior.

MOROCCAN MIGRANTS

Starting in the 1960s, migrant workers from the mountainous Rif area of northern Morocco were recruited to work in Dutch factories. Due to economic prosperity, these workers, as well as workers from other Mediterranean countries such as Turkey, Italy, and Spain, were needed to fill the demands of the labor market. The migrants saved money and sent it to Morocco and demonstrated their newly gained wealth by leaving the countryside for a new house in the city. Even then, their ultimate return to Morocco seemed self-evident. However, although these first-generation Moroccans have always been strongly focused on the land of their birth, the majority still live in the Netherlands to this day. Indeed, contrary to early expectations, men sent for their wives and children, and families were reunited on Dutch soil. Their houses in Morocco were rented to relatives, and the migrant families returned to them only on holidays.

Eventually, though, economics changed, and many Moroccans lost their jobs. Nowadays, most Moroccan families have low incomes and live in the poor neighborhoods of Dutch cities. The first Moroccans to migrate to the Netherlands have become bitter, elderly men who often go to the mosque and shun Dutch society. They are analphabetic and speak Dutch poorly. Their wives, because of traditional Islamic rules, often do not leave the house. As a consequence, these parents are in a poor position to assist and guide their children in their daily lives. As a matter of fact, a form of role reversal often occurs, as Moroccan children accompany their parents and translate when visiting a doctor, counselor, or civil servant.

The Local Problem

Since 1998, Amsterdam has had fifteen "city parts," and these formal geographical units have their own councils. Amsterdam-West is a 35-km^2 suburban area on the outskirts of Amsterdam that consists of four city parts. These four city parts have also been amalgamated into a single police district. The total number of inhabitants in West is 162,500, while the city of Amsterdam has 735,000 inhabitants. Most of West was built in the 1950s and 1960s, when the population was growing and cheap housing was needed. In the beginning, Dutch families with children came to live in West. The children grew up and left, but the parents stayed. As a result, West has a relatively large number of elderly residents. Another relevant demographic factor is the influx since the 1970s of low-income migrant families drawn to West by the prevalence of cheap houses for rent. These latter families often have many young children. These factors have created a decidedly bimodal age distribution in West's population.

This research was done in the section of West for which we use the pseudonym Waterveld. Because Waterveld is home to a disproportionate number of ethnic minorities, the overall population is heterogeneous. As in the other three city parts of West, Moroccans constitute a relatively large portion, over 12 percent, of the population of Waterveld. In Amsterdam as a whole, they make up only 7.8 percent. Waterveld is not a ghetto, and neighborhoods within it are not considered "no-go" areas. Another aspect of the American stereotype that does not apply is the fact that this city part has many public agencies. While neighborhoods where migrants live often are poor and look bad, there is no dilapidated housing in Waterveld, it is quite green, and the streets are clean. Indeed, the streets where the boys from Windmill Square hang out are part of a busy shopping area visited by thousands of people everyday.

The Moroccan boys from Windmill Square are sons of migrant workers, and their family background is relatively common in Waterveld. The Windmill Square group is not the first group of Moroccan boys that has drawn public attention. In Amsterdam since the mid-1980s, newspapers have printed reports based on police observations that mention the criminal activities of several groups. In 1985 in Waterveld, a Moroccan group of eleven boys was apprehended; they had committed 170 offenses in only one-half year's time. Their victims were often homosexual men who were robbed after they invited the boys into their homes. These men did not go to the police because they feared this would mean more trouble. In December 1988, a newspaper article that mentioned Moroccan gangs in the inner city of Amsterdam drew considerable attention. It gave a frightening picture of two to three hundred youngsters who were said to work in a hierarchical organization with ten to fifteen leaders. They terrorized the inner city, it was said. This article provoked critical reactions because of its stigmatizing effect.

On April 23, 1998, a small incident between a Moroccan boy and a policeman in August Allebéplein, a square in Amsterdam-West, grew into a massive conflict between the police and Moroccans from the neighborhood. Because of the barricades in the streets and the vigor of these unexpected "riots," every newspaper in the Netherlands reported on this event, which proved to be a turning point. In the following weeks, there were new confrontations in several other parts of the city between the police and Moroccan boys. Again, articles and life reports were in the media. The city council initiated an investigation into these conflicts. The resultant research examined the circumstances that had led to these unexpected outbursts (Crisis Onderzoek Team 1998) and their broader context, mainly focusing on welfare and social security facilities (Stuurgroep Jeugdproblematiek Amsterdam West/Nieuw-West 1998). The Amsterdam police reacted by forming a special unit tasked with investigating and mapping youth groups, with an emphasis on North African (Moroccan) involvement.

The neighborhoods where the conflicts emerged also reacted in positive ways. Projects were initiated to help youngsters spend their free time prosocially. As part of one of these projects, Moroccan youths from Amsterdam visited a poor hospital in Morocco, where the youths worked and repaired furniture. International attention was drawn to the self-appointed Moroccan Neighborhood Fathers, who set out to broaden social control by walking through the neighborhood on a daily basis, talking to youngsters, and correcting them if necessary.

Thus, Moroccan jeugdbendes in Amsterdam have been mentioned in the media and public discourse throughout the last few years. In the beginning, these groups were operating in a twilight zone; later, they became more visible, and open confrontations drew more attention. Yet, even though positive initiatives have evolved, Moroccan youth groups remain a serious problem.

Our research supports this position. The boys from the group we examined hang out in several places in the neighborhood, all in the public sphere. When their presence in one location brings about too many conflicts, the police can send them away. Four police reports about the Windmill Square group, dating from December 1998 to January 2002, credit the group with a lot of criminal activity. Every report cites a number of offenses, such as assault, theft, vandalism, threats, nuisance, and arson. According to the last three reports, the boys also committed street robberies and stickups. All reports show thirty to fifty offenses within a few months' time.

It also appears that the Windmill Square group has been getting into more and more conflicts within the neighborhood. Neighborhood citizens and shopkeepers who once opposed the boys and tried to correct them have largely ceased their involvement as a result of insults and intimidation. On a few occasions, violence has been used against them. Mostly blows are exchanged, but sometimes knife use is reported, although there are no reports of serious injuries. In a typical conflict scenario, the boys confront those who have taken a stand against them or their activities. When there is an argument, the boys use threats to get the other party to retreat. "We know where you live" is a common declaration. Because the boys act as a group, such intimidation has a big impact. The following excerpt from our field notes is illustrative:

> In the supermarket a small boy is caught while stealing a can of soda, and the police are called. In the meantime, a large group of twenty to forty boys gathers in front of the store; they want to free the boy before the police arrive. Shouting and cursing, they all enter the store, threaten the personnel, and within seconds steal money from a candy counter. When the police arrive, they have to wait for backup before they can transport the young boy to the bureau.

Repeatedly, property is damaged, but there is seldom proof of who is responsible. While most people in the neighborhood know about the Windmill Square group, the individual boys are anonymous. "They all look alike," victims often respond when asked for offender descriptions. Shopkeepers are especially vulnerable to the group's behavior, as broken windows and stolen goods directly affect their income. One shopkeeper said he never parked his car in the vicinity of his shop. "If they know what car is mine, I need new tires every week." Boys get so bold that they sometimes enter a shop and threaten a cashier before stealing something from the store.

Neighborhood residents and businesses often believe they have little recourse. It is felt that the police often come too late and are not effective. As a consequence of intimidation and a lack of faith in the ability of the police to resolve the situation, people try not to get involved in conflicts with the group. When talking to the police, they say they will not stand as witnesses, and charges are not filed, which makes it even harder for the police to do their job.

Group

The Windmill Square group is mentioned in police reports dating from 1998, indicating that the group has existed for at least seven years. In these reports, the police produce a list of members who are criminally active. While individual names on these lists have changed over the years, at least ten boys' names have remained constant, and about twenty-five members are listed on average. This makes it safe to say that although some boys come and go, a number of boys remain in the group for a long time. Boys range between sixteen and twenty years of age, with an average age of eighteen. This average age has not changed much over the years; in 1999 it was 17.5. In the Dutch context, the age of twenty seems rather old for a boy to belong to a street-oriented group.

From the police reports and our observations, it seems clear that the group consists entirely of boys. While we found that every now and then some of the boys have girlfriends, these girls are not brought to places where the group meets. Of the twenty-four members whom we could identify as regular visitors to the hangouts, all are Moroccan with the exception of a Dutch, a Surinamese, and a Dutch-Philippine boy. Thus, the group is seen as a Moroccan group, and the three non-Moroccan boys are "Moroccanized" in the sense that their conduct is the same as the rest of the group.

The police first coined the name "Windmill Square group" after the square where the boys meet; the boys themselves do not use a name when they talk about their group. Boys from the group cannot be identified as members through the use of distinctive symbols. There are no typical jackets, caps, shoes, or other pieces of clothing that distinguish them from other boys. Nor do the boys have tattoos, piercings, special hairdos, or other body symbols unique to group members. The group also does not use graffiti with special wording. However, these facts do not mean that the group does not use symbols. To the contrary, they use a lot of symbols, but all of them are taken from global youth styles. Hip-hop music and gangsta rap has many fans. Tupac is a hero in Amsterdam-West, and one can read his name in graffiti and hear his lyrics where youngsters play music. The English gangster argot has become part of the vocabulary of youngsters all over the world, and Moroccan boys of this particular group are no exception. In the community center where the Windmill Square group often meets, a text on the wall reads, "I wonder if heaven got a ghetto."

While the boys get into altercations with neighborhood citizens and shop-keepers, there are no conflicts with other youth groups, no gang wars. Some-times boys from other parts of town who know somebody in the group come and visit. This is not a problem since there is no sense of territoriality. The places where they hang out have no clear boundaries. Where they meet is de-termined by such practical matters as transport; it has nothing to do with group rules.

The group is egalitarian. It has no ranks nor does it have subgroups that are formalized in any sense. When asked, the boys say the group has no leader. Of course, this does not mean the boys are all the same or that they all behave in the same way. Some boys are older and stronger than others, and they will not allow the younger ones to beat them in a game or to make fun of them. On the other hand, younger boys will not obey the older ones. There is no one in the group who can tell another boy what to do. Still, in certain situations, boys can take a steering role, and some boys are more likely to play those roles than others. We observed situations that ended in conflict when a certain boy would act as a catalyst to pull the group beyond neutrality. This would typi-cally occur when a boy got into an argument with someone. At that point, other group members present could intervene if they so chose. However, if the boy confronted the other party and got into a one-on-one fight, the others could not stand idly by. In this situation, they would have to join in and help the boy. Certain boys do this over and over again, and they are not respected for it. On the one hand, when they are around something is bound to happen and that means boredom is unlikely. On the other hand, most boys have learned that these members get the group into trouble, and they hate to get in contact with the police for something stupid. The problem is, once again, that the individual cannot be told what to do. He will not listen because, within this group, a docile, obedient person counts for nothing.

The boys spend a lot of time together, but, of course, some individuals go together better than others. Some boys say they have friends within the group. When asked what this means, they say that when in trouble, they expect help from only a few boys. They do not fully trust all the other boys, and they will not lend money to members they do not consider friends. This does not weaken the group because it is not a surprise. As a matter of fact, the boys know very well what to expect from each other. In the neighborhood where they are located, this equals security. "I have known him for so long," they often say when expressing what group members mean to them. Most of these boys have grown up together in the neighborhood. They have few other contacts, and this seems to make the group their main podium for social interaction, fun, and gratification.

Individuals

The twenty-four boys mostly come from big families with low incomes. Two boys come from a family of ten children, and another boy has seven brothers and sisters. At least eight boys come from broken families where the father or mother is not present and lives in Morocco. Four boys come from "problem families," in which other family members, besides the boy, have police contacts. The mother of a non-Moroccan boy is a drug addict.

Most of these Moroccan families are traditional in terms of gender roles. Girls have little freedom and are strictly supervised, as their conduct (i.e., losing their virginity) can seriously damage the honor of the family. Boys have no tasks at home and spend a lot of time on the streets because the house is considered the domain of women. The boys can damage the family reputation if word gets out that they have been in contact with the police. Fathers may react by punishing them, but this seldom changes the situation. Sons simply try to avoid meeting their fathers. On the other hand, the boys may be considered nontraditional in terms of religious practice. When asked, most say religion is something for when they are older.

At school and in work, these boys are not successful. They drop out of school very easily and find themselves on the labor market with few qualifications. Although economic conditions have been good in the few last years, and the boys have found work now and then through temping agencies, none of them has managed to get a steady job. Their lack of discipline to get up early and the fact that they get bored easily with doing the same, simple work for a long period are the main reasons for their unemployment.

All boys in the group have had at least one police contact, and most of them have had several. Police registration shows that they are not all equally known to the police. One boy is mentioned in 5 files, while another's name pops up 202 times. Their offending behaviors are diverse. A wide range of activities makes for a cafeteria-style pattern of crime, from shoplifting and burglary, to theft, street robbery, and stickups. There seems to be no specialization. Although Moroccan boys in other Dutch cities often have been active in drug dealing, this is not the case in Amsterdam-West. Since the police are aware of many of their offenses, the boys have all been brought to court at least once. However, they seldom received serious punishment. The judges typically handed out fines, labor-and-learning sentences, or both, although in some cases, boys have been sent to jail as a result of multiple-offense charges.

At least eight boys have had contacts with social workers. The results, however, were poor because the boys are "institution wise" and only participated for their own short-term benefit. Some programs considered successful in general could not bring about any positive changes in boys from this group, who left the programs prior to completion. They seem to be resistant to good intentions. Still, it seems clear that these boys are in need of intervention. They get into trouble easily, not only because of crime but also because of the unexpected financial consequences of repeated fines and the consequences of being uninsured. Thus, it would appear that important help could come in the form of assistance in dealing with debts.

Upon reaching maturity, Moroccan boys become "quiet" and "serious," and they change their ways. Although maturing out can be seen as a general process, for a Moroccan boy this can happen suddenly. Afterwards, he may seem like a completely different person. Nevertheless, some of these boys mature years later than nonmembers. This delay leaves them with few opportunities and discouraging comments from others. The following excerpt from field notes provides an example:

> A twenty-year-old boy was telling about the time that he would be a trucker. He would make long international journeys, and visit countries while being his own boss. Another one who heard part of his monologue killed the dream by simply asking when he would take his first driving lesson.

Thus, although the group from Windmill Square may be strong when opposing citizens and shopkeepers, once on their own, the individual members are insecure and ill prepared for a role in society.

Crime and Nuisance

The Windmill Square group is criminally active. By January 1, 2002, the police had registered 158 different offenses. As previously discussed, these criminal activities are diverse, and there seems to be no specialization within the group. Yet, this does not mean that certain boys, over some period, do not focus on a specific act they find rewarding. Even so, police numbers do not present such a pattern.

Co-offending happens regularly. Of the 158 registered offenses, more than one offender is documented in 68 cases. Seven boys have committed offenses with others relatively often (five or six times), while other boys have done so only a few times. These official figures probably underestimate the prevalence of co-offending because the boys, as a rule, do not talk when they are apprehended. Ratting on a companion is taboo. Indeed, they have no reason to behave differently as they have learned that keeping still after being caught will put them back on the street within a few hours. Within the Dutch justice system, immediate punishment for a non serious crime is nonexistent.

A lot of the offenses committed by the boys from the group are not seen as group-related offenses simply because the offender acted alone or in a non recognized pair. These individuals or pairs are not acting on behalf of the group or are acting without the group's knowledge. For example, shoplifting and burglary are secret acts.

However, when it comes to nuisance, the story is quite different. In these cases, behavior is viewed as a group phenomenon and is very public. The Windmill Square group has earned a reputation for being highly confrontational, especially in nuisance situations. The following excerpt is illustrative:

> Rowdy because of too much alcohol, three boys cross the square. They are followed by a bunch of others, who feel something is bound to happen. The three shout, curse and harass bystanders. Police officers warn them to stop, but one of them won't listen. The officers decide to arrest him, but a growing number of boys is entering the scene. By pulling the boy and shouting, they obstruct the arrest.

By acting as a group when opposing others, the boys from Windmill Square are not easy to deal with. The group uses its physical power. The boys learn how to use this to their own benefit, and opponents in the neighborhood know from experience that individual group members will be backed up by the group. The group's physical power and reputation allows it to prevent acts of opposition by, for example, obstructing arrests, as in the case above, or dissuading victims from reporting members to the police. Moreover, if an incident is reported, the group can intimidate complainants and witnesses. Our field notes capture one such situation:

> Two young boys on the street have a quarrel and fight. A boy from the Windmill Square group who is a few years older sees them and gets involved. He chooses sides and takes on one of the boys. He uses a lot of force, hitting and kicking the boy who is totally overpowered. The victim later tells his parents what happened. They go to the police, and this can have serious consequences for the older boy who is on parole. Not long afterwards, a number of boys show up at the house of the victim. They enter the garden and look through the windows. This threatening behavior is meant to put pressure: withdraw your charges.

The group's reputation, particularly with regard to nuisance behavior, has spread outside its neighborhood. Amsterdam-West has no discotheques, so when boys want to go out, they go to the center of town. In several parts of the inner city, boys from this group are known for bad behavior and causing fights. Bouncers have had several conflicts with them, and the police in these parts of Amsterdam know about "Moroccans from West." Outside Amsterdam, Moroccans from West are also known in Zandvoort, a small city on the coast about 20 km from the capital. In sunny weather, boys go there to hang on the boulevard. As a rule, they drink much and become very loud. Here, too, they get into conflicts easily. Newspaper reports included in our field notes provide an example:

> After the first warm day of 2001, newspaper articles mention a group of Moroccan boys harassing women in public places and in the train when coming from Zandvoort. They are loud and obnoxious, and one of the Windmill Square boys, with his pants down, sits on the lap of an elderly lady. When leaving the train, they are arrested.

Culture

Culture is the sum of experiences, knowledge, norms, values, meanings, and symbols that members of a group share with each other. In discussions of the culture of Moroccan youngsters in the Netherlands, ethnicity is often highlighted. Almost all of the Windmill Square boys have parents who spent most of their lives in Morocco. How these parents raised their offspring is undoubtedly influenced by their own history. On the other hand, the children themselves were not born in North Africa and did not grow up there. They played in Dutch streets, went to Dutch schools, and learned the Dutch language better than their parents did. In explanations of why some Moroccan boys go astray, the notion of culture conflict is often brought up. According to this perspective, these youngsters have to deal with conflicting Dutch and Moroccan cultural elements; the children cannot choose between them and fall into a state of normlessness. This is a deterministic and simplistic notion as it sees norms as autonomous, neglecting individual choice. Moreover, it makes culture into a static entity with no relation to context. In our view, the opposite is true. Culture is dynamic, reproduced and shaped in a constant process of adaptation to its context. In trying to understand the culture of the Windmill Square group, we have found Moroccan and Dutch aspects relevant; however, so, too, are other influences, such as global youth culture. As shown above, the latter are easily traced through symbols in clothing, speech, and gestures. Here, our focus in not on what is passed down through generations but rather on the everyday experiences of the boys and how these experiences affect the way they view the world around them.

Part of this understanding requires acknowledging that the Windmill Square group is isolated. The boys live on the edge of town, seemingly cut off from the rest of the city. "There is nothing to do here for us," they continuously complain. At the same time, they do not go to school or hold steady jobs, and they are not members of any clubs. Furthermore, those contacts they have with outsiders are often antagonistic. This leaves the group inside-oriented, and nonmembers are distrusted. As has been said, ratting on someone is a sin. In the group, issues are dealt with using one-liners and mainly through shouting. This leads to a situation where the group, after simplification, comes to dominant opinions with no shades of gray and a strong perspective of "us versus them." The common association of Moroccans with crime in the Netherlands is believed to be the result of misjudgment on the part of non-Moroccans. The boys believe that the media only focuses on what goes wrong and that Moroccans are stigmatized without good reason. Even though this group is responsible for much crime and nuisance, they seem convinced that others are really to blame.

They do not read newspapers and would rather watch a film than the news, which would seem to indicate that they are uninterested in or disconnected from world events and politics. Yet, in politics, their stance is clear and firm. Although born and raised in the Netherlands, as Moroccans these boys choose the side of the Arab world. They are anti-America and anti-Israel, and in this respect, they differ from most people in the Netherlands. When they are angry and feel the outside world is against them, they use one single word that stands for the enemy: *Jews.*

In many respects, the boys are very similar to one another. Their personal histories have parallels, not least because they have shared experiences as a consequence of being part of the Windmill Square group. This does not mean, though, that the boys are close friends or that they trust each other. On the contrary, they are alert not to leave valuables in their coats with others around, and they do not lend other boys money, thinking they might not get it back. This may sound negative, but there is another side. The group has no explicit rules, with the possible exception of codes regarding betrayal. Yet, they know very well what to expect from each other. As noted above, "I have known him for so long" is an expression of security. There are situations where the boys act as a group to oppose others. They do this mainly through intimidation, but, if necessary, they also use force, even against the police. This can only work if they know what the others will do.

The boys are aware that the group means power. On the other hand, being part of the group diminishes their chances. It leaves them with a police record and otherwise almost empty-handed. This is partly the outcome of group dynamics that we observed during fieldwork. These group dynamics are related to characteristics of the Windmill Square group, such as the egalitarian relations between the Moroccan boys and the absence of leadership. Even though there are no explicit rules, patterns in conduct emerge. Events unfold along the same lines.

Among their fellows, boys witness illegal behavior and see that this meets with little disapproval. In a group like the one from Windmill Square, it is a small step to participate in criminal activities. In some instances, criminal acts are normal, as illustrated in the comment of one boy:

> The group prepares to go on an excursion with youth workers, and two of the boys have a task in organizing. They are aware of the risks when taking the

whole group, and they think ahead of what might happen when they travel with two small rented buses. One boy suggests that the "difficult" boys should not all be together in one vehicle. The other says they should not stop on the way and recalls what happened on an earlier excursion. Then, the bus had stopped for gas and the whole group got out, and in less than a minute, they stole a lot of things from the shop at the gas station. "You could have known this was bound to happen," he stated.

Criminal acts can also be the result of group dynamics. While an individual boy cannot be told what to do or corrected in front of others, paradoxically, he can manipulate the group. Individual actions repeatedly draw the group into risky situations where members have to take sides. This typically happens when certain boys seek confrontation and pull the others into it; this is comparable to "disturbed leadership" (Yablonsky 1959). The following question-and-answer exchange reflects the normalcy of this process:

Q: When a boy from the group is rude and annoys someone, what do you do?
A: We go over and try to make him stop.
Q: When a boy gets into a fight?
A: We help him. We have to help him.
Q: Even though it is his own fault?
A: That doesn't matter. We help him.

Group members can easily identify those who cause conflicts, but there is not much they believe they can do to change this. The troublemakers simply will not listen, and sanctions do not exist. The only thing left to do is to avoid meeting such troublemakers, but given daily routines, this is not very effective. As one boy expounded on this dilemma, "When he comes to the square, what can I do? I cannot tell him to go away. The street is not mine." In this isolated group, these group dynamics have a predictable outcome.

In the end, the Moroccan boys are left with fewer chances than they had before they became group members. Sooner or later, boys look around and see what they have achieved. Some realize that being part of the group will not get them ahead in society. Youth workers all say that individual members can be open and reasonable, but when others are around, they show a different side. Fellow group members can also hold a boy back, as illustrated in our field notes:

When a boy tells one of the researchers about his plan to apply for a job, another one is quick to comment: "You are stupid. What do you think? They will help you? No, you won't make it."

The boys think that the outside world is against Moroccan boys. This leads them to believe that they have few chances in society. Most individual boys lack the strength to go their own way against the dominant group opinion. Thus, the grim forecast becomes a self-fulfilling prophecy.

CONCLUSION

The Windmill Square boys form a durable street-oriented youth group whose involvement in illegal activity is part of their group identity. The Windmill Square group consists of twenty-four boys who are the steady members and a number of others that have less stable positions. Girls are not part of the group. It is a predominantly Moroccan group, with only a few non-Moroccan members. The group has been around for at least seven years; during that period, new boys have joined and others have retired. The group has no leaders, but in certain situations, some boys can play the role of instigator. The group has no name, no specific symbols, no territory, and there are no wars with other youth groups. We reached this and other conclusions by combining data from different sources: interviews and police archives, as well as informal conversations and observation.

The boys have few contacts outside the group, and this makes the group their main podium for social interaction, fun, and gratification. Criminal activities and nuisance behaviors bring them into conflict with neighborhood citizens and shopkeepers. The boys intimidate these outsiders and have built a reputation for not backing down. People feel vulnerable, and fear of retaliation keeps them from reporting the group's illegal activities to the police.

Within the group, isolation and simplification lead to a black-and-white picture of the group and the outside world: us versus them. Being part of the group means power because the group can oppose outsiders who might harm individual members. On the other hand, while being in the group, the individuals have seen their opportunities in Dutch society shrink. Group dynamics make it hard for the individual to take solo steps away from the group for their own benefit. At the same time, some boys can lead the group into trouble, with the other boys feeling they have no choice but to follow this negative route. In the end, this may lead to violence, and it often means breaking the law.

The Windmill Square group is a street gang. Even though some in the Netherlands are hesitant to use the term *jeugdbende*, or *gang*, the Eurogang definition clearly applies to this group. Of course, this does not mean that all Moroccan groups are gangs. When looking at the group dynamics and culture, an intriguing paradox comes into view. As a group, the boys can act against outside forces and are able to build a considerable power base. On the other hand, the individuals spend a lot of time together, yet have loose relations colored by distrust. It seems that knowing what to expect is more important to them than explicit rules or confidence in one another. As such, we conclude that American stereotypes that stress brotherhood or codes of honor offer poor guidance. Simultaneously, these findings raise important, unanswered questions about the nature of cohesion and its appropriate definition.

REFERENCES

Bovenkerk, F. 2003. Paniekreacties op de criminaliteit van allochtone jongeren in Australië en Nederland. In *Stigma: Marokkaan!* ed. S. Harchaoui and C. Huinder. Utrecht, Netherlands: Forum.

Crisis Onderzoek Team. 1998. *Verslag van interviews van het Crisis Onderzoek Team inzake onderzoek naar incidenten en ongeregeldheden Amsterdam West, 23 April 1998: Marokkaanse jongeren, politie en bestuur.* Leiden, Netherlands: Crisis Onderzoek Team.

van Gemert, F. 1998. *Ieder voor zich; Kansen, cultuur en criminaliteit van Marokkaanse jongens.* Amsterdam: Het Spinhuis.

———. 2002. Moeizame Marokkaanse medewerking; Cultuur als verklaring voor methodologische obstakels. In *Interviewen in een multiculturele samenleving; Problemen en oplossingen*, ed. H. Houtkoop-Steenstra and J. Veenman. Assen, Netherlands: Van Gorcum.

———. 2004. Gedeelde observatie is dubbele observatie. *Kwalon* 9 (1): 33–38.

Junger, M., and M. Zeilstra. 1989. *Deviant gedrag en slachtofferschap onder jongens uit etnische minderheden I.* Arnhem, Netherlands: Gouda Quint.

Kaufman, P., and H. Verbraeck. 1986. *Marokkaan en verslaafd.* Utrecht, Netherlands: Gemeente Utrecht.

Klein, M. W. 2001. Resolving the Eurogang Paradox. In *The Eurogang Paradox: Street gangs and youth groups in the U.S. and Europe*, ed. M. W. Klein, H. J. Kerner, C. L. Maxson, and E. G. M. Weitekamp. Dordrecht, Netherlands: Kluwer.

Stuurgroep Jeugdproblematiek Amsterdam West/Nieuw-West. 1998. *Door jongeren uitgedaagd; Voorstel voor aanpak jeugdproblematiek Amsterdam West/Nieuw-West.* Amsterdam: n.p.

Van der Torre, E. J. 1996. *Drugstoeristen en kooplieden; Een onderzoek naar Franse drugstoeristen, Marokkaanse drugsrunners en het beheer van dealpanden in Rotterdam.* Arnhem, Netherlands: Gouda Quint.

Van Gelder, P., and J. Sijtsma. 1988. *Horse, coke en kansen; Sociale risico's en kansen onder Marokkaanse hardruggebruikers in Amsterdam.* Amsterdam: Inst. voor Sociale Geografie, Universiteit van Amsterdam.

Viskil, I. 1999. *In een stad waar niemand je kent, kun je doen wat je wilt: Noord-Afrikaanse jongeren in een Amsterdamse coffeeshop.* Amsterdam: Het Spinhuis.

Werdmölder, H. 1986. *Van vriendenkring tot randgroep; Marokkaanse jongeren in een oude stadswijk.* Houten, Netherlands: Het wereldvenster.

———. 1990. *Een generatie op drift; De geschiedenis van een Marokkaanse randgroep.* Arnhem, Netherlands: Gouda Quint.

Yablonsky, L. 1959. The delinquent gang as a near-group. *Social Problems* 7: 108–17.

2

Criminal Gangs and Their Connections: Metaphors, Definitions, and Structures

INGER-LIESE LIEN

THE CONTAINER CONCEPT AND THE NETWORK METAPHOR

"We are hard men, like iron."

These are Pakistani boys, fourteen to fifteen years old, expressing their group (or gang) identity. The iron metaphor is their own, and they use it to show the strength of their determination, their pride, and their readiness to act. They hold that only something hard and solid, like iron, could get the best of them. "Only iron cuts iron," they say, referring to a Punjabi proverb.

In their account of gangs in a Norwegian city, my colleagues Tore Bjørgo, Yngve Carlsson, and Thomas Haaland (2001) adopted the magnet as a metaphor to indicate the attraction gangs exerted on some youngsters. Based on this model, they made a distinction between people who were easily magnetized—and easily recruited—and people who were totally unaffected by the presence of gangs in the neighborhood. They tried to identify the magnetic substance, that is, the factors that created the gangs' appeal. They found that symbolic markers of identity such as clothes, tattoos, and hairstyles could trigger violent reactions, polarizing local youngsters' attitudes, attracting some while repulsing others. Neutral clothing, naturally, did not have this effect.

In what follows, I make use of a number of metaphors to organize our understanding and analysis of the phenomenon we are studying. What is this phenomenon called a gang? What would be the best metaphor? The term *gang* has many definitions, all of which highlight different aspects of gang life. Such aspects are age span, use of symbols, self-definition, territory, continuity, norms, types of violence, and types of crime. Some researchers utilize broad definitions and include several criteria, while others take a more focused approach. Most researchers, though, see a need to include crime in their definitions (e.g., Decker and Van Winkle 1996; Huff 1991; Maxson and Klein 1985). They do so to differentiate between street gangs and many other types of youth assemblages, such as basketball or football teams, because the latter share many of the same elements of the former. In fact, the only difference is that they are not involved with antisocial behavior, violence, and crime. The Eurogang project defines a *gang* as "any durable, street-oriented youth group whose involvement in illegal activity is part of their group identity." Here we have durability, hanging around in the streets, and group identity as defining criteria. Only by adding the term *crime* to these attributes can we single out the group in which we are interested.

H. L. A. Hart (1994) holds that any meaningful term has a core meaning determined by very wide usage. In addition to this core meaning, a term will have a penumbra of indeterminate meanings. He maintains that a court of law cannot decide a case on legal grounds when the facts of the case fall into the penumbra (i.e., when there is uncertainty or disagreement among competent users of the language about the application of the relevant term). When it comes to the concept of the gang, the core, threefold meaning must include the attributes of crime, violence, and youth. Other incidental factors, common to many other subcultural groups, will fall more or less into the penumbra. Such factors include age span, duration, size, territory, use of symbols, a common name, a strong sense of identity, and so forth.

Most of the time, the metaphors used to understand gangs have been based on an avocado or an egg metaphor and employed a center-periphery way of thinking (i.e., hard core/soft margins, active/passive, closeness/distance to the core). Gangs are seen as being held together by an outer skin, creating a close and bounded entity, separate from their surroundings. Many of our concepts are based on this type of container metaphor, which posits an inside and outside demarcated by a clear boundary. The structure is topological, and the boundary can be made smaller or larger, even distorted, and still remain a boundary in the container schema (Lakoff and Johnson 1999).

In their typology of gangs, M. Klein et al. (2001) define five wide gang containers: the *traditional gang*, the *neotraditional gang*, the *compressed gang*, the *collective gang*, and the *specialized gang*. Their typology is based on formal criteria, like size, duration, and age range, that can be applied to all kinds of groups rather than on substantive criteria, like specific crime activities. Therefore, most of their defining criteria fall into the penumbra. Within the traditional gang, which has an average of 182 members (Klein et al. 2001), we can imagine that there will be numerous subgroupings and team groups, each of which could be defined as a separate gang in its own right, requiring a smaller conceptual container within the bigger container. Problems of leadership, organization, and social structure will be more urgent for large gangs than for small gangs and could lead to the crystallization of autonomous subgroupings through conflicts and tensions. Since such conflicts need to be solved at higher levels, they would spur the introduction of a more formal system of leadership and hierarchy. What should we call these smaller units: subgroups? subgangs? Specialized groups within a traditional group may not necessarily be mutually exclusive. As S. H. Decker (2001) and Klein (1995) have mentioned, gangs are usually poorly and informally organized. Decker argues that in an emergent gang city, the level of organization seems to be less than that in a city with a longer gang history. However, organization and gang structure may be influenced not only by history, but also by kinship factors and different types of networks. In certain conditions where kinship relations overlap with gang relations, kinship may provide the gang's organizational framework and stability. To understand how kinship interacts with gang connections, we need a network approach that extends beyond the closed and bounded concept of the gang.

The influence of the container metaphor on our understanding of gangs is also evident in the marginalization hypothesis. P. Bourgois (1996), together with J. D. Vigil (1996, 2002), holds that crime and gang formation are matters of marginalization. We think of something "marginal" as being excluded from or existing outside of mainstream society (i.e., to pursue the metaphor, not contained by society). The membrane that separates one container from another illustrates the disconnectedness of the part from the whole. A community is on the margins of the city, and a gang is on the margins of the community and separated from the family. The idea of a possible separation, of something being moved toward the outskirts and in the process of being pushed through the skin, is an important container-metaphor image of marginalization as well as of gangs with regard to the community structure.

Yet, despite its prevalence, social workers and social scientists often feel that the container model is not always useful for understanding the dynamics of connections and ties within, between, and beyond gangs. In the following, we see that a network metaphor can add a different dimension to our understanding of how gang members connect to their community. It can also help us reflect critically about the image of a gang whose state of marginality is like a container perched perilously on the edge of a cliff in imminent danger of tipping over or falling off.

One of the first to use the network model in the study of social relations was the social anthropologist J. A. Barnes (1954), who described and analyzed informal relationships between people living in a small Norwegian village. He found that a web of connections that had no clear leadership structure tied them together and connected them to the wider society. J. C. Mitchell (1969) developed this network metaphor further and introduced a complex set of analytical tools to describe the qualitative and quantitative dimensions of networks, such as density, range, anchorage, reachability, content, direction, durability, and frequency. He made a distinction between partial and complete networks based on individual (ego-centered) networks and networks of families, businesses, and friendships. The idea was to put the emphasis on interpersonal social relations *between* actors rather than *on* actors or *on* groups themselves. This shift of attention from group to network is a profound perceptual event. It resembles the changes that occur in connection with the well-known woman/rabbit picture described in perceptual psychology where background can become foreground and vice versa, engendering a paradigmatic transformation of meaning.

A network structure has elements of what could be described as a source-path-goal schema (Lakoff and Johnson 1999), where the network is conceived of as a web composed of several paths or threads with many crisscrossing goals and directions. The paths are imaginary as well as real and are conceptualized as linelike "trails." When we think of a web or network, a spider's web or fishing net easily comes to mind. These metaphors are illuminating when applied to gangs because they capture the connectedness and ties that exist between individuals and enable us to see them both as separate, visible units and as units linked together, as autonomous and connected at the same time.

In his study of the Freemont Hustler gang, Mark Fleisher (2002) prefers to use an ego-centered network approach, finding that gang members are never tied up only with other gang members within their in-group but also have connections outside the gang. Through this, they are able to bridge different resources in spite of the fact that a gang usually has a scarcity of what Fleisher terms *bridging capital.* Jerzy Sarnecki (2001) has also found it useful to apply a network analysis in his research on co-offending youths in Stockholm. By doing so, he was able to find that the most criminally active youths often commit offenses with their best friends. The network analysis is limited in time to six months: only youths committing illegal acts together within this time frame are included in the material. Sarnecki argues for this framing on methodological grounds in order to understand co-offending. However, networks can be dormant and invisible, then suddenly appear and become active. To better understand the people who commit illegal acts, their interrelations, and how gangs as entities operate to bridge and utilize different types of capital, we need a network approach that is open in terms of time and space. We need further to apply a thick-description methodology (Geertz 1976) to the structures and webs to avoid turning the network model into just another container metaphor.

For methodological reasons, researchers have often preferred the ego-centered network to the sociocentric model, which considers the network as a whole. The ego-centeredness of networks makes it easier to impose a container model on the structures, with different boxes representing different cliques, crowds, or gangs. Yet, while it may sometimes be necessary to see networks in this restricted way, the sociocentric version is superior in that it allows us to see both the container and the wider web simultaneously. As G. Simmel (1968) once discovered, all social life is made up of building blocks of dyads and triads. Between a mere one hundred people there are potentially ninety-nine hundred dyadic relations (Barth 1978). Therefore, the gang-as-container concept may be too broad and closed to allow us to discover the internal dyads and triads and too limited to understand those that extend beyond the container. According to the Manchester school, a social network or structure should be studied as a set of interdependent and connected roles, as role sets that extend widely. Along these connections are flows and interchanges of information between individuals as well as transfers of material goods and services between people (Scott 1991). Thus, gangs are not the opposite of networks. Rather, they are part of a continuous network, a cluster of connections that vary by complexity, density, and multiplicity. Scale is also a dimension of gangs (Grønhaug 1978), implying extension in social space and numbers of personnel and role complexity in the social system. If we circumscribe gangs, close them in as bounded entities, we will perceive them incorrectly or only partially and lose sight of the scale dimension.

This chapter examines gang structures using three Pakistani gangs as examples. At different periods—of two and three months' duration—in 1998, 1999, 2000, and 2002, fieldwork was conducted in Oslo, an ethnographic survey was completed in the Pakistani community, and court cases were followed. I have been doing anthropological research in the immigrant community in Oslo for twenty years since 1980, and I have personally known several of the parents of gang members for years. Informal, unstructured interviews with some members of the gangs were conducted at coffee places, and members of the police force, lawyers, and social workers were also interviewed for this study. Protocols, indictments, and court transcripts of the trials were also reviewed. Information gathered from this multitude of sources provides a clearer insight into how the gangs are integrated into the local and wider community. In the following, I maintain that the network structure of gangs interacts with the network structure of kinship, the structure of other types of networks such as of friendships and community relations in general, and finally, with the structure of the welfare system. These structures are dealt with separately.

THE STRUCTURE OF THREE OSLO GANGS
The Young Guns are friends from the Pakistani community in Oslo that have developed into a gang. The group came to the attention of the media and the public during the 1980s due to a series of fights with other gangs. In the 1990s, they fused with a gang of younger Pakistani boys who called themselves the A-gang. The resulting expanded gang perpetuated the name of the A-gang and includes the Young Guns as a subgroup. When the police and the media talk about the A-gang, Young Guns are included under that reference. The young A-gang boys were around fourteen years old when they started their criminal activities. Today, the age span in the A-gang is between twenty and thirty, while the oldest members in the Young Guns are reaching close to forty. The oldest members of the Young Guns have been active for almost fifteen years.

The two groups usually support each other, and they collaborate so intimately that they are often regarded as one group.

The A-gang criminal network is wide, extending to other gangs with whom its members party or work on particular jobs. The gang has connections with the Norwegian motorcycle gangs, Hells Angels, and Bandidos and is also involved in drug trafficking with Kosovo Albanians and ex-Yugoslavians who control the drug trade in Norway.

The members of the B-gang, the third gang, come from various suburbs on the east side of Oslo (Lørenskog, Stovner, and Furuset). Some met each other at the council youth clubs, others because their parents were friends. They have at least three cellular phones each, which they use for different purposes, and they have begun using the Internet as a form of communication. While the A-gang uses a few restaurants in Oslo as regular meeting places, the B-gang is very mobile and moves easily from town to town by car. It is not a territorial gang.

The B-gang uses the media actively to promote its image as tough guys. Members are often interviewed by both men's and women's magazines. The gang's activities in town and its fights with the A-gang are frequently cited in the most important national newspapers, with images of their golden chains and Ferraris displayed on the front pages. They seem to have won the fight against the A-gang, which has been weakened as a result of internal dissension and the generation gap between uncles in the Young Guns and their nephews in the young A-gang.

The police have recorded the names of about fifty members of what they call the A-gang, which is actually the conglomeration of the A-gang and the Young Guns, which we will call the "Big A-gang." In 2000, 1,173 charges were brought against the Big A-gang, which is an average of 24.4 offenses per member. The police divided the Big A-gang members into four categories: two leaders, ten intermediate leaders, twenty-two runners, and a fourth category containing fourteen people whose roles were unclear. The Big A-gang was charged with one murder, and the B-gang had twelve charges against them for attempts to murder. In January 2001, a homicide took place, which will be discussed below. The B-gang numbers around one hundred people, mostly between twenty and thirty years old, and has obtained the position it has today over a period of eight years. Notably, seven brothers from one family are involved in this gang. In 2001, the B-gang was charged with 2,463 felonies, mostly for property crime, drugs, violence, threats, and robbery. The gang model used by the Norwegian police is closed and bounded, based on a center-periphery egg or container metaphor.

When members of these gangs perform criminal acts, they generally do so in small groups numbering three or four people, sometimes only two. The relationships between the clusters of smaller units, the dyads and triads, and the gang as a whole are often contentious. Units may choose to share their experiences of successful jobs only with a few select others, leaving the rest of the group in the dark. The continual hostilities between the gang's substructural elements need to be examined in greater detail to understand the internal workings of gang structure and balances between relationships. Nevertheless, having an external enemy helps reduce antagonism between the more permanently functioning team groups, uniting and galvanizing them at a higher level in fights against the enemy.

The majority of the gang members in these groups are Pakistani, but there are at least a couple of Indian and Vietnamese supporters as well. The Pakistanis in the gangs belong to different castes, but the gangs are not divided along caste lines. For example, there is a group of Jat brothers, a group of Raja brothers and cousins, and a group of Gujr brothers in the A-gang. In Pakistan, these castes are endogamous, prohibiting intermarriage between different *biraderies*, also called in Urdu *quom* ("race"), *jati* ("Punjabi"), or *zat*. *Biraderi* comes from the term *bradr*, which means "brother." This implies that the caste conceives of itself as a consanguineous brotherhood, separate from other castes with which it has no bonds of kinship. In Pakistan, cousins are usually deemed preferable friends, as they are perceived as brothers with whom one ought to maintain connections and spend time.

The members of the Big A-gang are also united in a fictive brotherhood construct that extends across blood and caste boundaries. In this sense, they are modern, multicultural, cross-caste oriented and tolerant. They address each other as *bai* ("brother") and speak Punjabi among themselves.

As we see below, there are kinship connections between the two groupings of the Big A-gang, with older members of the Young Guns having younger nephews in the A-gang. There is a kind of generation gap between these two groups. The model in figure 2.1 is based on a container metaphor, but the network structure is also important, as people are connected to each other through team groups and through kinship connections.

The model in figure 2.1 is illustrative of the way connections work, although it does not cover all of the members of the gangs. The gray circles

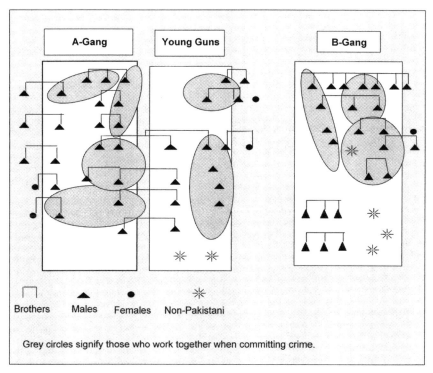

FIGURE 2.1
Structure of the Big A-Gang and B-Gang

show that team groups cut across kinship lines. The importance of team groups in the gang literature has been given too little attention as a basis of loyalty and friendship. The bigger gang units have attracted most of the attention. Transport vehicles (cars with five seats) and the criminal acts themselves are constraints that determine the size of a team in operation. Consequently, not more than three or four people are generally involved in a single crime act. As such, some units share experiences of successful crime acts that are not shared with the rest of the group. Furthermore, within a gang clusters of smaller units can often be in conflict with each other and also with the larger unit.

THE MEANING OF KINSHIP IN THE NETWORK STRUCTURE OF GANGS

Kinship is a durable network structure that lasts for life. In gangs whose structures are mainly based on kinship, other dynamics must maintain durability and ensure recruitment than those found in gang structures based on nonkin affiliations. In the case of the A- and B-gangs, kinship overrides and strengthens participation in the gang structure. For instance, all of Mr. Khan's seven sons are members of the B-gang, and the fact that there are many Khans in the gang has strengthened the position of all brothers from that family. In this sense, kinship confers status in the gang network. It is also important in terms of recruitment, as the brothers joined thanks to links of kinship. In several instances, kinship bonds outside the gang have interfered with intergang relationships. Related brothers and nephews exist as a shadow structure within the gang and can be activated when required. Because of chain migration from some particular villages in Pakistan, clusters of relatives have migrated and established themselves in Oslo. Pakistanis from some villages can have up to four hundred relatives that they identify and interact with frequently. These extensive kinship networks can be drawn into intra- and intergang conflicts. For example, in an internal fight between two members of the A-gang, a so-called nonmember, a taxi driver, was recently beaten up and severely injured because he was the cousin of one of the antagonists. One family member later told the press that the whole *biraderi* of forty people staying in Norway were at risk of being beaten up merely because of their blood relations to the A-gang member. It is this tapestry of interrelations that makes it difficult to delineate the source of a problem and to identify problem ownership (i.e., is it a family problem, a gang problem, or both?). Case 1 illustrates the confusion that can arise.

Case 1

One winter evening in January 2001, four young men were driving into a parking lot in Oslo's old town. These were (1) Asif, a member of the A-gang, (2) his cousin Mumtaz, a taxi driver, (3) Mohammed, a friend and medical student at the University of Oslo, and (4) Ali, a young boy recently arrived from Pakistan.

Entering the parking lot, Asif recognized some members of the B-gang waiting in two cars.

Asif got out of his car carrying an iron rod in his hand because he expected trouble. His cousin Mumtaz, the taxi driver, got worried, so he took his knife with him as he left the car. They all understood that the B-gang men were intent on trouble. Then, Asif discovered that the men were carrying pistols and other weapons. He shouted to his friends to run back to the car.

Left behind and alone, cousin Mumtaz tried to defend himself with his knife, stabbed one of the members of the B-gang twice, then tried to run away. He was shot in the back, and when he turned round, he was shot in the front—he was shot seven times in all. The seven members of the B-gang ran from the place in different directions. Asif returned to the parking lot to pick up his cousin, only to discover he had been shot and killed.

Asif told journalists later that this assault was due to the fact that the B-gang was insulted that he had left their gang and joined the A-gang. He was their intended target, but they shot his cousin instead. Through this murder, however, they had managed to destroy him, he said.

Every day Asif's father, three uncles, two cousins, and some friends sat in court, depressed. They were planning to take revenge, they told me, but at the moment, it was not completely clear who was responsible and which of the groups—the family, the *biraderi,* or the gang—should take action.

This case demonstrates the inadequacy of the container metaphor in shedding light on the way these Pakistani criminal groups work. Asif is connected to both a gang structure and a kinship system. He must demonstrate that he has the ability to defend and avenge his blood relatives as much as his fictive kin, the gang. In the Pakistani context, manhood rests heavily on the kinship structure as relations and connections are hierarchical and the concept of honor demands that a man defend his blood relations. If he does not, he is nothing. Even though some gang members defy their fathers and see them as weak, illiterate, and unable to speak Norwegian, all the same, expressing respect for them publicly is seen as a necessity. "A man who does not respect his father is nothing. When the father is nothing, the son is nothing." The gang structure interacts with the kinship structure in many different ways, and the concept of honor is applied to integrate the two structures at the symbolic level. Brothers and cousins who are not involved in crime and violence become easy targets for the rival gangs as a consequence of being an integral part of the sphere that the honor concept encapsulates for the gang members. Honor for a man revolves around the ability to defend (Black-Michaud 1975), so a man must demonstrate that he has the power and ability to defend blood relatives and fellow gang members. If he does not, he loses honor and respect and is ridiculed. This is why kinship relations become important targets for the enemy. Most murder cases involving the two Pakistani gangs in Oslo have followed a similar pattern where the wrong man, an innocent cousin, uncle, or brother of the intended victim, is shot or stabbed.

This demonstrates part of the problem of delineation and separation of gang from kinship, and it shows that when one person is hit, the honor of the individual gang member, of the gang as a whole, and of the family are all affected. Often, the gang structure encapsulates the family structure, as the words of a mother of three A-gang members illustrate: "We obey their demands. That is our duty." She lived in an apartment that her sons had furnished with modern, very expensive furniture. The illiterate mother was part of a logistic structure around the gang and cooked for both sons and friends and catered to their needs in many ways. Their father, who was ill and illiterate, took daily refuge in the mosque nearby, keeping to his old routines, pretending nothing was wrong. One of the three brothers was in prison, convicted of murder. During a period in which conflicts between the A- and B-gangs were escalating, their father tried to organize arbitration meetings with the parents of the B-gang members and some influential imams and men with *chowdry* (of or relating to the class of landowning men) reputations. However, these efforts to intervene proved unsuccessful.

Much of the literature on gangs stresses the importance of the gang as a substitute family, explaining this as an effect of dysfunctional families that are not tightly knit or have problems in other areas. I will not deny that malfunctioning families can ease children's paths into gangs, but Pakistanis do not make the gang a family substitute. Blood is still thicker than mud, as E. Anderson (1999) has pointed out. Pakistani gang members in Oslo are closely connected within their family network and spend a lot of time there. Indeed, over time, gang membership seems to encompass the whole family in some cases.

Recruitment often results from kinship connections. One member of the B-gang, Omar, told the court at a trial how he had tried to make a serious attempt to study at high school to create a better future for himself instead of following his brothers' example. However, he was constantly beaten up and harassed by older boys from the A-gang who had unfinished business of some kind with his elder brothers, who were members of the B-gang. They attacked Omar as he was the youngest person in the kinship structure and thus the most vulnerable. When he told his brothers at home about the harassment, they were furious and started to plan revenge. In their treatment of Omar, it seems that the A-gang wanted to communicate to the B-gang brothers that they had no honor since they were unable to prevent the bullying of their little brother at school. The need to protect small brothers is one of the reasons why A- and B-gang members hang around elementary and secondary schools as well as youth clubs. Several incidents involving bullying and more serious offenses, such as kidnapping, caused innocent Omar to become a more active participant in the B-gang against his own will. The kinship connections between gang members and the connections to relatives outside need to be highlighted and examined in order to understand the organizational structure of the gangs and their recruitment.

THE GANG IN THE COMMUNITY AND WELFARE STRUCTURE

In his descriptions of Chinese gangs in the United States, Ko-Lin Chin (2001) shows how closely they are tied to the social and economic organization of their communities. The gangs he studied often extort members of their communities, and extortion is also common in Oslo. Some Pakistani shopkeepers, particularly owners of small kebab takeouts, have been victims of extortion. People who have cheated the tax system or committed some paltry offense are especially vulnerable to threats and naturally become less inclined to report problems to the police. Immigrants and refugees in general are often ambivalent toward the system of justice, frequently due to negative experiences with their home country's system or because they have something to hide. Yet, when ethnic communities have gang problems, everybody is affected in some way. Mothers and fathers are afraid their sons will be recruited or become victims of crime and violence. The gang problem creates fear and distrust everywhere, and people start taking the law into their own hands to protect themselves. Codes of honor develop when the agents of the state are rendered impotent in the community.

Honor is a matter of power, morality, and family connections. Elaborating on the link between social structure and morality, A. Blok (2001, 21) argues that personal honor is related to a low level of state formation in the societies where it exists. Survival becomes dependent on the control of resources. Physical force and violence are used to compensate for the lack of a strong state. Men have to make themselves respected, and a moral code of personal and family honor develops as a necessity under conditions of political weakness and insecurity. The irony is that honor codes seem to develop within strong states as well, in pockets of urban cities. The code of the street described by Anderson (1999) within a U.S. city resembles a traditional honor code. The mafia (Elster 1989), neo-Nazi gangs (Bjørgo 1997), motorcycle gangs (Bay 2002), and immigrant gangs in European cities (Lien 2002) abide by various codes of honor that symbolically encompass their organizational structure. The gangs take the law into their own hands for the sake of honor and even try to manipulate their connections to the state institutions and the police, thereby actively weakening the influence and power of these institutions in their neighborhoods.

Honor concerns are the reason why some men in the ethnic community see the system of justice as a competitor, as something it is dishonorable to get mixed up with. This approach to honor characterizes the A- and B-gangs as well. While earning money illegally, they simultaneously see themselves as people who help their family and the community and who can be called upon to rectify wrongs. They compete with both the police and the *chowdries* ("landowning men") in the community. The *chowdries*, their fathers, and their uncles, who back in the villages used to arrange arbitration meetings, now face competition from gang members whose power and respect are derived from their sense of honor and loyalty, as well as their threats, violence, and sheer numbers. As one Pakistani father told me, "We have a huge family with many family members. We can fight the gangs only because we are so many that they dare not insult us. Businessmen with fewer family ties are weaker and more easily targeted by the gangs."

In his analysis of social control and deviance in a Pakistani ethnic community in Edinburgh, Ali Wardak (2000) develops a four-part typology of people based on their strategies for dealing with social control imposed by the community. He calls the first group *conformists*: these individuals make clear distinctions between right and wrong and are obedient to the values of their families and the mosque. The second group is the *accommodists*: these people have adopted a few Western values and made a few situational compromises, but they are basically loyal to the fundamental religious and cultural values of their community. The third group is the *part-time conformists*: these people attend the mosque, make sure that everybody sees them while they are there, then go to nightclubs with Western girlfriends, drink alcohol, and do the things regarded unlawful and *harem* by the community. The fourth group, the *rebels*, is the most deviant in respect of community values. These people want to have fun, enjoy life, and break away from the core values in their ethnic communities. They have become Westernized and act immorally according to community values. Often, they marry Western girls and leave their homes to live apart from their families. Some use drugs and are involved in violence and crime. The parents regard violence and crime to be un-Islamic and therefore a consequence of Western influences.

If we were to apply Wardak's categories to our A- and B-gangs, "part-time conformist" would probably be the best category for most, with the "rebel" label covering the rest. One of the leaders of the A-gang rebelled against the norms of his community and his imam father. He married a Norwegian girl, observed no food or drink injunctions, and turned to Buddhism for a while. The family regarded him as polluted by Western values and his criminal career as a result of this Westernization. However, most members of the Pakistani gangs share the core values of the Pakistani community and take part in religious festivals and ceremonies, visit friends for *afsos*[1] and *khattam*,[2] attend weddings, and visit the mosque once in a while. They combine these Muslim duties with gambling and visiting discotheques and nightclubs, just like the part-time conformists in Wardak's typology. They are well behaved and generous to their supporters, but their supporters fear them as much as they respect them. As one of my informants said, "They are nice to me. People are careful about me because they know that I am a friend of many of them."

Through their legal and illegal activities the gang members are connected to society at large. They have a multitude of connections among the police and in the welfare system, including to youth workers, social workers, teachers, bureaucrats, and even politicians and journalists. They are not marginalized in a conventional way but rather are linked and connected to influential elites. They are even invited to talk with ministry officials about youth problems. For example, in 1989, several of the Young Guns were invited by Minister of Internal Affairs Kjell Borgen to discuss youth policy. Then they were invited for a second time by the next minister, William Engseth, to discuss policy issues related to Oslo. The A- and B-gangs have also negotiated at the town hall together with several local politicians of Norwegian and Pakistani descent. These meetings have been reported in the media.

The gang members have many connections in the media and have taken journalists with them on their rides through the city. They have also invited them to restaurants and given many interviews. Two B-gang members, together with two members of the Hells Angels, were honored guests at a prestigious media conference in Trondheim, Norway (April 6–7, 2002). They have taken part in programs and films shown on television. They are always defended by the best and most proficient lawyers in the country and enjoy close links to them. In one of the areas where they live, the local subcouncil leader took a special interest in them, and a new youth club was opened in the 1980s in an attempt to wean youngsters off gangs.

Gang members have become adept at using these connections to their benefit. In case 2, two boys managed to mobilize both the kinship system and the welfare system in order to escape the police.

Case 2

Once, two men, apparently A-gang members, tried to shoot two other men in a car in the center of Oslo. Nobody was killed. The perpetrators ran off down the street and took refuge in a youth center run by a woman who had worked for years trying to integrate immigrant youths and help delinquent boys out of trouble. She knew these two men from the A-gang and was very happy to see them as, in her opinion, they were charismatic, sympathetic, and charming. Over and over again, she had tried to get them to leave their gang. Now, they were asking her to help them apply for a job because they wanted to start a new life, they explained. And she was so eager to help. She found them a little nervous and wary and quite sweaty. While they were sitting there, impatient and restless, she scanned the Internet for jobs. She was unaware that the police were outside looking in. Her friends told her that they had decided to live a decent life, which made her happy. After a while, they asked to use her phone. They called an uncle to come and fetch them. The uncle came, and they left in a hurry. It took days for the police to find them.

Gang members have connections within the welfare apparatus. They have frequented the youth clubs and know the workers. Sometimes these people become innocent helpers in transactions of which they themselves are unaware. For example, the child-protection authorities wanted to get Imran out of the neighborhood and send him away to another town because he had been involved with so much fighting that he was considered a threat to himself. This was not part of Imran's plans for his life, and he did not want to leave his parents and friends. He complained to a social worker in the youth club, who had a liking for him. She fought the child-protection authorities tooth and nail to help the boy stay in the community. Imran managed to play one part of the system against the other.

The same strategy is used against the police. Young and newly educated policemen often feel insecure when gang members refer to agreements made with officers higher up the chain of command, a ploy they often resort to when stopped in the street. Frequently, knowledge obtained from a long career in the system is used to beat the system, and acquaintances from one part of the system are played against authorities in other parts of the system. Lessons learned from appearances in court and contact with lawyers are used to fight the system and get milder sentences. Gang members have closer and more highly placed connections in the welfare system and know many more experts than other teenagers who have never been in trouble. They use this knowledge to get out of problems and fight the system when needed. Sometimes, one part of the welfare system will act as an advocate for the gang member against other parts eager to pin him down. Gang members have a very ambivalent relationship with agents of the welfare state. On the one hand, they are afraid of both the police and the child-protection authorities. On the other hand, such authorities can be very important to them whenever they get into trouble. One gang leader told me, "I was very careful with the child-protection authorities, and very polite to them. I always get them to do it my way. My friends in the gang are delighted I have this experience because it means we can do our work without interference. I have helped my friends a lot because I know the social worker Birgitte very well."

While normal children or youths have very little contact with lawyers, the social security system, youth workers, or school boards, gang members acquire ties and connections with officials in these systems very early in life. Most members of the society are not connected to the state through lawyers and the social security system and go, instead, through other channels. The route to influential politicians is shorter for many gang members, which may be why the A- and B-gangs are the heroes of many youngsters from immigrant backgrounds in Oslo. The problem is not that the gangs are disconnected from the structures of power and fame; rather, it is that they are too well connected to specific parts of it.

CONCLUSION

Metaphors and definitions are analytical tools used to understand processes in the real world. Different conceptualizations provide us with images we can use to understand processes of interaction. In this chapter, we have seen that the container concept of gangs restricts our understanding of the wider web of connections. The container metaphor probably affects our understanding of marginalization by reducing it to a matter of either/or, inside/outside. Gangs may actually have too many contacts in parts of the system and too few elsewhere. When thinking in terms of networks and connections, we get a mental image of a multitude of intersecting strands constituting a three-dimensional space in which signals are sent in several directions at the same time. Some go underground; others go above. The avocado model of gangs with its hard core and soft periphery contained within a skin is a more stable image and is sometimes very useful, but it needs to be supplemented with a cybernetic multidimensional network model that allows for more contingencies and a broader reach.

The gang structure presented here intersects with (1) the kinship structure and (2) the structure of the community (imams, *chowderies*, friends, and teachers). At the same time, gang members have relations—visible and invisible—with (1) parts of the welfare system through youth workers and social workers; (2) the juridical apparatus (i.e., the police and lawyers); (3) the media through newspaper, radio, and television journalists; (4) politicians; and (5) researchers. They are also connected internationally to their network of relatives in the villages of their parents' home country and often escape to Pakistan when in trouble. Through these connections, they can bridge resources (Fleisher 2002) in their effort to solve their different kinds of problems. It is through the open-ended and wide-ranging network model that we have been able to identify these ties, and in a globalized world, networks will become an increasingly important instrument in the social scientist's bag of conceptual tools.

For the purpose of improving our metaphors, we can fuse the network model with the image of a subway system (e.g., the London Underground). Just as tracks go up into the open, then down underground, sometimes the connections are visible, and sometimes they are invisible. The trains move between stations, which are sometimes busy and sometimes tranquil, uninteresting, and dormant, until suddenly a train arrives, creating a lot of activity and exchanging of goods and services that sparks our attention. Such are the gangs and their connections, visible and invisible, active and passive, sometimes exhibiting a high flow of information and services, sometimes not. The gang's connections are further linked to other hubs of friends, kin, schoolmates, and the welfare system, granting the gang a global extension, even though it is not visible to all.

NOTES

1. These are visits in connection with dead friends and relatives.

2. These are ceremonies held for the dead to improve their chances on Judgment Day. They are arranged forty days after the funeral.

REFERENCES

Anderson, E. 1999. *Code of the street: Decency, violence, and the moral life of the inner city.* New York: W. W. Norton.

Barnes, J. A. 1954. Class and committees in a Norwegian island parish. *Human Relations* 7: 39–59.

Barth, F. 1978. Scale and network in urban Western society. In *Scale and social organization*, ed. F. Barth. Oslo: Universitetsforlaget.

Bay, J. 2002. Honor and revenge in the culture of Danish outlaw bikers. In *Tournament of power: Honor and revenge in the contemporary world*, ed. T. Aase. Aldershot, United Kingdom: Ashgate.

Bjørgo, T. 1997. *Racist and right wing violence in Scandinavia.* Oslo: Tano Aschehoug.

Bjørgo, T., with Yngve Carlsson and Thomas Haaland. 2001. *Generalisert hat—polarisert fellesskap. Om konflikter mellom ungdomsmiljøer i en norsk by.* Oslo: NIBRs Pluss-serie 4.

Black-Michaud, J. 1975. *Cohesive force: Feud in the Mediterranean and the Middle East.* Oxford: Blackwell.

Blok, A. 2001. *Honour and violence.* Cambridge, United Kingdom: Polity.

Bourgois, P. 1996. In search of masculinity: Violence, respect and sexuality among Puerto Rican crack dealers in East Harlem. *British Journal of Criminology* 36 (3).

Chin, K.-L. 2001. Chinese gangs and extortion. In *Modern gang reader*, ed. J. Miller with C. L. Maxson and M. W. Klein, 134–44. Los Angeles: Roxbury Publishing.

Decker, S. H. 2001. The impact of organizational features on gang activities and relationships. In *The Eurogang Paradox: Street gangs and youth groups in the U.S. and Europe*, ed. M. W. Klein, H.-J. Kerner, C. L. Maxson, and E. G. M. Weitekamp. Dordrecht, Netherlands: Kluwer.

Decker, S. H., and B. Van Winkle. 1996. *Life in the gang.* Cambridge: Cambridge University Press.

Elster, J. 1989. *The cement of society.* Cambridge: Cambridge University Press.

Fleisher, M. 2002. Doing field research on diverse gangs: Interpreting youth gangs as social networks. In *Gangs in America*, ed. C. R. Huff. Newbury Park, CA: Sage Publications.

Geertz, C. 1976. From the natives' point of view: On the nature of anthropological understanding. In *Meaning in anthropology*, ed. K. H. Basso and H. A. Selby. Albuquerque, NM: Albuquerque School of American Research.

Grønhaug, R. 1978. Scale as a variable in analysis: Fields in social organization in Herat, Northwest Afghanistan. In *Scale and social organization*, ed. F. Barth. Oslo: Universitetsforlaget.

Hart, H. L. A. 1994 [1961]. *The concept of law.* Oxford: Clarendon Press.

Huff, C. R. 1991. *Gangs in America.* Newbury Park: Sage.

Klein, M. W. 1995. *The American street gang: Its nature, prevalence, and control.* New York: Oxford University Press.

Klein, M. W., H.-J. Kerner, C. L. Maxson, and E. G. M. Weitekamp. 2001. *The Eurogang Paradox: Street gangs and youth groups in the U.S. and Europe.* Dordrecht, Netherlands: Kluwer.

Lakoff, G., and M. Johnson. 1999. *Philosophy in the flesh: The embodied mind and its challenge to Western thought.* New York: Basic Books.

Lien, I.-L. 2002. The dynamics of honor in violence and cultural change. In *Tournament of power: Honor and revenge in the contemporary world*, ed. T. Aase. Aldershot, United Kingdom: Ashgate.

Maxson, C., and M. Klein. 1985. Differences between gang and nongang homicides. *Criminology* 23: 209–22.

Mitchell, J. C. 1969. *Social networks in urban situations.* Manchester, United Kingdom: Manchester University Press.

Sarnecki, J. 2001. *Delinquent networks: Youth co-offending in Stockholm.* Cambridge: Cambridge University Press.

Scott, J. 1991. *Social network analysis.* London: Sage Publications.

Simmel, G. 1968 [1908]. *Soziologie.* Berlin: Dunker and Humbolt.

Vigil, J. D. 1996. Street baptism: Chicano gang initiation. *Human Organization* 55 (2).

———. 2002. *A rainbow of gangs: Street cultures in the mega-city.* Austin: University of Texas Press.

Wardak, A. 2000. Social control and deviance: A South Asian community in Scotland. Aldershot, United Kingdom: Ashgate.

3

An Old-Fashioned Youth Gang in Genoa

UBERTO GATTI, FRANCESCA ANGELINI,
GILBERTO MARENGO, NATALIA MELCHIORRE,
AND MARCELLO SASSO

In Italy, criminologists and psychologists have often observed that juvenile delinquency is frequently a group behavior and that delinquent youths do not usually act alone. According to data published in 1999, of one hundred minors reported to the judicial authorities, 67 percent committed crimes with other people, usually minors. The percentage is higher when we consider just property crime (e.g., theft, robbery).

The mass media publicize the most shocking crimes committed by youth gangs, and there is general concern about juvenile group violence. Public concern also centers on the involvement of juveniles in organized crime, mainly in the south of Italy, and the possible exploitation of minors in Mafia crime. In spite of this social alarm, few empirical studies have been conducted, and no large systematic study has investigated juvenile gangs in Italy.

Some empirical studies have focused on particular kinds of juvenile phenomena, such as violence in sport and hooliganism. According to an ethnographic study on football supporters conducted by A. Dal Lago (1990), hooliganism in Italy seems to be less "deviant" and less violent than in other European countries. Similar results emerged from the studies conducted by A. Francia (1990) and by D. Gaddi and E. Calvanese (1993), who interviewed samples of football supporters. According to A. Roversi (2002), football hooliganism

GATTI, ANGELINI, MARENGO, MELCHIORRE, AND SASSO

is often tinged with political ideology, mainly (but not only) of the extreme right. Another form of youth group deviance that has been investigated is political violence, particularly with regard to the so-called skinheads. Having carried out a participant observation study on Italian skinheads with a violent ideology (e.g., racism, xenophobia), A. Castellani (1994) noted that the phenomenon involved only a small minority of youths.

The Ministry of Justice, Office of Social Services for Minors conducted an investigation aimed at providing an overview of youth gangs in Italy in 2002. To gather information on youths prosecuted along with other codefendants, ministry researchers conducted semistructured telephone interviews with twenty-eight social workers (one for each of the twenty-eight social services offices for minors in the country). They also analyzed the 1999 dossiers of the state prosecutors of the juvenile courts of a few large cities. The analysis was restricted to youths prosecuted together with at least three codefendants for crimes in which no adults had been involved. In reality, this study used the term *gang* to refer to the phenomenon of co-offending minors. Although it took into account the social and family conditions of the youths involved, the study did not consider the gang as an autonomous entity.

Another study that indirectly touched upon the issue of gangs was carried out by A. Dal Lago and E. Quadrelli (2002), within the framework of a broader investigation that used the ethnographic method in order to examine the crime situation in Genoa in the 1970s. By interviewing members of the criminal fraternity, the authors strove, retrospectively, to understand not only the peculiarities of the individuals interviewed (e.g., thieves, prostitutes) but also the mentality that characterized problem neighborhoods. These areas of the city were home to "neighbourhood youth gangs, which in some cases [would] evolve into something more serious," that is, into *microgangs* of two or three members that emerged on the streets and comprised the children of southern Italian immigrants who indulged in fighting with other gangs and committed petty thefts. They hated the police and young people from middle-class neighborhoods, whom they liked to torment. They had a culture of revenge, especially toward anyone who dared to report their crimes to the police, and attached great importance to respect and trust, which were regarded as fundamental values in social relationships. While the investigation carried out by Dal Lago and Quadrelli provides useful information that can help us to understand these 1970s gangs, their questions focused on the criminal careers of individuals, not on the life of a gang.

In Italy, a great deal of research has focused on the issue of the so-called *Coree*, those densely populated urban districts studied by F. Alasia and D. Montaldi (1960) where immigrants from the south came to settle during the years of the industrial boom. However, no studies have dealt with youth gangs in their own right. Moreover, even those researchers who have examined aspects of youth culture (e.g., the music that the young listen to and its underlying meanings) have used the term *gang* as a synonym for *group, gathering, casual company*, or, as we have seen, *co-offenders in crime*.

A. Colombo (1998) carried out an in-depth study of a very particular environment. For a year and a half, he frequented Porta Venezia railway station in Milan, where he interviewed Algerian immigrants, both young and old. As he himself has pointed out, this research was conducted *among*, not *on*, the subjects concerned. By living among them and frequenting their haunts, he was able to construct a very detailed view of their life stories and habits. One of the topics he looked at was the social groupings of these people.

These groups were underpinned by three elements. The first concerned bonds of friendship that had already been forged in their home country, the second regarded relationships founded on their common origin, and the third stemmed from the shared experience of life as an immigrant. These three props, however, are rarely found in their pure form. Often, they occur spuriously, conditioned by the degree of importance that the individual attaches to the group. Once the group has been formed, it confers certain advantages on its members. In addition to providing leisure-time company, it becomes a resource for the individual. A new arrival can exploit the group's experience, and a member who commits a crime can obtain help and reassurance from his companions, thereby suffering less from loneliness or feelings of guilt at having broken the law. While such groups do not have leaders, they do display a strong sense of solidarity toward members who have been arrested, especially if that member's arrest enables the other members of the group to escape arrest. A necessary condition, however, is that this solidarity be negotiated beforehand among the members, given that the group is not a cohesive unit.

The few Italian studies that have approached the subject of youth gangs have not generally examined this phenomenon directly. As such, a considerable gap exists in our knowledge base, and this gap undermines our ability to understand and respond effectively to gangs. This study attempts to begin filling this gap. The definition of a *youth gang* as "any stable, street-oriented youth group whose identity includes involvement in antisocial activity" is generally accepted within the sphere of the Eurogang network (Klein et al. 2001). On the basis of this definition, we identified a number of youth gangs in Genoa. Our aim was to investigate in detail the characteristics and history of one of these, which is active on a housing estate on the northwest outskirts of Genoa.

RESEARCH METHODS

Through our contacts with social workers operating in deprived areas of Genoa, we became aware of the existence of several youth gangs for which social integration programs were being implemented. One of these, which had been known to social workers for many years and was active in the Sperone neighborhood northwest of Genoa, had also been the subject of alarming articles in the local newspapers. Based on this preliminary information, we decided to focus our attention on Sperone youth.

First, we gathered information on the Sperone neighborhood through interviews with functionaries of the municipality and by examining written documents. Subsequently, we interviewed first a social worker who knew the gang well, then other adults selected by means of the "snowball method." These interviewees included other social workers, educators involved in two street-oriented projects, the local parish priest, a former teacher, officers of the carabinieri who policed the area, and the social workers of the Department of Social Services for Minors of the Ministry of Justice. A total of thirteen interviews were conducted, each lasting from forty-five minutes to an hour and a half.

During the same period, interviews were conducted with four of the five stable members of the gang who had for years made up the nucleus around which numerous other youths had gathered in a transitory fashion (the fifth refused to be interviewed), as well as with four transient gang members and three girls linked in some way to the gang. The gang members were picked out and interviewed by an educator who worked in the neighborhood and had gained the trust of these youths. The youths interviewed were between nineteen and twenty-two years old. All had lived in Sperone for many years. The interviewer knew the youths and had a stable relationship with them. The respondents were informed of the purpose of the interview and gave their consent. The interview was semistructured, lasted about an hour, and focused on the history and structure of the gang, the characteristics of its members, their relationship with society, and any deviant behavior or crimes that they had committed. All the interviews, both with adults and youths, were recorded and transcribed.

While not discussed in this chapter, an additional phase of this research project has been planned. A young researcher is currently in contact with the educators working in the neighborhood, and preparations are being made for her to get to know the members of the gang. Once contact and trust has been established, she will undertake a period of participant observation. As of this writing, it is believed that this phase should begin in the next few months.

NEIGHBORHOOD CHARACTERISTICS

As of 2003, the city of Genoa had a population of 620,000, spread somewhat unevenly over an area of about 240 km², mainly comprising a long coastal strip situated between the sea and the mountains and two valleys running perpendicular to it. These geographical features have strongly conditioned the city's urban and socioeconomic development by restricting the space available for expansion and influencing building criteria. The outskirts, unlike those of many other cities, are made up of decentralized urban areas rather than a belt of satellite municipalities.

Construction of the Sperone housing estate, the home turf of the gang that we studied, began in the 1970s in a hilly suburban area in response to the demand for low-cost housing. The pressing need to house a considerable number of people who were under eviction orders led to the building of low-quality residential complexes. The modular approach to the construction of these homes, which involved replicating a basic housing unit many times over, gave rise in some cases to inordinately large, uniform blocks of flats. Even in the planning stage, suspicions were voiced that the resulting climate would be one of anonymity and a scant feeling of belonging on the part of the inhabitants. The total area of Sperone, about 35,000 m², houses about 16,000 people. The hillside location of the estate means that all road access to the 3.5 km of the neighborhood's streets can easily be kept under surveillance. This thwarts control by the police, who are spotted well before they arrive.

For several years, Sperone and other such districts constituted a source of labor for nearby industries. Now, however, in the wake of the deindustrialization process that has affected the entire city, these employment opportunities have dwindled. The impact on the community has been decidedly negative.

Many of the neighborhood's housing complexes are owned by public bodies. Originally, they housed problem families from run-down urban areas. Most of these families consisted of first- and second-generation immigrants from the poor regions of the south of Italy, particularly Calabria and Sicily. Allocation of low-rent public housing was, and still is, based on family income and the size and structure of the family nucleus.

That these families have remained fairly cut off from the rest of the city is highlighted by the strong southern accents heard even among those who were born in Genoa. In the last few years, the number of non–European Union (EU) citizens—from North Africa, Albania, and Romania—has grown, although these are still only a small minority. Many of them squat in flats that are left empty either because they have been deemed unfit for habitation on health grounds—and therefore cannot be allocated—or because ever fewer people are prepared to move into them. Just as the immigrants who arrived in Genoa sixty years ago were met with mistrust, intolerance, and even hostility, today the same reception is given to non-EU citizens and drug (heroin) addicts in Sperone.

The open spaces in the neighborhood mainly consist of unkempt grassy areas, which, here and there, have become rubbish dumps. The remaining areas are asphalted for use by motor traffic. There are no pedestrian areas or walkways. Although a public bus service connects Sperone with the rest of the city, most residents use private motor vehicles. There are no shops, bars, or cinemas, but there is a supermarket and a pharmacy.

The blocks of flats are very large and linear. Dubbed "The Block," the most conspicuous of these is twenty stories high and almost 600m long. The Block is home to the gang members that we interviewed. Inside, a maze of corridors and gangways runs from one end of the block to the other. Teenagers used these passages—even those on the upper floors—as motorcycle tracks until recent structural modifications brought some measure of compartmentalization. Storage areas for tenants are situated on the tenth floor and can be reached through passageways created on the sides of the hills running alongside the building.

At ground level, unfinished, doorless garages are used as a dumping space for unwanted household items and the abandoned carcasses of cars and motorcycles. These spaces also lend themselves to illicit activities. Their poor state of hygiene and maintenance has turned them into a kind of no-man's-land, frequented by the ill intentioned and scrupulously avoided by "normal" residents. The fact that considerable areas of the buildings communicate directly with the outside means that tenants do not take responsibility for them. Consequently, they fall into neglect.

The buildings are designed in such a way that corridors and staircases link the various parts and connect these with the outside. This feature facilitates acts of vandalism and other illicit activities. Moreover, vandalism aggravates problems stemming from the poor quality of the materials used in construction and the difficulty of maintaining the buildings. Elderly residents living on the upper floors or those who have difficulty walking may be effectively confined to their homes because the control panels of the lifts have been vandalized. Staircases and long, tortuous passageways, which are frequently unlit (the lighting system being a favorite target for vandals), present blind spots where malefactors might lurk. Some residents have isolated small groups of contiguous apartments by installing gates or metal grilles (without authorization) in an attempt to keep the vandals out, thereby creating barriers that may prove dangerous in the event of a fire. The risk of fire is hardly a remote one, as particularly deprived families and squatters often improvise devices for heating or cooking.

Living on welfare is so widespread as to be practically the rule. Indeed, in many cases, the Social Services Department has been providing financial support for successive generations of the same family. The rate of unemployment is very high, and the level of education is somewhat low, due in part to the high early dropout rate from school. Many of the families have members with criminal records, some of whom are under house arrest. In short, the neighborhood has a very bad reputation.

YOUTH INTERVIEWS

Through the interviews with the gang members, we were able to glean information both on the life stories of these young people and on the evolution and characteristics of the gang. This information is presented in four categories: history and local setting, group description, individual gang members, and gang culture.

History and Local Setting

This gang has been in existence since 1995, when its members were twelve or thirteen years old. However, the youths have known each other since 1992, when their families were assigned to this public housing project. Relationships with other residents in the neighborhood have never been easy because "we made too much noise in the evening. . . . They looked down on us. . . . We rowed with all of them." In general, the local residents dislike having these youths around on account of their violent behavior and the risk of being targeted for revenge if they report their misdeeds to the police.

Group Description

The gang is composed of two types of members: (1) those who make up the stable nucleus and have stuck together for eight years, and (2) those who remain in the gang for shorter periods and have looser connections. The core is made up of five individuals who have known each other since they were small, went through school together, and spend their free time together. They are linked by a strong bond of affection and regard one another as "friends, those that you can count on the fingers of one hand; the others . . . are all just people you know." About fifteen other young people gravitate around this nucleus, primarily acquaintances, girlfriends, and occasional members who stay in the gang for a few months.

The boys usually hang out in the street or in local bars. They do not have a specific place with which they identify, but they always know where to meet up. Whether they meet at a bar or a mutual-aid society makes no difference. What matters is that it is "a quiet place where nobody gets on your tits." To meet up, they just ask around, "Where's Mauro?" (the leader at the time when the interviews were conducted), then, simply go and join him. The stable nucleus does not vary because a bond of affection links its members. These core members see themselves as loyal (i.e., they would never betray their friends and would be worthy of being "best man at a friend's wedding"). Some concern emerges for the future of these "brothers, even if not in blood." In particular, they are all worried about one member who seems determined to continue along the criminal pathway, while the others express an intention to change their lives, get a job, and raise a family. These youths have shared the experiences of failure at school, family breakdown, and lawbreaking. Their particular relationship is privileged and exclusive. Occasional gang members are ultimately excluded from it, even though they may be temporarily welcomed because of the benefits they bring with them (i.e., a scooter or a helping hand in a crime).

A girlfriend seems to be, in their eyes, a custodian of tradition and future prospects and must therefore be protected. All four of the hard-core members interviewed agree that their girlfriends have brought some order into their lives and enabled them to plan for the future. In the life of the gang, girls figure in only as someone's companion. They never take on a lasting individual role. According to some notion of division of labor, girls do not take part in the commission of crimes. According to the boys, females should be kept out of trouble, unless they are "runaways," and the girls "don't arse around like that." At the most, they might go for a ride in a stolen car. A girlfriend may be one reason why a gang member spends less time with his companions and commits fewer crimes, as his time is spent with her and his life becomes quieter.

The gang has a leader, although no one admits this. On the contrary, all members seem to deny the existence of a dominant figure in the group. When asked if the gang has a leader, all say no. As the conversations continue, however, it becomes apparent that one member is always present, takes the initiative, and is, in effect, the linchpin of the group. Obviously, he is one of the five core members. Another of these five also appears to play a leadership role, although one that involves counseling rather than decision making. The other members of the gang are likely to turn to him for advice or to talk over their personal problems confidentially.

The respondents do not report having intergroup relationships, although they do mention socializing with the individual members of other groups. Likewise, they do not indulge in gang battles, although they do fight with individuals who offend a friend. As one youth explained, "You hit me, right? I go back home all swollen up, and they say 'what happened?' And the team gets together and, like, ten of you go round there and sort it out." They do not travel far from home, frequenting only those districts adjacent to their own. They do not regard Genoa as their city, do not know it well, and show no interest in it. Their point of reference is the Sperone neighborhood, even to the extent that it is hard for them to imagine living elsewhere: "Our friends are here; this is where we hang out. Even if I go and live somewhere else, I'll always come back here. This is where we grew up."

Individual Gang Members

Stable Gang Members: Their families all originate in the south of Italy, particularly Sicily and Calabria, and have disintegrated. Of the four youths interviewed, one has no family (his father died when he was eight years old; his mother, a drug addict, was unable to look after him; his grandmother, who took him in for various periods, had his name removed from the official register of her family members when he reached the age of majority). The other three have parents who are separated. Two of the three live with their mothers, while the other lives with his girlfriend and her family and has a baby daughter. Their fathers are described as workers and friends, but the youths are reluctant to talk about their family backgrounds. We got the impression that they are unwilling to divulge shameful information about their parents. Before moving to Sperone, these families lived in the historical center of Genoa in the years when that part of the city was in its most dilapidated state. All four youths come from deprived families in which the parents work only occasionally. Whenever they have a lot of money in their pockets, it is the result of crime. And they spend it right away.

All four respondents have had dealings with the social services, and one spent some time in a group home for minors with family difficulties. This youth's memory of the group home is quite negative. He describes an environment of solitude and violence from which the only means of escape was to run away. All of the youths look upon social workers as villains who take children away from their families, although those who do their job well are depicted as exceptions to the rule. What they see as lacking in the social services, apart from these exceptional individuals, is a relationship of affection and sincere interest. Educators are seen in a positive light, although they are described as incomprehensible as the youths do not understand why anyone would wish to have a job helping others. They are all particularly fond of one "street" educator and speak of her with affection, which they regard as mutual.

The four youths had disastrous school careers. They all finished middle school, but some did not take a diploma. They do not look upon this as a problem since they see education as unnecessary. They did not accept school rules and, if these were imposed, it was considered to be an injustice. They tend to scorn education, the typical assertion being, "I had a good laugh at school, never used to do a tap."

The interviewees have all been imprisoned, first as minors, then as adults. They describe the juvenile prison as a place where you have to stand up for yourself and hit before being hit because it is important to show that no one can push you around. One of the youths talks about episodes of violence to which he was subjected in the juvenile prison in Turin, where he spent three days in solitary confinement for having set fire to a mattress: "terrible it was. It was winter and I didn't have anything, no blankets, no shoes, no shoelaces. Did three days in there. It was a tiny little room. Even the door was low, made of re-inforced iron. And there was a sort of little toilet next to the wall, a foam rubber mattress on the ground . . . without any blankets, only a pillow. I did three days in there, with half an hour out for a breath of fresh air, on my own though; it was separate air. . . . Three days is a long time." Survival in the adult prison depends on a concept that is well known in the logic of the neighborhood: respect. The inmate not only has to earn respect, but he also must show respect. In this way, he is seen to be "a regular guy." As one youth put it, "You can't just walk in and start throwing your weight around because it's another world in there." Fellow prisoners are described as "good lads" and "all right," and the only non-EU citizens who are accepted are cellmates who are also "all right" and who bring the coffee at eight o'clock in the morning on the first day.

The gang members occasionally work as manual laborers (on building sites or asphalting), and working is perceived as a way of becoming "regular" and abandoning crime. In most cases, this work is unofficial, and the low pay is not enough to live on. Therefore, if they have children to support, they live together with their own family nucleus or that of their companion.

Their criminal activities began very early and are carried out exclusively in the company of the group. One youth talks about their "baby gang," which "started with us, a group of four or five lads" and " did more damage than a hurricane." The group has been involved in theft, robbery, fighting, and even attempted murder. They never use firearms, and only rarely do they use knives or other weapons such as chains, coshes (sticks), or crash helmets. In most cases, their crimes are not planned. For example, "You say, 'Let's go downtown and get something to eat.' Then you see a motorbike and you say 'F— me! I'm having that.' It's not like you go out to get yourself a bike." One crime that they mentioned involved the manipulation of a handicapped person. When they were very young, these youths made fun of a mentally retarded boy, going so far as to make him drink urine. The gang members use various types of drugs, including cannabis, cocaine, ecstasy, and amphetamines, but not heroin. They do not regard themselves as drug addicts.

Transient Gang Members: Four of the youths interviewed associate with the core members of the gang but have never been stable members themselves.

They have shared outings, recreational activities, and occasional holidays with the core members but have never been involved with them in committing crimes, nor have they been prosecuted or detained with them.

These four youths live with their families and are not of southern Italian origin. They do not frequent the core group on a regular basis, either because they have known its members for only a short time or because—like Sandro— they look down on them and aspire to a different social status: "None of the girls I've had belonged to the group. . . . And if you listen to the things they say, they're always going on about football. They smoke joints and they never do nothing; they don't know the score, where it's at."

Sandro describes the gang as a tightly knit group; it is difficult to get into and relatively easy to get expelled from, especially if you show too much interest in someone else's girlfriend. He does not, however, refer to the concept of *shamefulness* as the main cause of ostracism. Gianni does not use the term *shamefulness* either, while Marco and Matteo state that this is the chief reason for expulsion from the gang: "Like you get out of line; you know, you make out with another guy's moll; you shame him somehow." They all agree, however, that to get into the gang, you have to have some relationship with the neighborhood or be linked to the gang members through bonds of family or friendship.

They also agree that women occupy a secondary role: "The girls aren't part of the group; they're your friends' molls, not your friends," says Marco, while Stefano points out that a girl has to be decent and presentable, and that "it's out of order" for a girl to turn up or be invited out for a meal with the boys when no other girls are present.

With regard to dress, the youths stress the importance of having designer clothes, although Sandro scorns this attitude.

These youths do not talk about crimes that they have committed, nor does it appear that they have experienced any form of detention. Moreover, they do not see drug addiction as warranting ostracism; indeed, they have a much more tolerant attitude than the stable gang members toward Mauro, a former stable member who got hooked on drugs and who is now doing time for theft. They do not condemn him for his addiction, and, unlike the core members of the gang, who have abandoned their former companion, they continue to write to him in prison.

These youths also see violence as a legitimate means of meting out justice for wrongdoing, although their attitude is not nearly so harsh as that of the core gang members or the girls.

Girls: The three girls interviewed are linked to the gang members by bonds of affection. One is twenty-seven years old and the other two are nineteen years old. Two live with their partners, while the third is living with her parents while her boyfriend serves a few months' imprisonment for theft. She has a baby of a few months.

Donata depicts the gang in the same way as the boys do with regard to shamefulness, drugs, and the role of women: "They go over the top with this 'shamefulness' business. They show respect, but sometimes it's like they think they're in Sicily, in the Mafia. . . . Anyone who takes drugs has got no respect for anyone. Junkies are weaklings." Women take second place to men. To use Donata's definition, a woman is "a cow," who has to be defended from the at tentions of outsiders, by means of violence if need be. "The girls chase after them [the male gang members]. Sometimes they ride round in stolen cars with them. They follow them around. Sometimes fights start because someone starts pestering one of the girls. It's like I'm there dancing and some guy comes up to me, and even if my boyfriend's not there, one of the lads lets fly. It's this group thing, like they've got to stick together."

Donata points out that within the group it is not really possible to lead an independent life: the group provides important bonds, the neighborhood identity is very strong, and the southern Italian origin of the members' parents is deeply rooted: "You can have friends who are not part of the group, but you always tend to go back to your original group. . . . They have the southern code. It's a life code for us. . . . There's this culture of vendetta. . . . They're vindictive, and they talk about how they can take revenge."

As for relationships with the neighborhood, the members of the gang are described as being persecuted, stigmatized for their past mistakes. "The local residents are hostile towards the gang. They see this group as a bunch of criminals. They see you as what you've done; even if you've changed, you're marked."

Francesca, the girlfriend of Mauro, the ex-leader of the gang, also stresses the moral code of vendetta and the importance of shamefulness as a reason for expulsion from the group: "You can't be shameful, otherwise anyone can do what they like. You get your own back; that's what's at the bottom of everything. . . . There's loyalty and defense. I mean, you're out dancing and one of the boys gets into a spot of bother and the others all jump in. No one says, like, 'You shouldn't do that.' . . . To get into the gang, you've got to be someone's girl." Francesca has not associated with the Sperone gang for some months now since her boyfriend was imprisoned for theft and, especially, since he became a heroin addict: "I don't hang round with them now because my boyfriend's not there any more. He left them when he started to shoot up. He split and took up with people like himself. . . . When you get sent down, you get cut off, but when you come out they all come round to see you."

Francesca also reports that there are various reasons for expulsion from the gang: "If you're a man, it's because you're not like them, or because you've done something shameful; you've behaved badly." When talking about crime, Francesca is very precise in her use of juridical terminology. She does not, however, appear to regard violence as aggravating the crime: "crimes committed: theft, grievous bodily harm. . . . There's no violence; someone being robbed might put up a fight, so he gets hit."

By contrast, Monica is very reluctant to speak during the interview; she is afraid that by speaking frankly to the interviewer she might be accused of shamefulness. Nevertheless, it emerges from her account that there is another gang in an adjacent neighborhood that is rather different from the Sperone gang; the members' families are not of southern Italian origin, and they do not have a moral code typical of the Mafia culture. She claims that it is much easier to join or leave this other gang and that girls are not treated as inferior beings. The gang members from the adjacent neighborhood fear the Sperone gang, which they regard as very violent.

The girls are more reserved than their male counterparts, and very little of their personal history comes to light. One thing that does emerge from the accounts of all three girls, however, is that they all ran away from home several times at an early age and, after absconding, were put up by friends or stayed in community homes.

Gang Culture

As a bond of "affection" links these youths, there are no rites of initiation to the gang or typical behaviors. However, anyone who brings shame on himself will be expelled from the gang. All of the respondents agree as to what this means: shameful behavior is betraying a companion. They give the following example: "Like, maybe you do something with someone else and you get nicked. And then you squeal, and so, the other fellow gets nicked as well. It's just not on because if you thieve, you know, rob, like, if you choose that way of life, you've got to stick to the rules. That's the way it is. If you come to Sperone, that's the way they all look at it." Anyone who is guilty of this sort of treachery will be ostracized. No one will have anything more to do with him because he has broken a rule not only of the group but also of the community. However, the son of a "traitor" will not be blamed for the sins of his father unless he himself commits an act of treachery, in which case people will immediately say "It's in the blood." The use of violence to settle a score is quite normal. If a neighbor reports you to the police or a companion tries to take your girl, violence is justified. The degree of aggression, however, will vary in proportion to the trust you had in the traitor. If someone has reported you to the police, you burn his car. If someone tries to take your girl, you "kneecap" him.

The gang does not have particular symbols or badges. The members listen to both "techno" music and Neapolitan songs. They hate the police, whom they regard as unprincipled aliens. The state police, like the municipal police and the carabinieri, are considered to be violent and ill mannered, practically delinquents in uniform. They believe in God but do not practice their religion, although all claim that they would get married in church.

ADULT INTERVIEWS

From the interviews conducted with the social workers, parish priest, and carabinieri officers, an image of the gang emerges that only partially corresponds to the accounts given by the youths. The adults report that a gang has existed for several years, that it formed in the Sperone neighborhood, and that it has about thirty members, all of whom are Italian. The members used to meet up in a local bar, but after a time, were turned away because of the disturbance that they caused. All of the places that they frequent suffer acts of vandalism. While the youths report that gang membership is stable and reject the hypothesis that new, young members might be admitted, the social workers claim that in recent years the number of members has fluctuated. Moreover, they report that a group of five youths, four male and one female, has split off from the main gang and now behaves as a separate entity.

There is complete agreement between the two groups of respondents with regard to the geographical origin of the youths' families, their previous residence in the historical center of Genoa and in Biscione (a public housing estate on the hills behind the city), and the problems that they currently face. The adult respondents, however, add that at least one parent of each of these youths has been in trouble with the law or has been imprisoned. According to the carabinieri officers, almost 90 percent of the families in Sperone have a member with a criminal record.

Many youths have a long history of contact with the Social Services Department, often culminating in commitment to a group home. According to the social workers, the youths perceive this institution as a prison for children taken away from their parents from which they must escape. This impression is confirmed by one youth's account of his experience in a community home: "I was sent there when I was 15. . . . When I went for the interview, I was told it was another thing altogether. . . . I wanted to get out. I remember one of those educators, a right junkie he was as well. Went off his head, he did. Came at me, started slapping me around because I told him to f—— off because I wanted to get out. I mean it's like they follow you around all the time, even when you go for a piss. Anyway, I got this piece of iron from the workshop and hid it down my trousers. And that night, I broke the lock off the bathroom door, got away, and came back here. But that fellow, I would have loved to work out on him. It's okay for them to say 'come here, go there, do this, do that', but they don't understand that when I come out of there, I'm worse than when I went in."

Since families in Sperone tend to be large, many minors live in the neighborhood. Often, the younger ones are kept under control by their older siblings. The parents work from time to time. Fathers do the same kinds of jobs as their sons, while mothers work as home helps or assist the elderly. Our adult respondents point out that the youths often talk about their siblings but rarely about their parents. One educator claims that the physical absence of the father and the inadequacy of the mother in these families give rise to a great deal of confusion with regard to parental roles. Indeed, it is often the older siblings who lay down the rules for the younger ones to follow. This leads to enormous contradictions since they punish the younger ones for committing offenses, while committing similar offenses themselves. When the father is living at home, his is the main voice of authority. The problem, however, lies in the lack of continuity. After a month or so at home, the father is likely to disappear, either because he has been arrested or because he is on the run from the police. The mother is usually incapable of curbing the disorderly behavior of her children, either because she herself stays out late and does not have fixed hours or because she is resigned to the fact that her son will get into trouble with the law, just like her husband and brothers. In the most serious cases, it is alcohol that destroys the life of the family. Many couples in Sperone share this problem, often accompanied by drug abuse. Domestic violence frequently ensues. However, the signs of maltreatment are rarely seen on children. Likewise, it is very unusual for cases of sexual abuse to come to light.

Regardless of their problems, all of the youths are closely bound to their families. Indeed, they will tell the social services nothing about their parents that might be perceived as jeopardizing the family unit. Moreover, it is noteworthy that all the youths placed in communities choose to return to their families as soon as they reach the age of majority.

Almost all the youngsters in Sperone have difficulty at school, in part because the school fails to take much interest in them. In the upper middle school, they usually have to repeat one or more school years, and teachers tend to encourage them to stay at home on the grounds that they can take the middle school final exams in a private institution. Indeed, many of them obtain their middle school diploma only after taking the one-hundred-fifty-hour courses run by the municipality. Their participation in these courses is not, however, entirely welcome in that it tends to put off the highly motivated adults, often non-EU citizens, for whom the courses are designed. Hardly any of these youngsters enroll in high school.

The parish priest reports that many families are economically deprived and are provided with handouts from the parish "food counter." Many also receive assistance in paying their daily bills. Another indicator of the poverty and deprivation of this neighborhood is that squatters sometimes occupy vacant properties. These are often young couples who move into these flats and turn to the parish for help.

The adult respondents claim that the gang has a leader, who is replaced by a deputy in the event of arrest or imprisonment. Having been arrested, the leader may well continue to be present in the minds of the members, although the gang is destabilized by his absence and does not make decisions. This view conflicts with the accounts given by the gang members, who deny that the gang has a leader and do not mention any feeling of disorientation resulting from the arrest or imprisonment of any given member.

Girls play only a marginal role within the gang. They figure in as someone's girlfriend and are ready to defend their positions against outsiders. In attempting to understand how women are seen in Sperone, we came across conflicting opinions. It is agreed that their level of education is generally higher than that of males (all obtain a middle school diploma and many enroll in high school). However, while the educators reported that they have little freedom of movement and are not allowed out of the sight of their father and brothers, the parish priest noticed no difference in comparison with other young women of the same age. The social worker who runs support activities for girls in the neighborhood claimed that only boyish girls who owned scooters were considered worthy of respect, as they were perceived as males. Almost all of the boys have girlfriends, but never the same girl for long, and they speak of their girlfriends as sex objects. Conversely, a serious view of the couple emerges from the interviews with the youths. They never talk to the social workers about sexual matters or about diseases such as AIDS. It is taken for granted that the girls they frequent, being members of the group, cannot have contracted such diseases.

According to the adults, while there do not seem to be any rites of initiation into the gang, entry usually follows a sort of apprenticeship in the neighborhood's "baby gangs." The accounts given by the youths themselves, however, do not report any movement from a younger to an older gang. What they depict instead is the evolution over time of a stable nucleus that does not admit new members. Why a gang member might be expelled from the gang is not completely clear to the adults, although they all know the youths use the label "shameful" to identify those who are not wanted. The youths have a clear idea of what this label means. Indeed, the notion of shameful is understood in the whole neighborhood and is probably rooted in the cultural traditions of some areas of southern Italy.

According to the social workers, when a member of the gang is arrested, the rest of the group has to come to terms with the loss. If the period of detention is short, that member is not stigmatized as a deviant. If, however, the period of detention is longer, the arrested member will be perceived as a deviant and lose the respect of those who have never been incarcerated. The youths disagree. They say that arrest and detention do not undermine respect; rather, they are seen as a normal part of life. When a companion is released from prison, his fellow gang members will call in to see him. When he is in prison, it is their duty to write to him and to visit him. In their jargon, being imprisoned is referred to as "taking a holiday."

The youths' relationship with drugs is ambiguous. Cocaine is accepted, although its use is limited by its cost, while ecstasy and cannabis are frequently used with no perception of risk. Only heroin is regarded as addictive and is shunned. Heroin addicts are despised and ostracized unless personally known to the gang members, in which case, they are pitied. Although no one in the neighborhood seems to admit to using heroin, discarded syringes are commonplace.

The gang occasionally clashes with other groups, although members have friendly relations with the gangs from nearby neighborhoods, some of whose members are related to them. The parish priest claimed that gang fights are a thing of the past, and by and large, the gang members agreed. Fights are more common between individual members of different gangs who have some score to settle. In such cases, the offended party will explain to the leader of the offender's gang why he is seeking redress. If the leader judges that the complaint is justified, he will forbid the other members of the gang from joining in to defend their companion, and the two contenders will settle the matter. Violence is therefore a fundamental element in settling disputes and, as such, is in line with the Mafia-style code of conduct. Anyone who does not conform to this logic will be deemed shameful. Episodes of violence also take place outside the context of the gang, either for fun or for revenge. The parish priest mentioned some acts of violence against people and property, especially cases in which cars have been torched in order to punish people who have made complaints.

The gang does not seem to have any characteristic symbols or behaviors. The members' dress and the music they listen to are the same as those encountered in other deprived neighborhoods of the city. This prompts the social workers to believe that the youths do not see themselves as a gang but rather as a group of young people who have known each other for a long time and are bound together by shared experiences. The social workers claim that if these youths saw themselves as a gang, they would be able to list the members of that gang, while in reality they cannot do so. This assertion conflicts with the accounts given by the youths themselves, all four of whom counted and identified the same individuals as members.

Almost all of the youths own a motorcycle or scooter. Few have a car, as learning to drive and taking the driving test is fairly costly. Motorcycles and scooters are also associated with various offenses, such as underage driving, number-plate forgery, and the theft of spare parts, either for their own machines or to sell.

The social workers claim that the main interest of these youths is attracting the attention of the press in whatever way they can. The educators and the youths themselves disagree with this view. They also show an interest in "fashionable" clothes and Play Stations. It is not clear whether the youths have a characteristic language, although the interviewees mention certain typical expressions that they use.

The gang hangs out in the neighborhood but moves around out of necessity. Many of the locales that members used to frequent have closed down because of their presence. Others, including the discotheques nearest to Sperone, have barred them on account of their violent behavior.

Many members of the gang do odd jobs, mostly moonlighting, in the building industry or with relatives or acquaintances. They find it hard to hold down a steady job and often change employers. They do not have precise plans for the future and rarely save any of what they earn. Indeed, the desire to spend more than they earn often leads them into crime. This does not mean that all the gang members see themselves as deviants. Within the gang, some members have the reputation of being more delinquent than others, especially if they have been in prison, while some see themselves as normal youths. Even if they have a job, they all commit thefts, either for fun or to show off. Some commit more serious crimes, such as breaking and entering, robbery, and offenses against the person. Their ethical code demands that younger kids be defended and condemns sexual violence.

The gang has a deviant group identity because deviance is their rule, although they are aware that different lifestyles exist outside their neighborhood. They perceive the city of Genoa as remote from them. Indeed, during the G8 Economic Summit demonstrations in the city, few of them thought about what was happening and why. They do not practice any sports or attend any gymnasiums, although they tend to be physically strong as a result of their occasional manual labor.

In the opinion of the social workers, they do not have any political convictions (few understand the difference between "right" and "left"), they do not support any football team, and they have no religious faith, although all have taken their first communion. This view partly conflicts with the youths' own accounts. Indeed, during the interviews, they claimed that they supported a football team and went to the stadium to watch football matches. Moreover, two of them said that they believed in God, and all claimed that they would get married in church. They are superstitious and believe in ghosts. They hate squatters, punkish vagrants, foreigners, and homosexuals, although they accept lesbians. It is very difficult to organize any kind of activity with these youths as they are unwilling to participate or to make suggestions of their own.

The social workers claim that the gang members look upon officers of the police and carabinieri differently. The police are seen as "cops" and are despised, while the carabinieri are known and respected. Indeed, calling someone "marshal" (a carabinieri rank) is a sign of esteem. This difference did not emerge from the interviews with the gang members, who say that they hate both.

The relationship with other residents in the neighborhood seems to be one of conflict. Although the social workers claim that the neighborhood residents have a high threshold of tolerance, which stems from the fact that many of them are related to the gang members, the parish priest asserts that they are exasperated and intimidated, afraid to complain lest their cars be set on fire. Sperone is seen as a dangerous place, and anyone who can get out does so. This means that only the most deprived remain. The social workers report that many families have moved to Sperone from the historical center of Genoa. By contrast, the parish priest claims that families who can afford to do so are moving from Sperone to the historical center, which is perceived as safer and more integrated into the life of the city. This apparent contradiction, however, can be explained by the fact that Genoa's historical center has recently undergone vigorous restoration. The exodus from this area has left many flats empty, some of which squatters now occupy.

In addition to the gang in question, three gangs of twelve- to seventeen-year-olds have been identified in the neighborhood by social workers. These kids see themselves as deviants, and belonging to a gang is both a demonstration of strength and a means of acquiring an identity. In this respect, they are following the example of their elder brothers. These three gangs are composed of both boys and girls. The situation of these kids is practically identical to that of the members of the main gang examined. They come from problem families, drop out of school, and take the municipality's one-hundred-fifty-hour course in order to get their middle school diplomas. Unlike their older counterparts, who tend to spend their time in bars, the younger ones hang around the streets, which they regard as their exclusive domain. They commit acts of vandalism and annoy local residents. As they do not go to school, they keep different hours than those of kids the same age, going to bed and getting up much later, even compared to others in their neighborhood, where children of six or seven years of age can be seen in the streets as late as 11:30 p.m. Most of their time is spent doing nothing, in spite of the social workers' attempts to involve them in various activities. The Workshop, a center run by educators, is attended fairly regularly by fourteen- to sixteen-year-olds, who have twice stolen the tools as a reprisal (according to the educators) for some perceived offense.

INTERVENTION PROGRAMS

The Municipal Social Services Department has social workers and psychologists in Sperone who deal with problem minors and their families. Moreover, the Social Services Department of the Juvenile Court deals with minors who commit crimes. In addition to these basic services, the municipality has organized a range of programs aimed at the Sperone neighborhood, some of which have involved the members of the youth gang under examination. The Sperone Project, which began in November 2001, encompasses a number of programs aimed at assisting local residents. These include activities for children from broken homes who spend their time hanging around the streets. The aim of the project is to integrate resources and services in order to respond to the needs of the neighborhood, the idea being to implement intervention that has social, educational, and economic ramifications. The street educators are a fundamental resource in understanding the needs of the residents of Sperone. These are professionals who move around the area and have direct contact with the youth population.

The Workshop is a meeting point for adolescents and preadolescents, where kids can tinker with motorbikes and learn the basics of mechanics. In the last two years, it has become a place for spontaneous discussion, where minors can talk informally about subjects such as drugs and the need to respect the law and where they can fix their scooters without having to steal the necessary spare parts. It is frequented by minors aged twelve to eighteen years— the ages at which kids begin to form gangs and commit their first crimes. The Workshop has served its purpose of creating a relationship of trust between educators and minors. At the same time, however, it has highlighted the difficulty of penetrating gang dynamics. Indeed, the youths tend to protect the educators by keeping them in the dark about any crimes that have been committed. In line with the Mafia mentality that permeates Sperone, it is safer to know nothing.

The Occupati Project was created in response to the need for work and for local residents to regain possession of areas belonging to the community but long since abandoned. Work groups were drawn up to clean and restore communal areas, funds were allocated, and training courses were organized for local residents, who often complain that there is no work but do nothing to find it. One of the problems encountered by this project has been the large number of participants in the courses who have dropped out after only a few sessions, thereby hampering the creation of a stable work group. The project also provided gang members with various work grants consisting of payments in return for temporary work. The youths accepted these work grants and, according to the social workers' reports, completed the agreed period of work.

The Youth-Adult Group meets every evening from 9:30 p.m. to 12 a.m. Its activities are, of necessity, very flexible in that the venue sometimes changes and imprisonment takes its toll on attendance. The educators who participate in these meetings try to organize miniprojects with the youths, such as football tournaments or making a video about life in the neighborhood. During the meetings, the participants also discuss subjects such as the prevention of sexually transmitted diseases and the need to respect the law. In addition, issues such as delinquency and imprisonment are examined in informal meetings. Overall, the program attempts to foster a different way of thinking and living from that of delinquency and deprivation. This is an extremely elusive objective, as crime appears to be the rule rather than the exception in Sperone. The program's ability to achieve its goal is further hampered by the fact that it is difficult to organize any structured activity with these youths—even a football tournament.

Having worked in the field for two years, the social workers interviewed stressed how useful these projects are in creating a space for dialog and in raising awareness of an alternative to marginalization. The question arises, however, as to how far these projects have actually influenced the socialization of these youths. Then again, it must be borne in mind that the Sperone neighborhood is fraught with economic and social problems that are difficult to solve. It is therefore understandable that limited intervention in the lives of minors may yield some positive results while not providing a definitive solution.

THE PRESS IMAGE

In order to understand how the local press depicts the youths of Sperone to its readers, we examined all the issues of a local daily newspaper, *Il Secolo XIX*, published between April 2002 and March 2003. Ten articles from that period mention the Sperone gang, seven reporting the gang's involvement in fights and beatings and three dealing with the deprivation of the neighborhood's residents. In all of the articles, terms such as *gang* or *mob* are used in reference to the group. The newspaper portrays these youths as thugs from Sperone and the adjacent neighborhood who hang around the Baprix shopping center on the outskirts of the city, where they threaten or beat up other young people.

In one article, printed on April 22, 2002, under the headline "Mob Bent on Killing," the journalist clearly sets out to shock the public in his report of a case of attempted murder: "If he hadn't freed himself in time, they would have killed him. They would have thrown him from the seventh floor if he hadn't managed to hook his arm around the railings. There were ten of them, nearly all minors; ten kids against one young man. Savagely beaten because he complained about the din made by his noisy young neighbors; lifted bodily and thrust over the balcony. It happened in Via Verdi, in Sperone." The depiction is one of a bloodthirsty mob, and the article is accompanied by a photograph of three youths beating a fourth with sticks (reminiscent of Stanley Kubrick's *A Clockwork Orange*).

Two subsequent articles report on beatings meted out by the gang, and a third recounts the desperation of an elderly man who threatened gang members with a pistol. On October 10, 2002, the headline reads, "16-Year-Old Savagely Beaten by Baprix Mob." In this article, the gang members are described as kids without an interest, who roam the Baprix shopping center looking for trouble. On the same page, we read, "Sperone gang in action between Baprix and Via Guri," which reports that the police are looking for youths who are spreading fear throughout the neighborhood. A week later, a half-page article entitled "The Forgotten Tower Blocks. Desperate Tenants Write to Mayor" describes the very real problems afflicting the "Dike" and claims that the neighborhood's distress is chiefly caused by young "hooligans" who turn the lifts in the tower blocks into "lifts to hell." The story features an elderly man who, having survived a plane crash and the Vietnam War, refuses to surrender to the fury of the gang, which is depicted as an even greater threat. In the last of these articles, dated March 9, 2003, ample space is devoted to the problems of Sperone. This time, however, it is not only the youth gangs who cause trouble but also foreign immigrants, who squat in empty flats and dirty the landings and staircases, while the police stand idly by.

These articles paint a very different picture from that which emerges from the interviews with the youths. The youths' accounts describe thefts and occasional fights with other groups, emphasizing that they are chiefly involved in property crimes. Our interviews certainly do not evoke the image of a "gang one step away from murder" against which vigilante patrols need to be organized. The newspaper articles depict violence as a characteristic feature of the group. By contrast, it appears from the interviews that violence is used as a means of righting wrongs. The youths make no mention of roaming around in the afternoons looking for fights. On the contrary, their free time is spent with girlfriends or kicking a football around. Crimes are usually committed in the evenings, when they go out to steal cars or motorbikes.

In addition, all of the articles refer to a single gang. Clearly, however, the episodes reported involve various youth gangs. Moreover, the newspapers only focus on the strikingly violent aspects of these gangs, without investigating the complex social situation of the youths involved.

CONCLUSION

The various sources of information yielded a fairly detailed picture of the Sperone gang. The gang's characteristics and activities are well described in the interviews with the gang members, whose statements are partially confirmed by the adult respondents. By contrast, the picture painted by the newspapers appears to be somewhat distorted and sensationalized.

The gang that we examined is rather different from the gangs of young North African or Latin American immigrants that more frequently come to the public's attention. Indeed, the Sperone gang displays close connections with the culture of immigrants from southern Italy. Their values, habits, and language are very traditional, rooted in the original culture of their families. These youths share their families' sense of honor, code of secrecy, old-fashioned view of women, and hostility toward foreigners. The culture of the gang that we examined appears to stem from a sort of spatial and cultural isolation, a tendency to remain within the confines of one's own neighborhood, making it difficult to assimilate new values and attitudes. Although this group has no name and no particular badge of recognition, it can be regarded unequivocally as a gang in that it fulfils the criteria adopted by the Eurogang network. Having been in existence for eight years, it is a stable youth group that habitually gathers in the street and whose identity encompasses illegal activities, which are carried out with a certain frequency and constitute a characteristic feature of the group itself.

The bond that unites the members of the gang has strong connotations of affection and seems to be a kind of response to the family deprivation that they have all suffered. Rather than being a means of survival in a hostile environment, the gang seems to provide a way of filling the void in the family. Thus, it appears that affective ties are more important for this group than instrumental ties, which have been emphasized elsewhere in the gang literature.

The image of the Sperone gang is, in some respects, similar to that of the youth gangs described in U.S. studies, although significant differences can also be seen. The research conducted by M. Zatz and E. Portillos (2000) on gangs in South Phoenix, for instance, reveals that the gangs form primarily as a result of rivalries between Chicanos and Mexicans and as a means of protecting the community, since the police are considered to be totally inadequate. In this context, gangs are multigenerational. Even grandfathers report having belonged to gangs in their younger days, although they tend to define them as "good gangs" because they used chains instead of guns. While local men tend not to regard gangs as a problem, the women have formed a group called Mothers against Gangs in the wake of the killing of a few youths in gang clashes. As mentioned earlier, the Sperone neighborhood is one of the poorest areas of Genoa and is inhabited mainly by immigrants from southern Italy who moved to the northern cities during the period of industrial expansion. The families living in Sperone are mainly Sicilian and Calabrian and, partly as a result of the neighborhood's geographically isolated position, they tend to maintain their original culture, including its negative aspects. The concept of shame, the culture of honor, the code of secrecy (which is seen as a fundamental value), and the accent of these young people all belong to the south of Italy. The impression is that in this part of Genoa, nothing has changed since the first southerners arrived. Moreover, while not reaching the levels seen in the United States, violence and the culture of vendetta govern relationships among individuals, who are classified as either honorable or shameful. In Sperone as in South Phoenix, the police are looked upon as purveyors of violence hiding behind a uniform, even though no one has ever been killed in clashes with the police in Sperone. As in South Phoenix, women in Sperone have formed an association, although in their case, the main aim is to restore dilapidated buildings.

For the purposes of our analysis, the conclusions that emerged from the participant observation conducted over ten years by M. S. Jankowski (1991) are of interest. Having frequented thirty-seven gangs in Los Angeles, Boston, and New York, Jankowski puts forward various hypotheses to explain why youths join gangs. His analysis considers the relationships between the individual and the gang, the relationships between the gang and the community, and the gang as an organization. Starting from the assumption that living in a deprived community involves competing for scarce resources, Jankowski suggests that cooperation can increase the chances of success. The gang therefore emerges as a quasiprivate (not open to all), quasisecret social system governed by a leadership but without a bureaucracy. He lists six reasons for joining a gang, which are based on the individual's perception of increased success.

However, when we consider what prompted the youths of Sperone to form a gang, only one answer springs to mind: compensation for the common experiences of familial, economic, and social deprivation. Indeed, not only do all these youths come from southern Italian families but they also share similar problems of family breakdown, failure at school, and a history of property offenses. Their common history, southern culture, and sense of friendship have bound them together. In Sperone, everyone steals: "Straightaway, when you're a kid, like about fourteen, in our situation at least. Practically all the kids in Sperone do. You know, like, just for a laugh. Like you've got this scooter, so you go and knock off spare parts. Or else, what we used to do a lot, we used to pinch two or three cars and go racing up and down the hills. You know, just for kicks." Moreover, everyone in Sperone is familiar with the concept of shame: "When you come to a place like Sperone, everyone thinks like that." Alternative lifestyles can, however, be envisioned. Some manage to get a steady job, while others continue to break the law and frequently end up in prison.

In many respects, the Sperone gang does not fit the pattern described by Jankowski. Its members tend to break the law in random groups and do not use the gang directly as an instrument for committing crimes. Moreover, we cannot interpret their delinquent behavior as a desire either to conform to or to break with family tradition (although all of the youths interviewed would like their own children to have a different life). Nor does being in the gang offer them anonymity. In fact, the only features of Jankowski's pattern that can be discerned in the membership of the Sperone gang are the need for physical protection (since the gang helps its members to settle scores) and entertainment. This is a far cry from Jankowski's hypothesis of a contract of mutual need between the individual and the gang.

What emerges from the interviews with the Sperone youths is that their gang is characterized by the value of honor and the repudiation of shame. Their relationships and lifestyle are governed by a code of behavior that has been imported intact from the south of Italy by their parents and resembles the Mafia code. In a study of the informal rules governing relationships among members of some American gangs, E. Anderson (1994) notes that the use of violence in response to provocation is a fundamental norm. This code seems to stem from a deep-seated mistrust of the police and the judicial system and constitutes a sort of homemade justice. Families are headed by a single parent, usually a very young mother, who uses physical violence to solve conflicts and frequently leaves the children to their own devices for long periods. Thus, children learn at an early age that they have to look after themselves. They have no rules regarding what time to come home and end up spending most of their time on the streets. They learn to fight, often encouraged by their elders, who teach them that fear and passivity are wrong. By the time they are teenagers, they have assimilated this system of alternative norms and attach great importance to respect and virility, which are regarded as essential to survival. Having a gun, taking someone else's girl, and being the first to strike in a fight are trophies to be displayed proudly. Yet, committing crimes is not merely a show of strength but also a necessity in the face of unemployment.

The Sperone youths, however, often work. Moreover, they regard trying to steal someone else's girl as dishonorable behavior, and the betrayed boyfriend is called upon to reestablish order by teaching the interloper a lesson. One youth justifies the behavior of one of his friends who beat up another youth for trying to steal his girl: "He deserved it. I mean, going round with another guy's girl. That sort of thing doesn't go down well round here. I mean, when you see your girl with another guy, you just go off your head, don't you?"

The studies that seem best to explain the origin and dynamics of the gang that we observed are those that highlight the relationship between delinquency and the lack of so-called social capital (McCarthy, Hagan, and Martin

2002). According to this perspective, when the family is incapable of providing guidance and protection, the individual will look to the street environment for relationships of trust and understanding, which are seen as a resource. This is the condition of homeless youths who, bereft of family bonds, construct surrogate relationships in order to protect themselves and to stave off loneliness. The research conducted by B. McCarthy et al. (2002) among homeless young people in Toronto and Vancouver reveals the importance of having a nucleus that the individual can trust, a group with whom to establish relationships, which can be exploited as a resource. The gang is therefore perceived as offering advantages and protection in a dangerous neighborhood. When a youth joins a gang, the likelihood of his becoming a victim of crime diminishes since he can trust the members of his own gang to protect him against rival gangs. In this respect, the gang becomes an alternative source of social capital, a substitute for the legitimate source, the family. The Genoese gang that we examined appears to constitute a form of social capital that makes up for the shortcomings of the family. Rather than being used as a protection against danger, however, this social capital seems to be exploited as a source of support, friendship, shared values, and acceptance in an environment in which social esteem is difficult to achieve.

REFERENCES

Alasia, F., and D. Montaldi. 1960. *Milano corea*. Milan, Italy: Feltrinelli.

Anderson, E. 1994. *The code of the street: Decency, violence and moral life of the inner city*. New York: Norton.

Castellani, A. 1994. *Senza chioma né legge. Skins Italiani*. Rome: Manifestolibri.

Colombo, A. 1998. *Etnografia di un'economia clandestina. Immigrati algerini a Milano*. Bologna, Italy: Il Mulino.

Dal Lago, A. 1990. *Descrizione di una battaglia. I rituali del calcio*. Bologna: Il Mulino.

Dal Lago, A., and E. Quadrelli. 2002. Etnografia di una professione criminale. In *Un certo sguardo. Introduzione all'etnografia sociale*, ed. A. Dal Lago and R. De Biasi. Rome: Laterza.

Francia, A. 1990. Le caratteristiche socio—culturali di 100 tifosi "ultras," sostenitori del Pisa Sporting Club, rilevate mediante questionario. Dati preliminari. *Rassegna Italiana di Criminologia* 2: 231–47.

Gaddi, D., and E. Calvanese. 1993. Il tifo ultras. *Marginalità e società* 21: 79–103.

Jankowski, M. S. 1991. *Islands in the street: Gangs and American urban society*. Berkeley: University of California Press.

Klein M. W., H. Kerner, C. L. Maxson, and E. Weitekamp. 2001. *The Eurogang Paradox: Street gangs and youth groups in the U.S. and Europe.* Dordrecht, Netherlands: Kluwer.

McCarthy, B., J. Hagan, and M. J. Martin. 2002. In and out of harm's way: Violent victimization and the social capital of fictive street families. *Criminology* 40 (4): 831–66.

Roversi, A. 2002. La violenza negli stadi. In *La criminalità in Italia,* ed. M. Barbagli and U. Gatti. Bologna: Il Mulino.

Zatz, M., and E. Portillos. 2000. Voices from the barrio: Chicano/a gangs, families, and communities. *Criminology* 38 (2): 369–403.

4

Why Do Young Male Russians of German Descent Tend to Join or Form Violent Gangs?

Elmar G. M. Weitekamp, Kerstin Reich, and Hans-Jürgen Kerner

Over the last fifteen years, Russians of German descent (*Aussiedlers*) have consti-tuted the largest post–World War II immigrant group in Germany. There are some peculiarities connected with the immigrant status of Aussiedlers compared to that of other immigrant groups. The German constitution, the Grundgesetz ("basic law"), entitles settlers of German ancestry and their descendants to Ger-man citizenship immediately upon their arrival in Germany. Additionally, they receive, in contrast to other immigrant groups, extensive welfare support in or-der to smooth the hardship of migration and to provide support for integration.

For these reasons, among others, immigration and integration of Aussiedlers presented no particular problem for the German state, economy, and society in the past. Indeed, Russians of German descent were highly mo-tivated to integrate into the German society as quickly as possible and to avoid any trouble. This was mainly due to the preservation of German culture, tra-ditions, and language in the regions of the former Soviet Union where Aussiedlers lived in rather close communities, as well as to their conception of Germany as their homeland or motherland. Therefore, the integration of Eastern European immigrants of German descent was long perceived by na-tive Germans as a positive example and even as a model for other countries (Bade and Oltmer 1999).

This situation changed thoroughly and rapidly in the early 1990s, when the breakdown of the Eastern Bloc, the fall of the iron curtain, and the concomitant lessening of emigration restrictions caused an important upheaval with the arrival of hundreds of thousands of these ethnic Germans. This process started in 1987 and reached a peak in 1990, when nearly four hundred thousand immigrants from Romania, Poland, and the former Soviet Union arrived in Germany. The total number of those immigrants is by now far more than three million, and it is estimated that another two million people in these countries are still waiting to come to Germany. With the arrival of these massive numbers of people, a lot of problems emerged in the context of the immigration of Aussiedlers, for example, with regard to the labor and housing markets. Contrary to earlier Aussiedler immigration groups, the later groups were not equally embedded in German culture. Many of them did not speak the German language at all, causing unprecedented difficulties for their integration into German society. Presenting an additional, perhaps even greater, challenge for both the families of Russians of German descent and the host society, were some behavior patterns of the so-called *mitgenommene Generation* (literally, the "carried-on generation") (Deutsches Jugendinstitut 2002). This term refers to immigrant children and juveniles, who were typically not involved in the decision of their parents to leave home and emigrate to Germany. These youngsters not only had to cope with the consequences of migration to a new society but learned very quickly that promises of a land of milk and honey were false and that they would probably be deemed "losers" there. The resulting problems of failed integration, due to adjustment difficulties or refusal to integrate into German society socially, quickly became a great concern in the public eye. Over the last few years, it has become increasingly obvious that the young Aussiedlers remain in their own ethnic group, whether voluntarily or by force.

Consequently, the German public and some professionals often perceive young Aussiedlers as a violence-oriented and extremely brutal group that does not intend to integrate into German society and is highly involved in serious criminal activity. It appears that these behavioral phenomena often occur within gangs or violent youth groups whose members have the same ethnic background. In order to pursue these issues further, we will explore the following questions:

1. Do young Aussiedlers form street gangs or youth groups/cliques primarily because they became familiar with making friendships or bonding in this way in their country of origin? Or, do we have to interpret this behavior more as a reaction to social rejection by the native-born Germans and to processes of exclusion and marginalization in a growing "winner-loser" culture, where the Russians of German descent are clearly the losers?

2. When looking at deviant or delinquent behavior within immigrant Aussiedler groups, it is important to determine whether these activities are imported or homemade. By this, we mean to ask Do youngsters bring this problematic behavior with them, or do these patterns emerge after they immigrate to Germany? The latter would indicate that the immigration situation might lead to criminal behavior, the formation of gangs, and engagement in serious violent behavior.

In order to answer these questions and to identify some risk factors for joining gangs or problematic youth groups, this chapter describes the living conditions, common attitudes, and behavior patterns, especially those related to making friends and bonding to a clique, in their home countries. This is followed by a description of life circumstances after migration to Germany. To illustrate the perspectives of the young Aussiedlers better, we base our findings on data from our research project on the integration and dis-integration processes of young male Aussiedlers from the former Soviet Union. For this qualitative study, we conducted in-depth interviews of two different samples of Aussiedlers. One group consisted of forty incarcerated young Aussiedler men, the other of thirty-seven male Russians of German descent who had integrated well into German society or at least did not have official criminal records. All members of the samples were between eighteen and twenty-three years old at the time of the interview, and their average time of stay in Germany was five years. The aim of the study was to show which factors support, enhance, or prevent criminal behavior and how they influence integration and dis-integration processes.

CONCEPTUALIZATION AND THEORETICAL BACKGROUND: STREET-GANG FORMATION PROCESSES

Before we can properly discuss street gangs or violent youth groups, we must first elaborate upon what we mean by these terms. In this study, we use the definition of a gang or violent youth group developed by the Eurogang consortium through a reasonable consensus. The nominal operational definition is as follows: "A street gang or a troublesome youth group is a durable, street-oriented youth group whose own identity includes involvement in illegal activity." Whether these groups are labeled *gangs, youth groups,* or *Banden* is of less significance.

In order to better understand these groups and their origins, we draw upon C. L. Maxson and M. W. Klein's (1995) classification of street gangs, in which they differentiate between traditional, neotraditional, compressed, collective, and specialized gangs. Using this typology, A. Salagaev (2001) classifies gangs in Russia as *traditional gangs,* which are large, territorial, engaged in a wide variety of activities, have a history of self-generation, and have differentiated age or residence cliques. These gangs have a wide economic network, corrupt connections, and special security groups. They are hierarchically structured with strict norms and recruit their "fighters" from neighborhood youth. While they have a large pool of possible younger members, only a small number of them become active gang members. Their criminal gang activities include simple robbery, armed robbery, and drug trafficking, but their main business is "solving problems" for businessmen inside their territory. This link to organized crime, as described by Salagaev, was also found by J. O. Finckenauer and E. J. Waring (1998) in their study of the Russian mafia in America.

In contrast, the first assessments of E. G. M. Weitekamp (2001) and Weitekamp and K. Reich (2002) describe Aussiedler gangs and violent youth groups in Germany as neotraditional according to the classification system of Maxson and Klein (1995). The members usually hang out in segregated living areas that are often inhabited exclusively by Aussiedlers. They have a strong hierarchical order determined by age and experience the new country as an "enemy country" where their main task is to survive. Aussiedlers, especially in rural areas, often find that their only possible place to make friends is in these segregated living quarters. After families of Russian descent move out of these temporary special-housing units or segregated areas, older members of the Aussiedler gangs often come back. These older gang members then recruit younger Aussiedlers from the new arrivals and use them for their illegal activities. These newcomers admire those able to achieve status symbols, meaning consumer articles of the new environment, such as cars, electronic devices, clothes, and other items that indicate wealth. The gang and subculture members are involved in a variety of criminal activities, including robbery, extortion, simple and aggravated assault, sexual violence, and drug trafficking. In addition, the Aussiedler youths exhibit a very strong machismo culture and attitudes in which a high level of violence is considered normal (Reich et al. 1999). The latter attitudes have led Weitekamp and Reich (2002) to argue that the subculture of violence theory of M. E. Wolfgang and F. Ferracuti (1967) provides a useful vehicle for understanding these processes.

Research suggests that group behavior and the formation of gangs are nothing new for Russian youths who grew up in the former Soviet Union. According to R. Dobson (1990), Soviet youths experienced problems similar to those in Western nations before the iron curtain came down, but they were different in three aspects. First, political control over the young people was much stronger, and those who avoided and deviated from this control were considered political opponents. Second, the people of the former Soviet Union had to rely on the black market since the economy failed to provide sufficient consumer products. Third, the state was able to provide young people with jobs. Finckenauer and Kelly (1992) convincingly argue that these characteristics led to the emergence of subcultures in the former Soviet Union. As they point out, in the Soviet context, the concept of "youth" refers to people between the ages of fourteen and thirty, and instead of calling troublesome youth groups *youth subcultures*, the Soviets called them *informal youth associations*. These associations could be official as well as unofficial and, according to A. P. Fain (1990), engaged in activities developed by and serving its members rather than in activities ordered by officials. However, as M. Fel'dshtein (cited in Finckenauer and Kelly 1992) has pointed out, the informal youth associations engaged in behaviors that were not accepted and were quite distinct from those of mainstream society. The young people expressed their opposition toward officials and conforming citizens through differences in dress, behavior, and lifestyle. Part of that oppositional behavior could be delinquent and criminal, but, according to J. Bushnell (1990), the criminal behavior was not a central part of their activities. At first glance, these features fit the definition of the typical American street gang as defined by Klein et al. (2001). However, a major difference is the fact that the Soviet youth groups used these forms of behavior for political protest and to reject openly the customs and values of mainstream society.

Finckenauer and Kelly (1992) point out that an important distinction between the Soviet Union and other Western countries was that the Soviet Union
actively tried to socialize their youth into proper Communist citizens. The nation's youth organization, the Komsomol, was the main tool to achieve this goal.
Even though participation was voluntary, young people were forced to join if
they wanted to obtain higher education, better jobs, and promotions (Riordan
1989; Dobson 1990). According to Finckenauer and Kelly (1992), in the 1980s,
the Komsomol became too bureaucratic and corrupt and basically lost touch
with the needs of Soviet youth, leading to a loss of credibility and a search for
alternatives. Parallel to this development, the Soviet Union experienced an increasing pull toward consumerism and self-orientation. The Soviet economy's
inability to produce many sought-after goods led to black markets that became
attractive for young people and youth groups who could not find legitimate
jobs. According to Dobson (1990) and J. Riordan (1989), the alternatives to
state-organized activities and the failing state economy included youth groups
of rock music fans, hippies, neofascists, and hooligans, in addition to youth
gangs and vigilante groups. Many of these groups started to get involved in
criminal behavior. This constitutes quite a change from opposition to the dominant culture to the development of subcultures, where crime and violence become major features of daily life. V. S. Ovchinskii (1989) reports that almost half
of the leaders of these subcultures, gangs, and youth groups had spent time in a
correctional labor colony.

FRIENDSHIPS, BONDING PROCESSES, AND
CLIQUES IN THE COUNTRY OF ORIGIN

In the interviews, we were interested in finding out whether the youngsters
had been members of a clique/group or gang in their country of origin. We
also wanted to learn about the characteristics of these group or gangs, such as
the number and age of the members, how much time they spent together, and
what their main activities were. We classified subjects of our sample as *group
members* when their group of friends had existed over a certain period of time
and when the members reported spending a considerable part of their leisure
time together.

The overwhelming number of subjects in our sample reported belonging
to a group/clique or gang in their country of origin. This was true for 84 percent of the group in freedom and nearly 78 percent of the Aussiedlers who

were later incarcerated in Germany. Three Aussiedlers reported often changing cliques, and only five youngsters reported not belonging to a group/clique or gang. These results are supported by the studies of B. Dietz and H. Roll (1998) and C. Huber et al. (2001), which show that the great majority of young Aussiedlers belonged to a clique/group or gang in their country of origin (the studies report approximately 88 percent and 77 percent, respectively). The youngsters reported that group membership fulfilled various youth-specific needs and functions for them. Primarily, it provided protection against representatives of the state, who were considered to be enemies, especially in times of increasing national conflicts in the countries of origin. Membership also guaranteed fun, provided a variety of activities during leisure time, and had a stabilizing effect on forming their individual identities. In sum, to be in a clique/group or gang was a quite normal, widespread activity in the countries of origin and a manner of sharing friendship with other peers. This is not very amazing since it is a common experience for most adolescents; however, extraordinary for young Aussiedlers was the lack of orientation they experienced due to the political changes and the state's subsequent retreat from the tasks of education and support for the children. The families were not prepared to meet these educational needs, so the youths were forced to attach to groups that presented the only possibility to bridge that gap.

According to our analysis of the interviews, one has to consider these family factors in relationship with some characteristics of the group. An interesting finding was that the age of the group members played a key role with regard to attitudes and behavior patterns. Older peers served as role models for younger ones and influenced their attitudes substantially. When we compared the incarcerated group of Aussiedlers with those living in freedom, we found that almost half of the nonincarcerated subjects had younger peers or peers of the same age, as compared with one-third of the incarcerated subjects. A comparison of incarcerated and nonincarcerated Aussiedlers by the relative age of their group/clique members is shown in figure 4.1. We found an orientation toward older peers for Aussiedlers who were later incarcerated in Germany, and they were often involved in activities that are not typical for juveniles. Due to the greater mobility that resulted from the older peers' access to motorcycles and cars, the younger peers were able to visit discos or similar places to which they normally would not have access at their age. In addition, we found a strong relationship between the age of the peer group and the consumption of

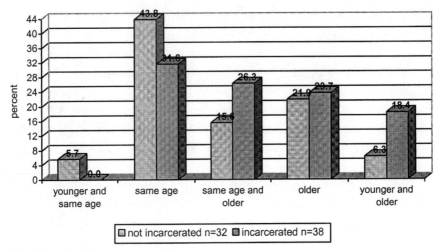

FIGURE 4.1
Overview of age of group/clique members in countries of origin

alcohol, drug use, and other deviant behaviors. Only four out of sixteen juveniles who consumed alcohol and soft drugs in their country of origin belonged to a peer group with the same age structure. A similar, close relationship was found for violent acts, especially aggravated assaults.

Some of these trends are illustrated in the following statements of one interviewee:[1]

I: How did you get to know your friends? Did they come from the same region or community your family was living in?

R09: We grew up together on the streets.

I: Did some schoolmates belong to the group? Did they attend the same classes as you did?

R09: Not from my class, but sometimes older or younger students from my school.

I: How much older were they?

R09: Two or three years, or so.

I: And you guys stayed together? How many of you were together, approximately?

R09: It depends on the day. Sometimes ten, twelve, or sometimes fifteen.

I: What did you normally do after school?

R09: Around 14:00 hours, we had usually already had some alcohol to drink.

I: Was that normal?

R09: Yes, but not much alcohol was involved.

I: What kind of alcohol did you drink?

R09: All kinds: beer, vodka, wine.

I: Where did you get the alcohol?

R09: We got the alcohol ourselves.

I: You bought the alcohol?

R09: Yes, bought and sold.

I: Did you have money?

R09: Yes, sometimes.

I: Where from? Did you have a job, or did you get it from your parents?

R09: No, stolen from families.

I: Hmm, in Germany you can only buy alcohol if you are sixteen years of age.

R09: There as well, but nobody cares.

I: If it does not matter, one can buy alcohol at fourteen years of age if one looks a little bit older? Or did the older friends buy alcohol for all?

R09: Yes, but I never drank as much as the others.

I: How much did you consume? Do you remember?

R09: Maybe a bottle of beer or so twice a week. Sometimes I did not drink for a whole month.

I: What did the others drink?

R09: How much or what?

I: Yes, how much and what?

R09: It was always different depending on how much was available. If ten bottles of vodka were available, then ten bottles were drunk, and two friends always wanted to have more, more, more.

The young Russians of German descent reported a high tendency to commit violent acts within their group of peers in their home countries. This attitude derived partly from an insecure environment, where violence was part of daily life, and partly from increasing national conflicts where the state usually represented the enemy and violence belonged to the daily repertoire of the state's activities. As a result, fighting was sometimes unavoidable, not only to maintain dominance over other groups but also for self-protection. Violent acts, especially fights between groups of youngsters, were also seen as "normal," as a common leisure-time activity like playing soccer. In this context, Huber et al. (2001) report that 81 percent of the juveniles in their study experienced violence and fights at their schools, and nearly 24 percent reported that they experienced this kind of behavior very often. The results for verbal violence and abuse were quite similar. The following statement is indicative of the normalcy of fighting for these youth:

I: With the other juveniles whom you constantly hung out with in your leisure time, was that a real group/clique or gang?

R06: Yes.

I: How many people hung out together normally?

R06: Fifteen or twenty. We often had in the group violent fights with other groups or played soccer with them. Our group or gang was named after the street we lived in, and we entered into fights or played soccer with groups or gangs from other streets.

I: So, the whole structure was organized according to the streets people lived in?

R06: Yes, we were proud to live in our street and to fight or play soccer for the street.

I: And what was the trigger for fighting each other or to engage in violent behavior?

R06: Yes, first we always had a soccer tournament in the street, but when one of our group/gang was beaten up in the street by somebody from another group/gang, we all went to him, and the other group got together as well. It was almost never one against one but always a group against a group.

I: Did you also get hurt at times?

R06: Yes, more than once.

I: How did this occur? Did somebody in the group/gang determine what to do and when to start it and if today one played soccer or started a fight? Who did determine that?

R06: Well, we did not have a leader or a boss. We were all very good friends, and perhaps, one came and said such-and-such street wants to play soccer with us, and then we did just that. On the other hand, if somebody came and said that he was beaten up somebody or others, lets go and have revenge.

I: And where did you meet for those kinds of activities?

R06: In the park.

I: How was it when a fight took place? Did you like it, or would you have preferred to do something else?

R06: When you were beating up somebody, it was a great feeling, but if you got hurt, it was no fun.

I: But these fights were some sort of leisure-time activity, and it was good
        fun as well?

R06:   Well, we did always have some sort of fights among the members of our
        group/gang as well. And it was to a certain degree also fun in order to
        avoid boredom. It was always about determining which member in the
        group was the strongest.

I: And who was the strongest?

R06:   Not me. He was two years older.

The importance of fights and the use of violence also becomes clear from
the following statement:

I: How is a fight judged in the group or gang?

R11:   In the past, it was much worse. In my country of origin, when you did not
        engage yourself in fights, you were out.

I: You were then considered to be a loser?

R11:   Much worse since nobody wanted to have anything to do with you. As a
        consequence, at all times, you had to defend yourself, your girlfriend, gee,
        you had to protect everybody yourself. How is that said? All for one, one
        for all, that works for the group.

The statements of our interviewees who were engaged in groups indicated
overwhelmingly that fights in a group context were seen as an appropriate,
sometimes the only, means for demonstrating strength, power, status, and,
above all, a traditional conception of masculinity. That those fights predominantly took place in a group context was a matter of honor. In accordance
with this opinion, Aussiedlers felt obliged to unconditional solidarity when a
member of the group was attacked by others. In such cases, a young male
Aussiedler had to defend the honor and reputation of the group. The use of
force was considered a particularly male attitude and seems to have been le-
gitimized.

FRIENDSHIP AND GROUPS/CLIQUES AND GANGS IN GERMANY

During adolescence, the peer group becomes increasingly important for juveniles. This is a normal developmental process, but one that entails specific
risks for young immigrants. Problems often begin as soon as the status of the
parents drops following immigration to Germany. The parents slowly lose
control over their sons as adolescence approaches, above all because the

youths more quickly acquire cultural—conventional or criminal—skills than their parents do. Therefore, friends or the peer group have to replace or over-take family functions.

In this aspect, too, young immigrants are confronted with a special situa-tion. When they emigrated, they had to leave behind their familiar friendship circle, peers, and clique/group. This means a painful loss for most of them. Finding new friends is not easy for several reasons. They not only suffer strongly from the loss of the social contacts, but they also struggle to com-municate successfully and to behave properly in a social environment differ-ent from that in which they grew up and to which they had become accustomed.

With this loss of familiarity comes the feeling of strangeness due to the pat-terns of communication and behavior of the native German youths. The situ-ation for the young Aussiedlers is a particularly difficult one. While in Russia, they were considered to be a minority group because of their German descent and often labeled as "German fascists." In Germany, even though they have a German passport, they are again a minority group, now labeled as "Russians." In addition to the minority status, they often have language problems and dif-ficulties in school. The schooling or job training they received in Russia is in-sufficient, even wholly inadequate, for the job market in their new country of residence, thus blocking legitimate opportunities and marginalizing them even more. In Germany, due to a lack of mutual understanding, it therefore comes as no surprise that these young people form or join youth groups, gangs, and subcultures in order to find a place where they belong and have others to identify with. Hanging out in groups was already very much a part of their culture when they lived in the former Soviet Union since, as explained earlier, it was often too dangerous there to hang out alone and to show one's opposition to the dominant society.

The Aussiedlers' perception of the Germans is apparent in the following statement:

> G23: The mentality is very important. In my opinion Germans grow up with a complete different mentality. They hate everything German. They do not know their own roots, and if you ask them where Germans are coming from, they answer, "Leave me alone," or "How should I know." They are not interested in their roots and their identity. They are inter-ested in parties and fun. There exist well-educated and knowledgeable

Germans, but they are rare in Germany. I compare the Germans with the situation of people in Russia. In Russia, people read lots of books, and you always have to deal, at least to a certain degree, with computers. In Germany, however, one has to deal with books a lot, but one absolutely does not read them.

Just as the young Aussiedler immigrants have negative feelings toward the native-born Germans, young Germans often hold similar low opinions of young Aussiedlers. For young Germans, it appears unattractive or even impossible to get in contact with this special immigrant group due to cultural differences, language problems, and certain social and behavioral manners attributed to Aussiedlers that many native-born Germans find distasteful. The negative social perceptions and attributes of the other group clearly overshadow the positive aspects. This particular kind of mutually disrespectful social perception is often the result of a lack of knowledge regarding the background, culture, and history of the other group. Obviously, these attitudes do not provide a good starting point for making contact with each other; rather, they fuel prejudices, stereotyping, and hate. Consequently, young Aussiedlers try to stay within their own ethnic group, as illustrated in figure 4.2.

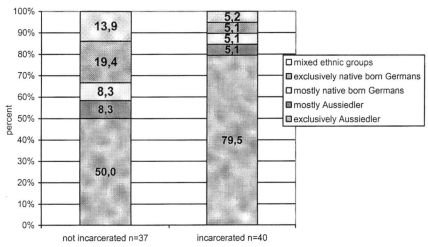

FIGURE 4.2
Overview of ethnic composition of peer groups in Germany

As figure 4.2 shows, ethnicity plays an important role in the selection of peer groups, especially for the incarcerated Aussiedlers, of whom nearly 80 percent report that their group/clique or gang is composed exclusively of other Aussiedlers, compared to 50 percent of the Aussiedlers in freedom. If we combine the "exclusively Aussiedler" and "mostly Aussiedler" categories, the percentage grows to 85 percent for the incarcerated group versus nearly 60 percent for the group in freedom. In contrast, when the "exclusively native-born Germans" and "mostly native-born Germans" categories are combined, the percentages rise to a little more than 27 percent for the nonincarcerated group and slightly more than 10 percent for the incarcerated group. Huber et al. (2001) report that the leisure-time activities of Aussiedlers changed dramatically upon immigration to Germany. Russians of German descent reported that while in the country of origin, they occupied their leisure time with family activities (25 percent) or spent it alone (8 percent) much less frequently than they reported occupying their time engaged in group and gang activities. In contrast, newly immigrated Aussiedlers reported engaging in activities with the family (94 percent) and spending the leisure time alone (87 percent) much more frequently, with group or gang activities playing a major role only after the respondent had lived for some time in the new country. These results further demonstrate the social isolation of the Russians of German descent.

One Aussiedler voiced his arguments for dissociation from native-born Germans as follows:

I: How was the situation with your friends? How did your peer group develop?

R22: I did not get along very well with the Germans. Their character differs. One could not get along with the natives. They have other jokes, different characters. With the other Russians of German descent one could get along very well since they have the same experiences and a similar character. And the Germans and their character, they achieve nothing, are lazy, play on computers all the time and, I don't know exactly, are different in their character. It didn't work. They have other interests than we have.

I: Is it so that as a Russian of German descent, you do not want to have contact? Or is it the case that the native Germans do not want to have any contact with Russians of German descent?

R22: Yes, that is the case. Well, it was so that they called me in my country of origin a "fascist," and here I am called a "Russian." And Germans have

other interests, have different characters. I always get along better with
Russians of German descent.

I: But in sports clubs you must have been together with native Germans?
       How did that work?

R22: Yes, we did play football but nothing else. I belong to a different group of
       friends.

Both self-dissociation and peer rejection from native-born Germans can lead
to social exclusion and to intensified grouping within the ethnic group. According to R. K. Silbereisen and E. Schmitt-Rodermund (1999), this situation can
also constitute a risk factor for attachment to delinquent groups. Another factor
that further prohibits better integration of young Aussiedlers and alienates them
from contacts with native Germans is their lack of opportunities to meet with
others and make new friends. Regardless of whether the new friends are Germans or other Aussiedlers, according to Huber et al. (2001), the majority (74
percent) of their opportunities occur within the temporary special-housing
units. Russians of German descent are assigned to these units by the state immediately after immigrating to Germany but should leave them, in theory, as
quickly as possible, according to F. Stoll (1999). In reality, however, families have
to spend an average of two years in these usually very crowded and poorly
equipped housing conditions. These are not good places for young people to
grow up in. They are forced to hang out in the hallways or outside the buildings,
and the people who live there generally have little privacy and few common
rooms that could be used for social activities. This environment represents their
"social home," so to speak, because it is the living environment of peers who
speak the same language, have common traditions and values, know the same
behavioral patterns from the country of origin, and, even more importantly,
face the same problems of rejection by the new culture, difficulty integrating,
and struggle to find their place in the new society.

So, how do young Aussiedlers come into contact with delinquent peers? On
the basis of the results of our study, we identified two possible pathways to
forming and belonging to groups/cliques or gangs that are involved in criminal behavior. The first pathway is a continuation of the social pattern from the
country of origin to seek out delinquent friends because it seems most attractive to be with them and extend the scope of normal activities. In these cases,
Aussiedlers predominantly look for older friends, meaning those who have

more experience, who supposedly are "winners" in the new society and belong to a group or gang in which serious delinquent behavior and violent acts, above all, are approved by the individual members.

The second pathway to getting involved with delinquent friends or cliques is a result of the life situation after immigration, which is, above all, characterized by deprivation in nearly every dimension of life, especially with regard to potential friendship and social contacts. This deprivation and isolation leads them not to assess offers of friendship critically. From our study interviews, we know that young Russian people of German descent who immigrated to Germany at an earlier time understand the problems, circumstances, and needs of newly arrived youngsters and know where to meet them. They use their insider knowledge and the situation of social deprivation to attract and recruit these young immigrants, asking them to join gangs for certain delinquent activities in order to combat migration-related problems and get on the winning side of society. They offer the young Aussiedlers what they miss the most: feelings of belonging, strength, power, control, attention, and acknowledgement, as well as fun, action, and success. Such groups, however, can advance and facilitate social exclusion even more because, instead of learning the values and norms of the German society and integrating them into their own behavior repertoire, they maneuver themselves further outside German society and into the subculture of delinquent outsiders.

The susceptibility to violent acts is high in such groups. As previously mentioned, in the country of origin, the use of violence was a common and recognized means of imposing one's interests and gaining highly esteemed male attributes like power, strength, and success. We revealed in our interviews that the interaction and dynamics within these groups/cliques or gangs, as well as the motivation and intentions behind violent acts, seem to remain the same in Germany. This, of course, is not particularly amazing since young people are not stripped of their behavioral habits upon departure from their home countries.

By further relying on behavior patterns proven to work successfully in the country of origin, the youngsters are able to gain back a feeling of control instead of feeling helpless in unknown or unclear social situations. Furthermore, the reinforcement patterns within the group are positioned in such a way that delinquent acts are rewarded and acknowledged; one can improve his status in the hierarchy of the group by committing crime, thus becoming a "winner" instead of a "loser."

In order to become a winner, Aussiedlers often get into fights with members of other minority groups in order to demonstrate their superior position in society. The following statement demonstrates that these fights rarely have an instrumental character:

R29: I was under the influence of alcohol and became somewhat frolicsome and started fights with Turks, who looked like people from Kazakhstan.

I: On which occasions?

R29: I don't know, maybe in the disco.

I: And then a fight started?

R29: Yes.

I: Did you look for a fight?

R29 Well, I do not know.

I: How did the fight get started?

R29: Well, most probably as it happened in the old times. You come, and then somebody shouts, "A fight is taking place. Come and help out." And then you run over there, even though you do not know anybody, and hit somebody (it doesn't matter whom), as you would have done in Russia.

It is always about honor, which is the center of interest in these conflicts and has to be defended unconditionally. Not only do the means for defending honor stay the same as in the country of origin, but so do the justifications for the use of violence. The following comments of one of our respondents illustrate how violence is deemed a justified response to perceived slights:

R36: We did come a second time, another misunderstanding since we took a cab, and the cab driver was a Turk, and I was with my girlfriend, and he stared at her, and I was drunk, and since I get very jealous, I beat him up.

I: Because he stared at your girlfriend?

R36: Yes, Turks always stare at our girls.

I: Does this happen always when you are under the influence of alcohol?

R36: Normally, yes. There were such misunderstandings. I did not understand the cab driver very well and thought all the time that he was laughing at me. He did ask me my name. I told him my name was Paul, and he thought it was Mustafa.

In order to supplement the picture, we must mention that the other young Aussiedlers represented in our control sample and those who did not attach to a delinquent group were not forced to acquire male attributes through violent acts. They were able to achieve acknowledgment and positive self-worth through pursuing personal goals, like obtaining a better education or the qualifications for highly valued or socially accepted jobs or, for example, having a family.

Of utmost importance also is the youngsters' dominant subcultural value that one always solves problems based on macho culture and attitudes: one never turns to the police but deals with all issues among the people or groups directly involved. J. Walter and G. Grübl (1999), drawing on first-hand knowledge from experiences in a German youth prison, reported that there is a close connection between conceptions of honor and masculinity and strong disapproval for regulating conflicts officially or involving official agents and their institutions in the problem-solving process. They report the following statement by a Russian inmate of German descent: "When you go to the police, you are a woman or an asshole." Echoing this sentiment, one of our subjects described the following experience:

> R19: Here, my first problem with the police was the following: I had a German friend, and he was a very good friend of mine, and we were together for about three to four years. He then beat up my little brother, and I told him, "Stop that and let me know what he did to you." However, he did beat him up again, and I warned him a second time. After the third incident, I asked him for money. After my brother reported another beating, I told him I would seriously beat him up if it ever happened again. He did beat my brother again, and I broke his jaw. He then filed charges against me with the police. Typically German!

YOUTH ABANDONMENT, DILEMMAS, SUBCULTURE, AND VIOLENCE

In order to place immigrant youth groups and the commission of violent acts in a broader perspective, we believe it is important to consider the general problem of youth abandonment. K. Polk and Weitekamp (1999) explain that young people use violence as a way to cope with youth abandonment. According to them, young people experience economic abandonment and are the "losers" in the contemporary "winner-loser" culture. Therefore, they are caught in a dreadful developmental trap. Polk and Weitekamp further point out that, historically, virtually all young people, at high, middle, and low points in the class structure, can look forward to a process of moving from childhood through schooling into adulthood, fulfilling some combination of work and family roles. These prospects are now less relevant, and the problem of abandonment is greater for those young people who leave school early and enter the labor force with little to offer in terms of qualifications, skills, or experience. W. J. Wilson (1996) describes a process in which work disappeared for the urban poor in America. He argues that a lack of full-time work leads to undesirable consequences, such as poverty and delays in both becoming independent from parents and establishing appropriate sexual relationships, marriages, and families. These individuals become stuck in a social and economic no-mans-land, where a central feature of their existence is that normal supports for adult identity are not available. Polk and Weitekamp (1999) contend that this situation forces young people to engage in complicated struggles and innovation in order to form their central identities as males or females. This development is even worse for members of minority groups by race, nationality, or ethnicity. F. Dubet and D. Lapeyronnie (1994) have investigated the "winner-loser" hypothesis in France and found that a significant shift has occurred in social problems, including crime trends. They conclude that the social exclusion of marginal groups had become the key problem of the 1990s. In addition, they consider the criminal acts of marginalized youngsters an expression of their helplessness, of their inability to live a normal life and gain access to society.

Here we can see the clear connection between violence and youth groups, gangs, and subcultures. The situation of abandoned youngsters is such that issues of status and manhood are problematic and cry out for solutions. According to Polk and Weitekamp (1999), the lack of traditional pathways for these youths to define themselves as men makes it appealing to form and join a youth group, gang, or subculture, especially when comparing their status to others'. These groups or cultures can change the rules of the game and make a "loser" into a "winner" again.

CONCLUSION

What Do We Know about Groups/Cliques and Gangs in Germany?

How can we judge the forming of delinquent groups/cliques or gangs, especially by Aussiedlers? Do Russians of German descent become active in criminal behavior because they have imported this behavior from their countries of origin, or can it be considered a reaction to the changes and life conditions they are confronted with upon arrival in Germany? After evaluating the formation of friendships, bonding behavior, and the formation of peer groups or gangs in the country of origin and Germany, both patterns seem to influence the emergence of delinquent groups and gangs in today's Germany.

In the country of origin, the formation of groups or gangs was a necessary process in order to survive in that society, and violence played a major role in youths' daily lives. In Germany, labeling processes result in the realization that they are outsiders, other, non-German. Strong experiences of rejection by their new "home" culture lead to the formation of strong ethnic-based groups and gangs. For some of them, this means finding in Germany the right platform to continue their criminal behavior and recruiting new arrivals for their criminal purposes. Others are pushed into criminal behavior and gangs since they were never given the opportunity to learn adequate, norm-conforming behavior and to succeed in the country they immigrated to. They are forced to rely on old, learned behaviors when problems and conflicts occur. Thus, the group or gang becomes their alternative and most important social frame, a network through which they hope to overcome the obstacles of the immigration process.

The situation of being abandoned is especially bad for young Russians of German descent since they are, so to speak, "double losers." They were outsiders in the former Soviet Union who could hardly succeed there; now, they are "losers" in the "promised land." The situation of abandoned youths thereby places them under a number of stresses, which are likely to increase their willingness to use violence. Caught in conflicts with others (native Germans and other immigrant groups such as the Turks), the abandoned young people cannot fall back on a wide network of other self-definitions as a way of asserting a self-concept that says, "This is who I am." Violence is an apparent, low-cost alternative, and gangs and subcultures can exert a strong attraction. Membership in a gang or subculture and the use of violence can change the rules of the game and make a "loser" into a "winner."

NOTES

This research was supported by grant We1445/6-1/6-2 from the German Research Foundation. Points of view or opinions expressed herein are our own and do not necessarily represent those of the German Research Foundation.

1. For the presentation of the statements out of our interviews, we use the abbreviation "I" for the interviewer and the combination of "R" with their sequential "number" for the individual respondents/interviewees.

REFERENCES

Attwood, L. 1996. Young people, sex and sexual identity. In *Gender, generation and identity in contemporary Russia*, ed. H. Pilkington. London: Routledge.

Bade, K., and J. Oltmer. 1999. *Aussiedler: Deutsche Einwanderer aus Osteuropa*. Osnabrueck, Germany: Universitätsverlag Rasch.

Borodin, S. V. 1990. Crime trends and directions in the criminal policy of the USSR. In *Soviet criminology update*, ed. UNICRI. Publication No. 38. Rome: UNICRI.

Bushnell, J. 1990. Introduction: The history and study of the Soviet youth subculture. *Soviet Sociology* 27 (1): 3–10.

Cao, L., A. Adams, and V. J. Jensen. 1997. A test of the black subculture of violence thesis: A research note. *Criminology* 35: 367–79.

Cloward, R. A., and L. E. Ohlin. 1960. *Delinquency and opportunity*. Glencoe, NY: Free Press of Glencoe.

Cohen, A. K. 1955. *Delinquent boys: The culture of the gang*. Glencoe, NY: Free Press of Glencoe.

Cohen, A. K., and J. F. Short Jr. 1958. Research on delinquent subcultures. *Journal of Social Issues* 14: 20–37.

Dashkov, G. V. 1992. Quantitative and qualitative changes in crime in the Soviet Union. *British Journal of Criminology* 32 (2): 160–66.

Deutsches Jugendinstitut. 2002. *Die mitgenommene Generation*. Munich, Germany: Deutsches Jugendinstitut e.V.

Dietz, B., and H. Roll. 1998. *Jugendliche Aussiedler—Portrait einer Zuwanderergeneration*. Frankfurt, Germany: Campus Verlag.

Dixson, J., and A. Lizotte. 1987. Gun ownership and the southern subculture of violence. *American Journal of Sociology* 93: 383–405.

Dmitrieva, E. 1996. Orientations, re-orientations or disorientations? Expectations of the future among Russian school-leavers. In *Gender, generation and identity in contemporary Russia*, ed. H. Pilkington. London: Routledge.

Dobson, R. 1990. Youth problems in the Soviet Union. In *Soviet social problems*, ed. A. Jones, W. D. Connor, and D. Powell. Boulder, CO: Westview Press.

Dubet, F., and D. Lapeyronnie. 1994. *Im Aus der Vorstaedte: der Zerfall der demokratischen Gesellschaft*. Stuttgart: Klett-Cotta Verlag.

Eckert, R., C. Reis, and T. A. Wetzstein. 1999. Bilder und Begegnungen: Konflikte zwischen einheimischen und Aussiedlerjugendlichen. In *Aussiedler: Deutsche Einwanderer aus Osteuropa*, ed. K. J. Bade and J. Oltmer. Osnabrück, Germany: Universitätsverlag Rasch.

Erlanger, H. S. 1974. The empirical status of the subcultures of violence thesis. *Social Problems* 22: 280–92.

Esbensen, F.-A., L. T. Winfree Jr., N. He, and T. J. Taylor. 2001. Youth gangs and definitional issues: When is a gang a gang, and why does it matter? *Crime and Delinquency* 47: 105–30.

Fain, A. P. 1990. Specific features of informal youth associations in large cities. *Soviet Sociology* 27 (1): 19–42.

Finckenauer, J. O., and L. Kelly. 1992. Juvenile delinquency and youth subcultures in the former Soviet Union. *International Journal of Comparative and Applied Criminal Justice* 16 (2): 247–61.

Finckenauer, J. O., and E. J. Waring. 1998. *Russian mafia in America: Immigration, culture and crime.* Boston: Northeastern University Press.

Hänze, M., and E.-D. Lantermann. 1999. Entwicklung und Anpassung. In *Aussiedler in Deutschland. Akkulturation von Persönlichkeit und Verhalten*, ed. R. K. Silbereisen, E.-D. Lantermann, and E. Schmitt-Rodermund. Opladen, Germany: Leske und Budrich.

Huber, C., K. Reich, E. G. M. Weitekamp, and H.-J. Kerner. 2001. Wenn aus Spass Ernst wird: Untersuchung zum Freizeitverhalten und den sozialen Beziehungen Jugendlicher Spätaussiedler. *Deutsche Vereinigung für Jugendgerichte und Jugendgerichtshilfen (Hrsg.) DVJJ-Journal* 4: 370–79.

Kennedy, L. W., and S. W. Baron. 1993. Routine activities and a subculture of violence: A study on the street. *Journal of Research in Crime and Delinquency* 30: 88–112.

Klein, M. W., H.-J. Kerner, C. L. Maxson, and E. G. M. Weitekamp. 2001. *The Eurogang Paradox: Street gangs and youth groups in the U.S. and Europe.* Dordrecht, Netherlands: Kluwer.

Maxson, C. L., and M. W. Klein. 1995. Investigating gang structure. *Journal of Gang Research* 3 (1): 33–40.

Miller, W. B. 1958. Lower-class culture as a generating milieu of gang delinquency. *Journal of Social Issues* 14, 5–19.

Noom, M. J., M. Dekovic, and W. H. J. Meeus. 1999. Autonomy, attachment and psychosocial adjustment during adolescence: A double-edged sword? *Journal of Adolescence* 22: 771–83.

Omel'chenko, E. 1996. Young women in provincial gang culture: A case study. In *Gender, generation and identity in contemporary Russia*, ed. H. Pilkington. London: Routledge.

Ovchinskii, V. S. 1989. Criminal tendencies in the youth environment. *Soviet Sociology* 27 (4): 88–91.

Pilkington, H. 1994. *Russia's youth and its culture.* London: Routledge.

Pilkington, H. ed. 1996. *Gender, generation and identity in contemporary Russia.* London: Routledge.

Polk, K., and E. G. M. Weitekamp. 1999. *Emerging patterns of youth violence.* Paper presented at the annual meeting of the American Society of Criminology, Toronto, Canada, November 17–20.

Pridmore, W. A. 2000. *Social structure and homicide in post-Soviet Russia.* Unpublished dissertation, School of Criminal Justice, Rockefeller College of Public Affairs and Policy, State University of New York, Albany.

———. 2001. Russia. In *Crime and crime control: A global view,* ed. G. Barak. Westport, CT: Greenwood Press.

Reich, K., E. G. M. Weitekamp, and H.-J. Kerner. 1999. Jugendliche Aussiedler: Probleme und Chancen im Integrationsprozess. *Bewährungshilfe* 46 (4): 335–59.

Riordan, J. 1989. *Soviet youth culture.* Bloomington: Indiana University Press.

Salagaev, A. 2001. Evolution of delinquent gangs in Russia. In *The Eurogang Paradox: Street gangs and youth groups in the U.S. and Europe,* ed. M. W. Klein, H.-J. Kerner, C. L. Maxson, and E. G. M. Weitekamp. Dordrecht, Netherlands: Kluwer.

Schagerl, S. 2000. Aussiedler-Jugendliche. Integrationsanforderungen-Bewältigungsstrategien-Gewaltprävention. In *Zuwanderung. Zugehörigkeit und Chancengleichheit für Kinder und Jugendliche,* ed. E. Gropper and H.-M. Zimmermann. Stuttgart, Germany: Aktion Jugendschutz Landesarbeitsstelle Baden-Württemberg.

Schmidt-Häuer, C. 1993. *Russland in Aufruhr: Innenansichten aus einem rechtlosen Reich.* Munich, Germany: Piper.

Schmitt-Rodermund, E., and R. K. Silbereisen. 1999. Differentielle Akkulturation von Entwicklungsorientierungen unter jugendlichen Aussiedlern. In *Aussiedler in Deutschland. Akkulturation von Persönlichkeit und Verhalten,* ed. R. K. Silbereisen, E.-D. Lantermann, and E. Schmitt-Rodermund. Opladen, Germany: Leske und Budrich.

Sellin, T. 1938. *Culture conflict and crime.* Bulletin no. 41. New York: Social Science Research Council.

Shelly, L. I. 1990. Crime in the Soviet Union. In *Soviet social problems,* ed. A. Jones, W. D. Connor, and D. Powell. Boulder, CO: Westview Press.

Shoemaker, D. J., and J. Sherwood. 1987. The subculture of violence and ethnicity. *Journal of Criminal Justice* 15: 461–72.

Silbereisen, R. K., and E. Schmitt-Rodermund. 1999. Wohlbefinden der jugendlichen Aussiedler. In *Aussiedler in Deutschland. Akkulturation von Persönlichkeit und Verhalten,* ed. R. K. Silbereisen, E. D. Lantermann, and E. Schmitt-Rodermund. Opladen, Germany: Leske und Budrich.

Singer, S. I. 1986. Victims of serious violence and their criminal behavior: Subcultural theory and beyond. *Violence and Victims* 1: 61–70.

Spiridonov, L. I. 1990. Social contradictions and anti-social manifestations. In *Soviet criminology update*, ed. UNICRI. Publication No. 38. Rome: UNICRI.

Stoll, F. 1999. *Von Russland nach Württemberg: Eine Studie zur Integration jugendlicher Spätaussiedler*. Unpublished master's thesis, University of Tübingen, Germany.

Strobl, R., and W. Kühnel. 2000. *Dazugehörig und ausgegrenzt: Analysen zu Integrationschancen junger Aussiedler*. Munich: Juventa.

Tertilt, H. 1995. *Turkish power boys: Ethnographie einer Jugendbande*. Frankfurt, Germany: Suhrkamp.

UNICRI. 1990. *Soviet criminology update*. Publication No. 38. Rome: UNICRI.

Walter, J., and G. Grübl. 1999. Junge Aussiedler im Jugendstrafvollzug. In *Aussiedler: Deutsche Einwanderer aus Osteuropa*, ed. K. J. Bade and J. Oltmer. Osnabrück, Germany: Universitätsverlag Rasch.

Waters, T. 1999. *Crime and immigrant youth*. Thousand Oaks, CA: Sage Publications.

Weitekamp, E. G. M. 2001. Gangs in Europe: Assessments at the millennium. In *The Eurogang Paradox: Street gangs and youth groups in the U.S. and Europe*, ed. M. W. Klein, H.-J. Kerner, C. L. Maxson, and E. G. M. Weitekamp. Dordrecht, Netherlands: Kluwer.

———. 2004. Straffällige junge Aussiedler—was kann die Justiz tun? In *Jugendstrafvollzug am Ende des 20. und zu Beginn des 21. Jahrhunderts*, ed. J. Walter. Godesberg, Germany: Forum Verlag.

Weitekamp, E. G. M., and K. Reich. 2002. Violence among Russian-Germans in the context of the subculture of violence theory. In *Crime and justice at the millennium: Essays by and in honor of Marvin E. Wolfgang*, ed. R. A. Silberman, T. P. Thornberry, B. Cohen, and B. Krisberg. Dordrecht, Netherlands: Kluwer.

Wilson, W. J. 1996. *When work disappears: The world of the new urban poor*. New York: Vintage Books.

Wolfgang, M. E., and F. Ferracuti. 1967. *The subculture of violence*. Beverly Hills, CA: Sage Publications.

Young, P. 1932. *The pilgrims of Russian-Town*. Chicago: University of Chicago Press.

Zabelina, T. 1996. Sexual violence towards women. In *Gender, generation and identity in contemporary Russia*, ed. H. Pilkington. London: Routledge

5

The Role of Crime Acts in Constituting the Gang's Mentality

INGER-LIESE LIEN

Crime is special and should have a central position in an analysis of gang be-havior. True, it may take five minutes to commit a robbery, but this temporally insignificant act has deep personal and social consequences. The worries, agita-tion, and tension that it gives rise to may last for days or years, both consciously and unconsciously. In spite of the importance of the crime act (Letkemann 1973), it is astonishing how little focus researchers of gangs have given it in their efforts to understand how gangs work. This article shows how crime acts gen-erate pride, shame, and fear that lead to a specific mental schema, a particular-istic morality, a dualistic way of thinking, a compartmentalized way of life, and the gang acting as moral therapy. A specific mindset is the outcome of a series of crime acts of robbery, extortion, violence, and drug dealing.

It is true that the appeal and the thrills of crime, as well as the moral and mental aspects of it, have been eminently described by others (Katz 1988; Tedeschi and Felson 1994). In *Seductions of Crime*, J. Katz (1988) takes a holis-tic approach, using several methods to discover a variety of emotional and mo-tivational aspects related to different types of crime and criminals. He argues that materialist theories have refused to confront *the spiritual challenge* repre-sented by crime, resting explanations of crime on a somewhat sentimental and reductionistic basis. E. Anderson (1999), on the other hand, takes ideology more seriously and finds the sources of normative values in what he terms "the code of the street," in ongoing daily activities within the dynamics and interactions taking place in the street between juveniles and others living in poverty- and crime-stricken neighborhoods. P. Bourgois (2003) and J. W. Moore (1991), together with J. D. Vigil (1999, 2002), find that crime and gang formation are matters of multiple forms of marginalization and a need for respect, with few legal ways to obtain it. They include both material and spiritual aspects in their explanations of the lifestyle in the street, using ethnographic methods in their studies of peer groups, families, the school, and the street. In this article, I use a narrower approach than the previous authors and dive into a situational and structural description of the mere crime act to analyze it as a microsystem and look at the different roles that are acted out. The description of the emotions, morals, and motivations that are generated, with short- and long-term effects, is anchored in the dynamics and structure of the crime act itself. The role of the perpetrator is of particular interest and central to the analysis.

Robbery and extortion are particular kinds of external events that will generate specific ways of thinking, a specific value system with particular morals that we can call a *mental schema*. J. M. Mandler (1984) describes a mental schema as organized experience that is built up in the course of interaction with external events. According to R. D'Andrade (1995, 180), the cognitive schema is used to represent something to reason with or to calculate from by mentally manipulating the parts of the model to solve some problem. This schema, then, is constituted by external events, generated to reason with and to solve problems developed in the course of events, but it also has *directive force*; it motivates actors, leading to new events. We will look more closely at the crime act in order to examine the development of a "thought community" and a compartmentalized way of life (Zerubavel 1997, 15).

The analysis in this chapter is based on material collected from interviews with members of several gangs in Oslo. The gangs are known under the names of the Bad Boys, Mafia Brothers, the A-gang, and the B-gang. Further interviews were conducted with family members and girlfriends between 1999 and 2001.

A SITUATIONAL ANALYSIS OF CRIME ACTS[1]
In his analysis of encounters, E. Goffman (1959, 1967) is particularly concerned with "impression management" and the central role of "face." Through situational analysis, he shows how participants are sensitive to the deference they re-

ceive and claim, and they use rituals of speech and gestures in everyday life to avoid embarrassment, maintain social bonds, and grant honor and respect to the recipients that they interact with. A crime act is different in its structure, feelings, and norms from an everyday encounter. It is a performance where the players must control information, undercommunicate weaknesses, and over-communicate determinacy. The perpetrator is not intent on maintaining positive social bonds with the victim. Rather, the opposite is the case. He aims at belittling the victim and reducing his or her self-respect in order to make the victim feel low enough to submit to the willpower of the perpetrator. This requires a particular game and role enactment from the perpetrator. The victim, on the other hand, has very little control over the situation and is expected to show deference and respect and to give away his or her possessions. The perpetrator must be alert to potential tricks and avoidance behavior from the victim and demand deference to his power and total submission in order to succeed.

For the perpetrator, the intention behind a crime act is to make an individual give away something that he or she is not legally or morally required to. The perpetrator enters an ongoing situation that is already defined, a situation where roles are set and interaction proceeds according to agreed-upon rules. As a newcomer, the perpetrator has to redefine the situation and quickly change established role patterns, turning equal relations into a power hierarchy where he is at the top and the people already in the situation are at the bottom. The perpetrator is short on time and only has a few means of constructing a situation of superiority and inferiority, of dominance and subordination. He must create respect based on fear. The instruments applied to produce fear are voice, dress, body stature, and pointing with a gun or knife, all of which indicate the willingness to use brutality or even to kill or injure in order to obtain the object. Pointing at the victim with a gun or knife is a way of communicating to the victim an image of decisiveness that says, "Nothing can stop me, so just give me what I want." It is a negative transaction in three stages, which has a tipping point in the middle of the act, where the victim subordinates him- or herself to the situation and gives away his or her possessions. The first stage is persuasion, the second is submission of the victim, and the last stage is the sortie. Each stage has its own problems and challenges for both the victim and the perpetrator. The persuasion stage requires that the perpetrator introduce his definition of the situation immediately and make the victim believe instantly that his claims are serious. "This is a robbery!" is a clear signal that produces fear and defines the situation. The perpetrator must establish his power in a convincing way and create so much fear that the victim feels there is no alternative to giving in. It is a way of trapping victims and making them experience the situation as a matter of life or death so that they will hand over what is demanded in order to survive as there seems to be no other solution. During the second stage, the victim accepts the definition, accepts his or her inferiority and the seriousness of the perpetrator, and submits to the expectations of the perpetrator. The third stage is the exit of the perpetrator, leaving the victim(s) behind.

To illustrate, we will look at some empirical cases described in court by members of several gangs. These cases illustrate many of the cognitive effects of crime acts.

Case 1

Cod is in a group of boys, about ten altogether, ranging between twelve and sixteen years old, who call themselves the Mafia Brothers. They used to rob children in the streets. Cod described one such incident and its psychological consequences.

> Ghost, Cod, Porridge, and Cucumber surrounded a Norwegian boy in the street, looked him straight in the eyes, and asked him to give them his cellphone and money. They told the boy that if he obeyed, they would not hurt him. He showed them his pocket. It was empty. They asked him if he had a credit card, and he said yes. They told him to go to the ATM at the corner and take all his money out. They followed him there to make sure he did not run away. Cod held his finger out under the jacket so that the boy all the time should think he had a knife there or a pistol. The boy stared at the finger under the jacket, got scared and gave away everything, 300 kroner. Then, they let him go, and they all ran from the place.

In conversations with me, Cod explained that the first robberies made him feel anxious and afraid but proud as well. He tried not to think of the victims. He and his friends went out and bought pizzas with the money they had stolen. They celebrated the incident and talked about it afterwards, especially about how stupidly the victim had reacted. But later, when Cod lay in his bed, he started to worry. His main concern was that his mother, someone at school, teachers, or youth workers would find out, and what would they say? His fear of being discovered became so great that it felt like a terrible pain in the chest. He was troubled for days, and his mother was worried because he was not eating properly. It took him a week to overcome this ache. It turned out that nobody found out about and confronted them with the crime act. After a week, he began to feel normal and relaxed. They did it again and again. And after every time they robbed, he felt less troubled. They got money. He could buy presents for his girlfriend, and he looked smart in his new trousers. He invited fellow students to McDonald's; they said things like, "You are such a nice guy, Cod, always giving." He told me that he felt trendy and superior. He got used to robbing. It allowed him to be generous. There was no other way he could maintain this reputation of bigheartedness. He was, in fact, very proud that he and his friends had been smart enough to elude the police every time. So, shame and fear turned into pride, and immorality in one sphere turned into morality in another—being defined as the good guy. However, the spheres had to be compartmentalized so that the truth of the one sphere would not leak into the other, which would lead to shame. "I would die of shame if my girlfriend and her friends knew," he told me.

Case 2

Riaz, Sulfiqar, Ijaz, Sungand, and I were sitting at home at my place. Then, we decided to rob someone. Then, we went down and waited until the shop closed—fifteen to twenty minutes. Then, we did it. Ijaz held the gun. I stood close by with the bottle of tear gas. I said nothing. Ijaz said something: give us the money, and things. Then, I sprayed with the bottle in the shop. After the robbery, we went home to my place and shared out the money. The hardware was buried in the flower box on the balcony and the gun too.

Case 3

Rashid and Hamid shut Mr. Mohammed in a room and kicked him in the face and in different places on his body. They struck his hands with a screwdriver and threatened to kill him. Rashid forced Mohammed to pay 5,000 kroner a month and a "fine" of 90,000 kroner. Then, he and Hamid forced Mohammed into a car and took him to an apartment where Rashid hit him several times, pointed his pistol at him and threatened to break all the bones in his body and kill him if he did not pay. The outcome was that Mohammed agreed to pay the required amount every month from the takings of his business.

Case 4

Fahim, a member of a Pakistani gang, threatened Mr. Quereshi, saying that he would shoot him in the leg if he did not pay 100,000 kroner. This threat persuaded Mr. Quereshi to pay 20,000 per month for a five-month period.

A GENERAL DESCRIPTION OF THE STRUCTURE OF CRIME ACTS

Any social situation can be described as both a communication system and as a deference-emotion system (Scheff 1990). The first system enables speakers to make their thoughts known to each other and the second, their evaluation of each other's status. T. J. Scheff argues, supporting a point made by both D. Sperber (1996) and N. Elias (1978), that the division between sociology and psychology has made it difficult to integrate emotions into structural analysis, as emotions now belong to the psychologist's department. This delineation is fruitful for neither the psychologists, who lose sight of the context of social life, nor the sociologists and criminologists, who need to understand emotions and motivations in order to understand social life both at the micro and macro levels. I have tried to overcome this gap by introducing emotions into the analysis of interaction in the crime situation. The crime acts described above are social systems that communicate deference and contempt with consequences for both individuals and groups. Crime acts construct feelings of ambivalence, pride, fear, and shame because of the problem of legitimacy and the neglect of the importance of the social bond in the crime situation. Another reason is that ordinary rules of conduct (Goffman 1959) are broken. The crime act is actually a destruction of the potential social bond between the victim and the perpetrator and an introduction of a new set of rules, where the deference-emotion system is now hierarchical and the perpetrator must use force and fear to obtain a kind of deference based on respect out of fear.

Gang members' cultural capital (Bourdieu 1986), in order to obtain deference during crime acts, is the ability to instill fear, block empathy, and create a hierarchical situation in which control is in their hands. Because the offender is on top, the situation may provide excitement and even joy. K. Rørhus (2000) says that most robbers are both exited and scared during the robbery, and their ability to think clearly is usually restricted because of the critical nature of the situation and their use of drugs. Use of violence during a robbery is connected to a feeling of lacking control, and panic may lead the robbers into impulsive behavior motivated by fear, self-defense, and the need to escape. D. Indremaur (1995) argues that violence is often introduced as a substitute for good planning. According to S. H. Decker and B. Van Winkle (1996, 144), gang members have a fatalistic attitude toward violence: "You gotta do what you gotta do." "We don't go looking for trouble." So, professionally, the ability to create convincing threats is more important than actually acting violently. Violence can occur, though, as the last resort when threats do not work properly in getting the victim(s) to accept the situational definition. J. W. Messerschmidt (1993) argues that a robbery is gendered into a masculine activity because it boosts power and self-esteem. Robbery yields both pleasure and money, which is why it is so difficult to end a career of crime.

Pride

The American psychiatrist Donald Nathanson (1992) argues that we should understand people and personal motivation according to what instills pride and what instills shame within a given context. A competent self is the one that evokes the happiest memories. "[C]an there be any real difference between the pride of a hunter bagging his quarry, the pride of a soldier who kills his enemy in battle, and the pride experienced by a terrorist when his bomb kills a busload of schoolchildren? I think not" (Nathanson 1992, 20). Crime is an act that requires a specific form of professionalism and competence; this is a source of pride that gives a heightened sense of self, even though it is an act that entails great ambivalence and may also lead to shame, as we will see later. According to Scheff's (1990) analysis of microsociology, pride is related to maintaining social bonds, and shame is a sign of a severed or threatened bond. I agree more with Nathanson's (1992) conception of pride as excitement linked to self-esteem and "competence pleasure" experienced by "the competent self." Of course, these factors are connected, as reputation and reward related to competence can be obtained from assessments of significant others. Recognition lies within a certain type of relation and not in all relations. For the perpetrator, the victim is not the significant other and may actually be irrelevant to his self-esteem, but other gang members are relevant as judges of his competence. Recognition that leads to pride can be obtained in the backstage of the crime act, when the perpetrator sits with his friends and boast about his role enactment. Robert Paine (1989), in his study of law-breaking activities in Pakistan, argues that through breaking the law, one gains a reputation for fearlessness, showing the world that one is above the rules. Norm-breaking activities add to a person's prestige and give him "a heightened sense of self or of being," while simultaneously increasing the status of the norms. The fact that perpetrators have managed to act professionally in a crime situation contributes to their feeling of pride in more or less the same way as the soldier, who feels proud upon receiving the recognition of his fellow soldiers for killing the enemy in battle.

Crime acts are high-risk activities that lead to a feeling of superiority and situational narcissism (Freud 1991, 304). The perpetrator may develop what J. D. Vigil (1999, 276) terms a *monster ego*—he feels superior because he is in control. "Crime is an exciting, thrilling game where criminals put their skills and personalities against the 'world out there.' The excitement makes it all worthwhile and each small success confirms the youth's belief that it is the only future worth pursuing. They are not pushed into crime; instead they rush headlong into it, lusting for the thrills and opportunities that come with it" (O'Kane 1992, 119).

Blocking of Empathy and Self-control

It is the rule of the game that in order to create a situation of fear, the perpetrator must act professionally and threateningly by raising his voice and creating a scary image persuasively, often with the help of a weapon. The inner self of the person, his compassion and care, must be numbed. The more brutal he looks and the scarier he makes the situation for the victim, the more successful and professional is the perpetrator, unless the victim switches over and behaves irrationally and disobediently as a consequence of his fear.

In this particular context, the perpetrator cannot be a compassionate and caring person. He must act with the opposite qualities: antagonism, cruelty, and anger. Physical training, muscle mass, and body size are important for this kind of occupation. So, too, is control of the eyes and body movements. The situation must be acted out to convince the victim and reveal no weakness. The greater the perceived threat, the greater the chance that the victim will cooperate.

These realities are understood well by gang members. Members of the A- and B-gangs in Oslo all take part in daily physical training at studios in Oslo. In this way, their self-discipline is admirable. To increase muscle mass, they take substances like Testoviron, Vistol, Pirmobolan, and Extraboline, as well as cocaine and Valium. The effects of these drugs can be observed in their faces and necks, which grow rounder and bigger. A Norwegian girl, who had recently become a member of a Vietnamese gang, told me, "I had to change a lot of what I had learned from my family. I needed to learn how to keep my face like my Vietnamese friends. You know, they can look you straight in your eyes and tell you lots of lies. The most important thing is to learn how to control your eyes and your face, and to tell lies." Echoing the same theme, when I asked a member of the B-gang in Oslo why his brother was not a member of the gang, he said that his brother was too innocent, naive, and stupid. "You know, he will always tell the truth. He is like a child. To be in this business, you need to control yourself, your face, even your eyes."

The Danish philosopher K. E. Løgstrup (1971, 1972) argues that trust is a *sovereign manifestation* of life. It is the basis of the positive responsibilities that people assume when they meet each other. Even strangers feel the sovereign manifestation of life, and their first inclination is toward positive responsibility and trust. This trust lies in seeing the face of the other (Levinas 1985). If this normative hypothesis is true, then being involved in crime could cause a person to work against his own natural inclinations, which may cause pain in the perpetrator. To act badly toward a stranger or to deceive and tell lies would not be the first preference for any person. Thus, a person who acts like this would go through a process of mental change as a consequence of the act. A former girlfriend of a gang member said, "Now his eyes are just black. They reveal nothing. He has changed so much. When he was a teenager, his eyes used to sparkle. And there was conscience in them. Now, there is nothing. If he has murdered a person or two, I do not know, but, well yes, I could believe it. His eyes are like that—empty."

Fear and Shame

Leaving the crime scene does not imply that the consequences are left behind, as Cod's narrative in case 1 tells us. The exit stage has not come to an end even though the perpetrator reaches home safely. There may be people looking for him. As a consequence of the act, his world is suddenly full of potential enemies—the police, witnesses, denouncers—who may inform on him so that his freedom will be taken away. He is also afraid that people who should not know about the act will find out. Cod, in the example above, is afraid that his girlfriend will find out. "I would die of shame," he says.

The act, therefore, hangs on to the person for days, weeks, months, or years not only because it is illegal but because it is unnatural and threatens the person's image of himself. It has the potential to create both shame and fear.

Gradually, fear infiltrates every aspect of the criminal's life. The armed rob-
ber, once he has the money, is afraid to leave the bank in case the police are
waiting outside to shoot him. He lives in daily fear. He feels constant stress and
becomes paranoid: "You're always on edge, on pills." "It's a strange life, too.
You're always nervous 'cause there's always something they can pin on you.
You never know what's gonna happen. That makes it exciting too, but it gets
you after a while" (West 1989, 186, in Cusson and Pinsonneault 1986, 77).

Gang members are usually connected to a lot of people and interact with ordinary people in the society, whom they do not necessarily want to have any
knowledge of their crime acts as this would cause embarrassment. These painful
feelings must be dealt with and reduced. H. B. Lewis (1971, 19) argues that shame
is an inhibitor of pride and misdeeds. "Shame is an acutely painful experience
about the self, and it feels as if 'it could die' or 'crawl through a hole.'" Perpetrators need to see themselves in a positive way, like everybody else. Therefore, the
feeling of shame needs to be repressed by avoiding people who may condemn
them, concealing information, and bracketing the event so as to single it out as
something unimportant. As one perpetrator said, "It took me only a few seconds
to stab him down. Should I be judged by these two seconds, when I have been a
good person most of the time?" Telling lies, using over- and undercommunica-
tive strategies, and concealing facts are ways of avoiding shame. Scheff (1990, 18)
argues that shame can become pathological when it is not acknowledged, which
may explain the hypersensitivity to insults that some gang members exhibit.
Some people develop a chronic shame state and react with exaggerated aggression. G. Sykes and D. Matza (1957) distinguish among five major techniques of
neutralization that criminals develop in order to live with their crime acts and reduce shame: (1) denial of responsibility (e.g., "I was drunk"), (2) denial of injury
(e.g., "Nobody got hurt"), (3) denial of victimization (e.g., "They deserved it"),
(4) condemnation of the condemners (e.g., "They're crooks themselves"), and
(5) appeal to higher loyalties (e.g., "I had to stick by my mates"). These kinds of
arguments give the perpetrator a heightened sense of self so that, in the end, he
can see himself as a good rather than a bad guy. Repetition also tends to make
crime acts more routine and normal. Another way of maintaining a positive self-
image is to use the gang as moral and psychological therapy. Hanging around
with like-minded people who also have criminal experience makes the person see
himself as normal and acceptable. By controlling information, compartmental-
izing, using dissimulation strategies, constructing narratives of justification, and

adopting techniques of neutralization, gang members can maintain a positive self-image among their friends and families. However, others usually see them as bad guys, and they often have to fight enemies.

Love and the Gang as Moral Therapy

Life in the gang can be described, in Goffman's terminology (1959), as the backstage for the crime acts. It is also a refuge, an extension of the exit stage where the bad guy of the crime act is turned into a good guy among friends. The leader of the A-gang, described in the newspapers as the most dangerous man in Norway due to his criminal acts, had a reputation among his friends for being a loyal, generous, and nice person. He would throw parties for his friends, dole out champagne, and lend money. He was a big man who gave his riches away and saved nothing. His generosity was enormous, his friends argued. Resources obtained illegally from one sphere were converted in another and invested in building the person's moral reputation among friends. The ideology of love and brotherhood was built in the group.

Some members of the A-gang are apparently serving time thanks to criminal activities committed by their "brothers." They are willing to sacrifice both their life and their freedom for the love of their friends, they argue. The ideology of sacrifice is based on moral arguments. One inmate, a member of a gang, told me,

> The fact that I had so much love for my friend that I would risk my life for him, was highly appreciated among the inmates that I met in prison. I would have killed the person and he was so badly beaten he looked like a chopped vegetable afterwards. I did it for my friends. Several of the inmates told me afterwards that they were impressed. I had proven myself a trustworthy person and not a coward. Therefore, a marvelous criminal career was waiting for me. They liked good guys like me, they said.

A particularistic morality for those who are inside the group develops around generosity, love, and sacrifice. Inside the group, one is considered a morally upstanding person even though he lies, steals, and may commit murder outside the group. Describing his attachment to his friends, another gang member told me, "It was love between us. Nothing could get in between. I told my girlfriend: if I must choose between you and them, I will choose them."

A gang, then, operates as a moral unit, and violent crime acts are given moral justification in the narratives constructed by the gangs. As long as the acts are justified by this way of thinking, it will be difficult to change gang members' criminal behavior. All groups who set themselves apart from society, such as gangs, other criminals, religious sects, and countercultural groups, develop *gemeinschaft*, immunization techniques, and a prickly suspicion that makes dialog with outsiders difficult and tense. Their scheme of thought could possibly be called an ideology, as it has logic, moral backing, and justification, benefits some and not others, and is immune to corrections (Skirbekk 1999).

Violence, Anger, and Hate

We will look at a competition between two Pakistani gangs in Oslo where honor, pride, and shame are at stake. The act presented in the court is described by one of the victims, who is particularly concerned with his embarrassment and shame, as we will see. This act led to several new acts of revenge, where members of the A-gang were shot at, and a murder occurred. Using the terminology of Goffman (1959), we may argue that this incident describes a *character play*.

A against B: A Case from Court

The following statement was made to the court by Fahim of the B-gang, twenty-one years of age, one of seven brothers:

> One day I was sent by my mother to buy some parts for our dishwasher that was broken. My little brother walked with me. Suddenly a car stopped close by, and three A-gang members came out and forced us in their car.
>
> Two more cars came. One was a Honda with three persons, and a Mercedes with four persons and then a pickup with two persons.
>
> They drove up to a deserted place near a lake. I was terrified all the time. There, they opened my mouth with their hands, and one of them put a pistol in my mouth: "Do as we want you to, or we'll kill you." I thought I was going to die, so I asked for forgiveness and said sorry. But they were not satisfied. They talked to each other all the time and were making several phone calls to their friends on their cell phones.
>
> Then, they forced us into the car again, and we drove further. They took us to a stall behind the shopping center at Stovner. I discovered that inside the stall, they had managed to gather a lot of Pakistani youth from the area, fifteen to twenty boys, everybody staring at me as we went in and making a circle around me. Ali in the A-gang said, "You must ask my little brother for forgiveness." Now, he forced me to bend down and touch the feet of his youngest brother, who is much younger than me. They had a camera and took two pictures. The Pakistani boys in the audience were laughing. It was so degrading.

First, I bent down and touched the knee of the boy, but they were not satisfied, so I had to bend even further down again and touch him at the tip of his shoe. They wanted to humiliate me and laugh at me. They wanted me to know for the rest of my life that I had touched the feet of the small boy. They have harmed and hit and molested lots of people before, but they have never ever before demanded that anybody should touch their feet. This is the worst thing that could happen. When they had taken the photos, we were told to get out quick, otherwise they would kill us, they shouted.

The kissing of feet is a tradition from Sufism, where disciples, out of respect for a holy man, bend down and kiss or touch his feet as a mark of total devotion. The act in this case denoted subordination of the older member of the B-gang to the young A-gang brother. When forced to touch the boy's shoes, the B-gang member showed that he was a devotee, increasing the value of the other at his own expense. It was an expression of superiority and hierarchy, showing the audience that the B-gang was bending its head before the A-gang. The photo was the evidence that this inferiority position was true. It created a terrible feeling of shame and humiliation in the B-gang member, as expressed in the sentence, "It was the worst thing that could happen."

In this case, the two members of the B-gang were forced into a kind of theater play in the stall with an audience of twenty Pakistani boys. Their roles were forced upon them with threats. The oldest B-gang member was forced into a metaphorical theater play based on the Islamic Sufi tradition regarding the inferiority and submission of a disciple to a holy man by touching his shoes. The staged play communicated symbolic power and strength, conceptualized as honor and talked about as respect. Gang fights can be described as plays directed toward an audience. There are several audiences here: the members of the two different gangs, the audience of ordinary Pakistani youth, and the audience of the Pakistani and Norwegian community. There is also an audience in the criminal network of Oslo, consisting of criminal superiors who need people and groups to "hire" or "employ." The shoe-touching act described above is a communicative play about position, power, competence, and emotion intended for many audiences. It is also a serious identity play directed toward the general public, telling Norwegians and Pakistanis alike that the A- and B-gangs are not to be taken lightly and that one of them is the most powerful, hence superior and qualified. In this situation, the A-gang showed itself to be superior.

Gang fights are between specific enemies, but they have other functions as well. They may lead to material gains at a later time as a reputation for being tough is necessary in extortion and the drug market. Perceived honor and respect make the job much easier. The A- and B-gangs in Oslo do not fight with other gangs; they fight with each other primarily because they are competing in the same market for the same goods. In his analysis of multicultural management, M. Maruyama (1994) argues that in business, diversity enables mutual benefit, and sameness causes war. When we look at gang wars in Norway between the motorcycle gangs, Bandidos and Hells Angels, and between the two Pakistani gangs, the A- and the B-gangs, the gangs that fight each other are astonishingly similar in terms of the crimes they commit, their activities and values, and their ethnic backgrounds.

R. Nisbett and L. Ross (1991), in the tradition of Kurt Lewin, argue that we should understand groups as being in a constant state of tension as they try to balance the factors at work to create equilibrium. Tension is produced as a result of conflict in the minds of individuals, of dissonance in attitudes and values, and of conflicts that need to be resolved within the groups in different situations. Retaliation is one way of converting tension into well-being for a person knocked off balance by wounded self-esteem. Retaliation feels good as it reduces the pain in an individual who has been put down. Retaliation has the added effect of boosting self-esteem within the group and enables the group to see itself as superior and competent.

A. T. Beck (1999) looks at the cognitive basis for strong feelings such as hate and acts of revenge and finds that a categorical, dualistic type of thinking characterizes the mentality. I would add to his understanding the point that the dualism is hierarchical. Beck diagnoses hate as a self-centered thinking disorder with only two positions, the good and the bad. So, when the A-gang attacks the B-gang in Oslo, the attack is justified in the gang's mental schema where hate is important. Both groups see themselves as the good guys and as superior to each other. They have morality on their side, and they are the innocent victims of, and attribute malice to, each other. Beck writes,

When this primal mode of thinking is triggered, he automatically prepares to attack—to defend his highly invested value. This hostile mode takes over the thinking apparatus and crowds out other human qualities such as empathy and morality. The same kind of thinking is activated whether the perpetrator is reacting as a member of a group or as an individual. Unless interrupted, the hostility sequence proceeds from perception of transgression to preparation to mobilization to actual attack. (1999, 22)

COGNITIVE SCHEMA OF THE GANG MEMBERS

L. Yablonsky (1967 and with M. Haskell [1990]), a criminologist concerned with the psychological dimensions of gangs, distinguishes among four different personality types. The first type is referred to as the *socialized* criminal, who is emotionally normal but becomes criminal as a result of learning. The second type is the *neurotic*, who becomes criminal as a result of a personality distortion. The third type is the *psychotic* criminal, who has a more severe personality disorder. The fourth is the *sociopathic* criminal, who is egocentric and has a less delusional and compelling personality disorder than the psychotic.

According to Yablonsky, the sociopathic youth is produced by the social milieu that trains him to develop sociopathic personality traits. "The youth with this type of sociopathic personality syndrome, living in the disorganized-slum neighborhood, is most prone to participation in the violent gang. . . . He is characteristically unable to experience the pain of the violence he may inflict on another, since he does not have the ability to identify or empathize with any others" (Yablonsky 1967, 217, 219). This type of person is further described as behaving irresponsibly, untruthfully, insincerely, and antisocially, without a shred of shame, remorse, or guilt.

However, my material shows that these characteristics are only situational and are contextually determined. Responsibility, loyalty, discipline, empathy, and love are universal emotions and motivations found in both gang members and nongang members. Yet, these emotions can be professionally blocked in crime situations and during encounters with enemies or the authorities. The competence involved in being able to block these emotions may lead to pride. It may also lead to a dualistic and particularistic way of thinking that is backed by a compartmentalized lifestyle within different social spheres. A mental schema motivating and supporting the ability to block empathy may be the aggregate outcome of repetitive crime acts. It will be built and developed in the mind of the gang members as a solution to tension, shame, and fear accumulated after a series of crime situations. The personality structure is not necessarily there before the crime acts, but it will be developed through repeated crime.

A model of a mental schema and the way it is institutionalized, reinforced, and internalized is presented in figure 5.1. We see that it starts with crime acts, which not only generate capital and pride but also fear, danger of arrest, and considerable

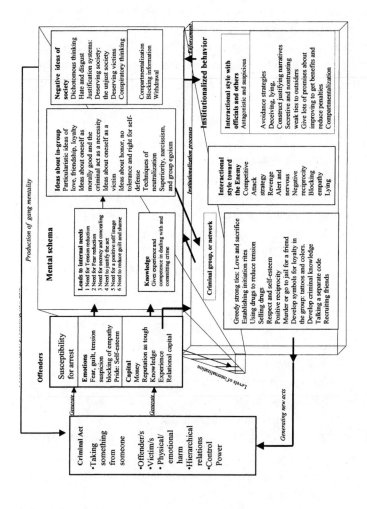

FIGURE 5.1
The social production of gang mentalities

emotional pain. For the offender, this experience leads to internal tension, and several emotional needs that must be dealt with. He has to alleviate tension and fear, control information through secrecy, and justify criminal acts, while at the same time acting the good guy role. He develops a dualistic, hierarchical, and particularistic way of thinking, with different moral standards for different categories of people and situations. He develops ideas of compassion, love, and sacrifice in relation to his friends, and he explains his acts through a construction of himself as a victim of society. The victimization point is necessary in order to justify the criminal act. He cannot be blamed, the act is heroic rather than evil, and the victims get what they deserve. He blocks his empathy not because of an emotional defect in his character but because of economic and situational need and the professionalism required during a crime situation. In the long run, however, a repetitive blocking of empathy may change his character permanently so that he truly becomes a sociopathic personality according to Yablonsky's definition. The gang member creates narratives about the crime act that make it into a requirement, a law of nature, unavoidable by any act of will on his part. By this twist in the prevailing logic, the act can be portrayed as good rather than bad. Ordinary social thinking is turned upside down to justify the perpetrator and the crime.

This way of thinking, converting the assailant into the victim, is an element of the cognitive psychology of crime acts through which the offender denies that he himself is to blame. The offender is sensitive to the violation of rules— the rules that he himself claims the other party should follow. But when the rules are used against him, it creates a sense of hurt and humiliation. "Because groups are biased in their perception of themselves and others, their people are likely to attribute better motives and more sterling character to members of their own group than to those of an out group. When things go wrong, people are likely to assign more blame to a member of an out group than to members of their own group" (Beck 1999, 151).

The mental schema is institutionalized and embedded in the behavioral patterns of all gang members, assailants and defenders alike. It can be described as a specific social form, aggregated by repetitive crime acts that only take a few minutes but must be concealed indefinitely. They organize themselves accordingly; they talk accordingly; their structure, economy, alliances, and opponents are constructed accordingly; and finding this mental schema replicated elsewhere provides positive feedback, fostering further internalization.

Beck (1999) argues that a dualistic way of thinking was beneficial for survival in a band society when people had to act quickly and make rapid decisions based on small amounts of information, as in hunting-and-gathering societies. Gangs live a life in a hostile environment that they themselves have created. They live in a modern, urban, band society. The police and other criminal gangs are actually after them, so they have to be alert to and suspicious of the intentions of others; attacks are easily mounted, and they have to react and process information very rapidly. They are caught in each other's web, and their actions toward each other reinforce their shared mental schema and make it stronger motivationally. The irony is that in order to survive, they are caught in a spiral of vengeance, which can lead to extinction in the long run. Their mutual similarity and knowledge of each other's background and aims make their thinking intelligent and rational rather than the other way around.

Individuals moving around in a hostile environment have to be alert and aware of the mentalities of others, which motivates them to internalize the code in use. This mentality can be internalized to different degrees, from a superficial, clichéd level to a highly motivational level (Spiro 1997). When the mentality is shared by many, as in a gang-dominated area, ignoring it would be senseless because it motivates the actions of both friends and enemies. The glove fits the hand. A person who associates with gangs and their members and is involved in crime activities has to understand the type of thinking employed; gradually, he internalizes it lock, stock, and barrel himself.

Criminals and gangs have more or less the same ambitions as most other people. They want recognition and are greedy for certain lifestyles and money like the rest of the population. Yet, they are also willing to break the law and to inflict harm, pain, and suffering on people to achieve their goals. In this way, they depart from the majority of the population, the "decent" portions of the community that may well be poor but do not use the same techniques to enrich themselves.

CONCLUSION

While many scientists have tried to find the causes of crime either in the character of the perpetrators themselves or in the environments where they live or have been brought up, such as the family, peer group, or surrounding socioeconomic structure, I have tried to look at the crime act as itself the cause of crime. The claim that crime creates a mindset that generates more crime may seem circular, but it is in fact a processual argument. I do not try to explain why youths turn to crime and become criminal in the first place. Rather, I ask what crime acts do to individuals. This question has led me to discover the pains and pleasures of crime and the mentalities that develop as an aftereffect of participating in crime acts. S. Yochelson and S. Samenow (1976), who very early discovered that criminal life has a special thought structure, seem to argue that this way of thinking is present before the crime acts begin. They use a concept like the "criminal child" to distinguish would-be criminals from other children and argue that their way of thinking causes crime, implying that the way of thinking preceded the actual crime acts. Yablonsky seems to fall into the same ditch, ranking crime acts as outcomes of personality traits either inherited or learned before perpetrators enter into crime situations. I do not share this perspective. On the contrary, I hold that criminal thinking occurs as an aftereffect of crime, then develops, matures, and becomes increasingly motivating as more crimes are perpetrated. Finally, it may reach a point of no return that alters the whole structure of thinking and motivation. This is a tipping-point theory of mind based on the aggregate outcome of a series of behaviors that need to be interpreted and justified. M. Klein (1995) particularly has pinpointed the quantitative dimension of crime acts in trying to distinguish gangs from juvenile groups. On the opposite sides of the tipping point, gangs and juvenile groups reside on a scale of crime acts where quantitative dimensions have created two qualitatively different categories with different mindsets and different ways of life. Repetitive criminal acts are therefore very forceful in producing the qualitative change. Perpetrators' need to see themselves as morally good in spite of their violent criminal careers are motors behind the building of justification systems and new mental schemas.

To counteract this process, we need to build programs that work not only on a structural level but also on the normative level to change the mentality and to reorient and reverse the value systems held by gang members. As these values and patterns of thinking have become very habitual and are often held with deep conviction, we should not be too naive about the ease of such processes of change. Despite the challenges of internal resistance, immunization, and information blocking, any program that deals with gang members and their crimes must take the mentality factor into account in the rehabilitation effort.

NOTE

1. In the following analysis, perpetrators will always be referred to with masculine pronouns, as all gang members interviewed were male. Victims, on the other hand, may be either male or female, as my research revealed that gang members' crime acts are committed against both sexes.

REFERENCES

Anderson, E. 1999. *Code of the street: Decency, violence, and the moral life of the inner city.* New York: W. W. Norton.

Beck, A. T. 1999. *Prisoners of hate: The cognitive basis of anger, hostility and violence.* New York: Perennial.

Bourdieu, P. 1986. *Det sociala rummet och dess omvandlingar. I Kultursociologiska texter. Utvalg av Donald Broady og Mikael Palme.* Lidingö, Sweden: Salamander.

Bourgois, P. 2003. *In search of respect: Selling crack in el barrio.* Cambridge: Cambridge University Press

Cusson, M., and P. Pinsonneault. 1986. The decision to give up crime. In *The reasoning criminal,* ed. C. B. Cornish and R. V. Clarke. New York: Springer-Verlag.

D'Andrade, R. 1995. *The development of cognitive anthropology.* Cambridge: Cambridge University Press.

Decker, S. H., and B. Van Winkle. 1996. *Life in the gang.* Cambridge: Cambridge University Press.

Elias, N. 1978. *The history of manners.* New York: Pantheon.

Freud, S. 1991[1930]. *Civilization and its discontents.* In *Civilization, society and religion,* ed. A. Dickson, Trans. and J. Strachey, Penguin Freud Library, vol. XII, 243–340. Harmondsworth, United Kingdom: Penguin Books.

Goffman, E. 1959. *The presentation of self in everyday life.* New York: Anchor.

———. 1967. *Interaction ritual.* Garden City, NY: Anchor.

Indremaur, D. 1995. *Violent property crime.* Sydney: Federation Press.

Katz, J. 1988. *Seductions of crime: Moral and sensual attractions in doing evil.* New York: Basic Books

Klein, M. 1995. *The American street gang.* New York: Oxford University Press.

Letkemann, P. 1973. *Crime as work.* Englewood Cliffs, NJ: Prentice Hall.

Levinas, E. 1985. *Ethics and infinity.* Pittsburgh, PA: Duquesne University Press.

Lewis, H. B. 1971. *Shame and guilt in neurosis.* New York: International Universities Press.

Løgstrup, K. E. 1971. *The ethical demand.* Philadelphia: Fortress Press.

———. 1972. *Norm og spontaneitet.* Copenhagen: Gyldendal.

Mandler, J. M. 1984. *Stories, scripts and scenes: Aspects of schema theory.* Hillsdale, NJ: Erlbaum.

Maruyama, M. 1994. *Mindscapes in management: Use of individual differences in multicultural management.* Aldershot, United Kingdom: Dartmouth Publishing.

Messerschmidt, J. W. 1993. *Masculinities and crime.* Lanham, MD: Rowman & Littlefield.

Moore, J. W. 1991. *Going down to the barrio: Homeboys and homegirls in change.* Philadelphia: Temple University Press

Nathanson, D. L. 1992. *Shame and pride: Affect, sex and the birth of the self.* New York: W. W. Norton and Company.

Nisbett, R., and L. Ross. 1991. *The person and the situation: Perspectives of social psychology.* New York: McGraw-Hill.

O'Kane, J. M. 1992. *The crooked ladder: Gangsters, ethnicity and the American dream.* New Brunswick, NJ: Transaction Publishers.

Paine, R. 1989. High-wire culture: Comparing two agonic systems of self-esteem. *Man* 24: 657–72.

Rørhus, K. 2000. *Ranere. En studie av raneres tenkemåte og mentalitet.* Oslo: PHS-series.

Scheff, T. J. 1990. *Microsociology: Discourse, emotion, and social structure.* Chicago: University of Chicago Press.

Skirbekk, S. 1999. *Ideologi, myte og tro ved slutten av et århundre.* Oslo: Tano Aschehoug.

Sperber, D. 1996. *Explaining culture: A naturalistic approach.* Oxford: Blackwell Publishers.

Spiro, M. E. 1997. *Gender ideology and psychological reality.* New Haven, CT: Yale University Press.

Sykes, G., and D. Matza. 1957. Techniques of neutralization: A theory of delinquency. *American Sociological Review* 22: 664–70.

Tedeschi, J. T., and R. B. Felson. 1994. *Violence, aggression and coercive actions.* Washington, D.C.: American Psychological Association.

Vigil, J. D. 1999. Streets and schools: How educators can help Chicano marginalized gang youth. *Human Educational Review* 69 (3) (Fall).

———. 2002. *A rainbow of gangs: Street cultures in the mega-city.* Austin: University of Texas Press.

West, W. G. 1989. The short-term careers of serious thieves. *Canadian Journal of Criminology* 20 (2): 169–90.

Yablonsky, L. 1967. *The violent gang.* Harmondsworth, United Kingdom: Penguin.

Yablonsky, L., and M. Haskell. 1990. *Criminology, crime and criminality.* New York: Harper and Row.

Yochelson, S., and S. Samenow. 1976. *The criminal personality: A profile for change.* New York: Aronson.

Zerubavel, E. 1997. *Social mindscapes: An invitation to cognitive sociology.* Cambridge, MA: Harvard University Press.

II

QUANTITATIVE APPROACHES

Identification and Self-identification: Using a Survey to Study Gangs in the Netherlands

FRANK M. WEERMAN

The use of youth surveys to study gangs is a relatively new phenomenon. Traditionally, studies of gangs have been descriptive, using ethnographic methods and interviews with key informants. These methods have resulted in profound insights into the nature and characteristics of gangs and gang members in the United States (see classics like Thrasher 1927, or recent ethnographies like Decker and Van Winkle 1996; Fleisher 1998; Hagedorn 1998; Miller 2001; Moore 1991; Vigil 1988). Comparable studies of gangs in Europe are scarce (examples include Patrick 1979; Tertilt 1995). Surveys of gang membership have been conducted in the past (i.e., Klein and Crawford 1967; Short and Strodtbeck 1965), but these were modest in scope and often used samples of already delinquent youth. Only since the beginning of the 1990s have general youth surveys become a significant source of information on gangs and gang members (see especially Esbensen and Huizinga 1993; Thornberry et al. 1993). In Europe, surveys have yet to become an established means of studying gangs or troublesome youth groups. Relatively few survey studies have included items about gangs or youth groups (some recent examples, however, include Bradshaw 2002; Haaland 2000; Huizinga and Schumann 2001).

While ethnographic studies provide depth and detail, the use of youth surveys to study gangs has its own unique selling points. Surveys provide information about the proportion of a population involved in youth gangs and enable comparisons and generalizations. They inform us about organizational characteristics of gangs at different sites (Esbensen and Peterson Lynskey 2001), about risk factors for gang membership (Thornberry 1998), and about the longitudinal development of gang members and nongang members (Hill et al. 1996; Thornberry et al. 2003). They also provide information about the unique contribution of gang membership to delinquent behavior, apart from the influence of delinquent friends (Thornberry et al. 1993; Battin et al. 1998).

One has to bear in mind, however, that surveys are usually based on samples of middle and high school students. This implies that the results are primarily valid for the population of youth. Ethnographies and statistics are also based on older members of gangs and youth groups. Moreover, ethnographic studies often rely on key informants who are core members of gangs, and statistics are based on the most delinquent, active parts of the gang spectrum. School surveys include more members from the periphery of gangs and wannabes. Surveys cover the less serious, but also more common, part of youth involvement in gangs and troublesome youth groups (see also Curry 2000).

To establish gang membership in youth surveys can be difficult. Ethnographies are usually restricted to clear cases of gang situations and use rich and varied sources of information. Youth surveys are necessarily based on a limited number of written questions. The identification of youth groups as gangs (or troublesome youth groups) is further complicated by definitional and operational problems with the gang concept. In many American surveys, this problem is avoided by relying on self-identification: respondents are simply asked, "Do you belong to a gang?" However, in this way, the researcher is not certain that the respondent has the same type of youth group in mind as he or she does. Usually, this problem is handled by asking control questions, for example, questions about the criminal activities of the respondents' gang (e.g., Esbensen and Peterson Lynskey 2001). This solution might work quite well in the American situation, where the concept of a gang is familiar to most respondents. In Europe, the use of the word *gang* or its synonyms (e.g., *jeugdbende, bande*) is less widespread and more ambiguous. Asking directly if a respondent belongs to a gang might result in less reliable answers than it would in the United States.

Within the Eurogang network, considerable energy and time have been devoted to finding common definitions and operationalizations of the gang concept. This effort has resulted in the development of a nominal definition of *gang* through the consensus of the U.S. and European researchers in the Eurogang network. In the School Survey Working Group within the Eurogang network, criteria and survey procedures have been developed to establish gang membership objectively among respondents. A funneling procedure leads respondents through a set of questions about formal and informal peer groups, the characteristics of these groups, illegal activities, and finally, whether respondents would call their group a gang (or its synonym in their own language). This technique offers objective criteria for the researcher to define whether a group is a gang under the Eurogang definition (e.g., based on their public orientation, makeup, and activities). At the same time, it incorporates the more subjective criterion of respondents' self-identification as members of a gang.

In this chapter, data from a school survey in the Netherlands is used to study gangs and gang membership among a sample of youth. The study is among the first to apply the Eurogang nominal definition of gangs, and it uses a questionnaire based on the funneling technique developed by the Eurogang network. It is the first study to apply survey methods to the subject of gangs and troublesome youth groups in the Netherlands. The data may offer insights into two important issues. The first is identification: if and how well gang members can be identified with the Eurogang definition and survey method. The second is self-identification: how members of youth groups refer to and view their groups themselves and how their views overlap with or differ from identifications based on the Eurogang methods.

RESEARCH METHOD

This study is part of a larger school-based research program (the School Project of the Netherlands Institute for the Study of Crime and Law Enforcement), which combines the collection of quantitative survey data and qualitative interview information at twelve secondary schools in and around The Hague. The research program covers subjects like peer influences, development, and school interventions and has a longitudinal design. Two cohorts, students in their first class of secondary school and those in their third class, are surveyed repeatedly. Data from the first wave (conducted in 2002) are used for this chapter. A second and third wave were conducted in 2003 and 2004, respectively.

Two goals guided the selection of respondents in our study. The first goal was to get a relatively high-risk sample with a substantive proportion of respondents involved in different kinds of problem behavior and delinquency. To accomplish this, we decided to oversample students with low education levels from places with clear inner city problems. We have chosen to focus on the area of The Hague, a multiethnic city with a reported presence in the past of troublesome youth groups and gangs (see Gruter and Versteegh 2001; van Gemert 2001). Our second goal was to get a great deal of variation in school contexts and student populations. To accomplish this, we selected schools from different neighborhoods in The Hague, as well as some schools from smaller cities in the vicinity. The sample also contains a school for agricultural education and a reformatory school, both contributing to the variety in school contexts. By combining the two seemingly contradictory goals, we managed to get a sample that is useful for analyzing problem behavior and delinquency. Although it is clearly not a random sample, it represents a cross-cut of Dutch youth (with low levels of education), especially in the area of The Hague. As such, it can be used to generate a general image of gangs and gang affiliation among adolescents in the Netherlands. An overview of the sample demographics is presented in table 6.1.

The total sample size is 1,978 respondents. Both genders are well represented in this study; the numbers of boys and girls in the sample are almost equal. Almost all respondents are between twelve and sixteen years old. Two age categories contain more respondents than the others (thirteen and fifteen years) due to the cohort design of the study (i.e., most first graders are thirteen years old, and most third graders are fifteen years old). The majority of respondents were recruited in The Hague,[1] a substantial minority lived in one of two medium-sized cities (about 120,000 inhabitants) nearby, and some respondents were recruited from a school in a small city. Compared with the general Dutch population, large and middle-sized cities are over-represented. Ethnic minorities are also relatively oversampled. More than one-third of the sample consists of respondents with a foreign background, but respondents with Dutch parents are still in the majority. Turkish, Surinamese, and Moroccan respondents are the ethnic categories best represented. There is also a number, although relatively small, of Antillean respondents. About 11 percent of the respondents have parents from mixed foreign countries (e.g., a Surinamese mother and a Turkish father). There is

Table 6.1.   Demographic Characteristics of the
Dutch Youth Sample

Total Sample Size	Percentage (number)
	100 (1,978)
Gender	
Male	55 (1,098)
Female	45 (880)
Age	
11	0 (1)
12	11 (210)
13	32 (624)
14	18 (347)
15	25 (490)
16	13 (252)
17	2 (45)
18	0 (2)
19	0 (1)
Location of school	
The Hague	58 (1,147)
Medium-sized city	34 (674)
Small town	8 (157)
Ethnicity*	
Dutch	62 (1,228)
Turkish	7 (148)
Surinamese	7 (132)
Moroccan	5 (101)
Antillean	2 (35)
Other country	6 (111)
Mixed	11 (223)

*Every operationalization of ethnicity has its shortcom-
ings and problems. In this study, ethnicity is based on
parental birthplace (most ethnic-minority youths are
second-generation immigrants). It is possible that some
ethnic-minority respondents are coded as Dutch even
though they have an ethnic-minority background, as
some respondents may be third-generation immigrants.

also a substantial category of respondents from a variety of other countries,
mainly Africa and the Middle East.

The questionnaire was administered in the classroom during normal
school hours. Respondents who completed the questionnaire received a reward (a check for $5 to spend in a music store) to stimulate current and fu-
ture participation. Parents were informed beforehand, and they could contact
us for information and refuse to allow their children to participate (this happened in only three cases). Two or three researchers were present during the
administration of the questionnaire. They introduced the research and answered questions from the respondents. Based on our experiences, we believe

our presence in the classroom was very important and necessary. In this way, we could control the situation (i.e., we could make sure that students filled out the questionnaire without consulting each other and preserve the respondents' anonymity by preventing inspection by other students or by teachers). We could also explain to respondents the intent of particular items and receive feedback regarding difficulties or ambiguities in the questionnaire. In a few cases, we identified respondents who did not cooperate seriously or who were obviously cheating. Thus, our presence enhanced the reliability of the data.

We used computers to administer the questionnaire instead of the usual paper-and-pencil method. All participating schools appeared to have computer classrooms, although the quality and quantity of the computers varied considerably. A program with our questionnaire was installed on the school network, and students could fill it in on one of the classroom computers. Output was coded on a diskette. In general, students were very comfortable with using the program. We had already tested a computer and a paper-and-pencil version of the questionnaire in a pilot survey (about one hundred fifty respondents), which revealed that there were no clear disadvantages to using the computer version. Indeed, it appeared that respondents liked it somewhat better than the written version. In addition to trying out the computer version, testing the questionnaire itself was also a goal of the pilot study. Based on our experiences and reliability analyses, several items and scales were improved in the definitive version.

The part of the questionnaire dealing with gangs and other youth groups was based on draft instruments developed by the Eurogang network and discussions during and after the fourth Eurogang meeting in Egmond, the Netherlands. The questionnaire followed a funneling procedure in which neutral questions were asked first and specific gang questions later. The first question asked if respondents belonged to any formal groups, like sport or scouting clubs.[2] After this introductory question, respondents were asked if they belonged to informal groups of youths who knew each other. If they confirmed that they did, they continued with a series of questions about their group. The first questions asked for the size, makeup, and duration of their group and about meeting places and group names. These were followed by questions about group characteristics. Respondents were asked to indicate whether certain characteristics were present in their group. One of the characteristics was whether they called the group a *jeugdbende* ("gang") themselves. The last series of questions dealt with risky and illegal activities by group members.

We applied the Eurogang nominal definition of a gang or troublesome youth group (see the introduction) to identify respondents as gang members. More specifically, we used an earlier version of this definition, which was slightly different in formulation and still had some ambiguities regarding operationalization. Therefore, our identification of gangs differed on some points from the procedure developed later. One difference was that we did not ask directly if groups were street oriented. Instead, we asked if groups had certain places where they usually were present; if the answer was yes, we asked where they were the most. Another difference was that we did not ask directly whether illegal activities were part of the group identity but instead asked questions about illegal activities by group members. As will become clear, these differences caused some difficulties but also provided interesting information about the problems that go with identifying gang membership.

IDENTIFICATION

Some 39 percent of respondents answered that they belonged to an informal group of youths who was not officially organized.[3] However, these groups were not always the kind of youth groups we were interested in, namely the "durable street-oriented youth groups" mentioned in the Eurogang nominal definition. A couple of additional analyses were carried out to see which respondents really belonged to such groups. These analyses are summarized in table 6.2.

First, answers about group members' ages were checked to control if all reported groups were really *youth* groups. One item asked respondents to identify the age range into which most members of the group fell. The age of thirty

Table 6.2.   Characteristics of Street-oriented Youth Groups Represented in Informal Groups

Characteristic	Percentage (Absolute Number)
Members have mean age of thirty or over	1 (7)
Group name and location indicate a church or sport club	4 (28)
The group is not an informal youth group otherwise	2 (18)
The group has existed less than three months	2 (18)
The group usually meets at home, in school, or at church	9 (70)
Durable street-oriented youth groups	82 (621)
Total respondents reporting informal groups	100 (762)

was chosen as a cutting point. Seven respondents were members of groups with a mean age higher than that. After this, group names and locations were analyzed to see if these items revealed clear indications that respondents were actually not reporting about *informal* groups of youths hanging out with each other. In a number of cases, it was clear that respondents were reporting about sport clubs: they reported the name of a certain sport team and a sport club or the soccer field as their meeting place. In some other cases, it was clear that respondents reported about a church group (giving religious names and church as the meeting place). A variety of other indications were found that respondents were not reporting about groups of youths hanging out with each other (the category "not an informal group otherwise"). Some respondents were talking about subcultures or supporters of a soccer team, which are categories instead of informal groups. Other respondents met at work (colleagues), on the Internet, or generally reported that they met youths at parties or in discos. There were also a few respondents reporting about only two people (hardly a "group"). After these apparently non–informal youth groups were filtered out, an item about the duration of the group was checked to see if it was a *durable* youth group. Eighteen groups that had existed for three months or less (following the operationalization of the Eurogang nominal definition) were categorized as nondurable. Further, the reported locations of the groups were analyzed to see if the groups were *street-oriented* youth groups. Respondents reporting that they meet with the group at school, in church, or in the homes of members were seen as belonging to groups that were clearly not street oriented. Respondents reporting that they met on the street, in a square, or in the park or who mentioned street or location names were seen as belonging to clearly street-oriented groups. Respondents who met at other places, like pubs, cafes, fences, neighborhood houses, or at a skate field, were also seen as belonging to street-oriented groups because these locations are public places. A problem was that many respondents (about one-third) reported that they did not have a fixed meeting place or did not mention the type of location. These respondents were not left out of the analyses as they probably met each other at different places in public, and there was no indication that they were not street oriented. Unfortunately, we did not ask directly if groups hung out or met each other in public places, which would have improved the identification of street-oriented groups.

Of the 762 respondents indicating that they had an informal group of friends meeting each other, 621 were identified as belonging to durable street-oriented youth groups. However, this was only the first step toward identifying gangs or troublesome youth groups according to the Eurogang definition. The second step was an analysis of the illegal behavior of group members. A scale of group delinquency consisted of six questions about offenses by group members (vandalism, assault, stealing less than € 5, stealing more than € 5, burglary, and robbery). Respondents were asked to indicate how many members (none, coded as 0; some, coded as 1; most, coded as 2) of their group were involved in these offenses. It was easy to distinguish the nondelinquent groups from the groups that were involved in illegal behavior, but the latter category varied between groups with some members involved in vandalism to groups with most members involved in stealing, burglary, and robbery. Therefore, we had to address the problem of deciding which groups were gangs according to the Eurogang definition (which holds that illegal activities must be part of the identity of the group). Exploratory analyses were carried out to define a cutting point: between three and four on the group delinquency scale, which ranged from zero to twelve, appeared to be a reasonable borderline. Most groups with at least one serious offense (stealing more than €5, burglary, and robbery) scored higher than three, and groups with only some members involved in illegal activity usually scored lower than four. The cutting point also implied that at least one of the less serious offenses was common in the group or that one of the serious offenses was committed by some group members. In either case, illegal activity could be seen as normal or accepted in the group.

Using these cutting points, the 621 respondents in durable street-oriented youth groups were classified as nondelinquent, lightly delinquent, and ganglike groups. The results are reported in table 6.3. The first column presents percentages within the category of respondents in durable street-oriented youth groups, and the second column presents percentages of the total sample.

Table 6.3 shows that about half of the youth groups reported by respondents in our sample were innocent (i.e., no members of these groups were involved in any of the offenses we asked about). A further 30 percent of the groups were lightly delinquent: their group delinquency was below the cutting point. Members of these groups were only sporadically involved in relatively light forms of delinquency. Nineteen percent of the youth groups were beyond the cutting point; they could be called gangs or troublesome youth groups according to the Eurogang definition. Thus, about one-fifth of the informal groups of adolescents in our sample could be called gangs, while the other groups were relatively harmless.

Table 6.3. Which of the Durable Street-oriented Youth Groups Are Gangs?

Group Delinquency	Percentage of Durable Street-oriented Youth Groups	Percentage of Total Sample	Absolute Numbers
Nondelinquent	51	16	315
Lightly delinquent	30	10	1189
Gang/troublesome youth groups	19	6	117
Total in durable street-oriented youth groups	100	31	621
Respondents not in durable street-oriented youth groups		69	1,357
Total sample		100	1,978

When we look at the third column in the table, we see that 117 out of 1,978 respondents are identified as gang members. This represents 6 percent of the total sample, a small minority but nevertheless a meaningful proportion. Gang membership appears not to be a widespread phenomenon, but it is clearly present.

SELF-IDENTIFICATION

We asked all respondents belonging to an informal youth group if their group had a name of its own, and if yes, what this name was. A large majority of these respondents, 83 percent, reported that their group had no name. The same was true for respondents who were identified as gang members, although the majority was less pronounced (70 percent). This is an interesting result because it departs from the situation in the United States, where most gangs have names, usually based on a location (e.g., 5th street) or a gang root name (e.g., Crips or Black Gangster Disciples).

The names that were mentioned also offer important information because they tell us something about the way in which youth group and gang members perceive and identify their groups. To analyze this qualitative information, a classification was made of the group names given by the respondents. Four broad categories of names were used. First, there was a category inspired by location names: street names and places such as Delftselaan ("alley of Delft"), plein ("square"), de loods ("the shed"), and the Little Overbos squad (Overbos is a neighborhood). Second, there was a category of names inspired by the word *gang*, sometimes names that were clearly based on U.S. gang culture. This category contained names like Gangsters, Westside Gangsters, Gangster Bitches, the Gangsta Bradaz, Bloods, and Moerwijkgang (Moerwijk is a neighborhood, so this name is actually a combination of the first and the second category). A third category was reserved for names that were not inspired by the word *gang* but were nevertheless clearly intended to have a dangerous or heavy meaning. These were names like Mafia, Petrusplein Mafia (Petrusplein is the name of a square), Black Hell, Born to Drink, and de Bende van Ellende (a quite poetic name which can be translated as "the gang of misery"). A fourth category was reserved for all other names that were relatively neutral, notwithstanding the fact that some of the names were also quite original. This neutral category contains names like Fanatik, the Simpson Boys, Bollywood Girls, and Kadeboeren ("farmers from the wharf"). Table 6.4 presents the distribution of group names for the respondents that were identified to be in a youth group. The table shows the distribution within the three different categories of group delinquency.

A number of interesting points can be made on the basis of table 6.4, although absolute numbers within the categories of names are quite small. First, the table shows that there are differences among the three categories of delinquency in the way that they name their groups.[4] As mentioned before, respondents in gangs more often had names for their groups than respondents in non- or lightly delinquent groups. They also used gang-inspired names and dangerous or heavy names more often than the other groups, as well as location names. This is what we would expect from gangs. However, another interesting finding is that gang-inspired and dangerous names were not restricted to the groups identified as gangs; some respondents in lightly delinquent and

Table 6.4.   The Relationship between Group Name and the Distribution of Delinquency for Three Categories of Youth Groups

	Percentage of Nondelinquent Youth Groups	Percentage of Lightly Delinquent Youth Groups	Percentage of Youth Groups That Are Gangs
Group has no name/name not mentioned	87 (275)	84 (159)	70 (82)
Location names	3 (10)	2 (3)	6 (7)
Gang-inspired names	2 (6)	4 (8)	7 (8)
Dangerous or heavy names	1 (3)	4 (7)	7 (8)
Neutral names	7 (21)	6 (12)	10 (12)
Total	100 (315)	100 (189)	100 (117)

even in nondelinquent groups had such names. In these cases, the self-image connected with the group names did not overlap with the reported behavior of group members, which suggests that a name indicating a gang or a trouble-some youth group is not always reflective of reality.

The question whether an informal youth group was a jeugdbende was answered affirmatively by 199 respondents, 32 percent of those who belonged to a street-oriented durable youth group.[5] These respondents could be seen as individuals who self-identified their group as a gang. Table 6.5 presents the proportions of respondents in groups that used the word *jeugdbende* and those who did not for each of the three delinquency categories. This information offers important insight into the relationship between identification and self-identification.

Table 6.5 reveals a couple of things. It shows that a majority of the respondents (57 percent) in the category of identified gangs also self-identified as belonging to a jeugdbende, and this figure differs from that of respondents in the other categories.[6] However, a substantial minority, almost one-half of the gang members, did not self-identify. In other words, many respondents identified as gang members did not call their group a jeugdbende. The table also shows that some of the respondents that were not in a gang, as defined here, did call their group a jeugdbende. This is true for about one-third of the light delinquents and for almost one-quarter of the respondents categorized in the nondelinquent groups. Here, many respondents identified as members of relatively innocent groups saw themselves quite differently. Summarized, table 6.5 shows that identification and self-identification do not overlap perfectly in this study. We can see this when we look at the identified gang members, almost one-half of whom did self-identify their group as jeugdbende. It is even clearer when we

Table 6.5.   Self-Identification as a *Jeugdbende* (Gang Member) and Delinquent Involvement

	Percentage of Nondelinquent Youth Groups	Percentage of Lightly Delinquent Youth Groups	Percentage of Youth Groups That Are Gangs
Group is a jeugdbende, per respondent	22 (70)	33 (62)	57 (67)
Group is not a jeugdbende, according to respondent	78 (245)	67 (127)	43 (50)
Total	100 (315)	100 (189)	100 (117)

look at it from the self-identification side. About two-thirds (132/199) of the respondents who used the word *jeugdbende* for their group were identified as nongang members.

DISCUSSION

The results and experiences of this study offer interesting insights into the identification and self-identification of gangs and gang membership in the Netherlands. First of all, our experiences show that it is possible to identify gangs and gang members using the funneling procedure developed by the Eurogang network. This is important because this procedure can be used to establish gang membership according to the Eurogang nominal definition without using the word *gang* or translations of it, terms that may be problematic. The funneling method worked quite well to lead respondents away from thinking about official groups, although it appeared that some sports teams and church clubs still slipped through. This implies that a control imposed afterwards is still necessary. The funneling method also helped in leading respondents easily through the more neutral questions toward questions about illegal group activities and the definition of the group as a gang (or, in our case, jeugdbende).

However, experiences with the questionnaire also point out some difficulties in defining the real nature of a group. In this study, we had to rely on information about the meeting places of groups, and we had some difficulty deciding which answers indicated street orientedness. This problem might be solved in the definitive survey instrument of Eurogang, which includes an item that asks directly about the street orientedness of groups. Another problem was the establishment of cutting lines between groups. Although we found a cutting line between gangs and other groups that worked quite well, our choice is still somewhat ambiguous. The problem is that the definition does not specify which level of illegal activity or delinquency is needed to make a group a gang. This difficulty remains, although the new survey instrument contains an item that asks if illegal activities are normal in the group.

The results show that 6 percent of the entire sample can be identified as belonging to a gang. This proportion, however, should not be seen as an exact estimate for the total youth population in gangs in the Netherlands. First, our sample does not exactly mirror Dutch youth. It does not contain older adolescents and young adults. The sample is also not random, although it is quite representative of young adolescents in an urbanized region. More important, the sample does not contain dropouts and truants, which might be particularly prone to gang membership. Second, our identification procedure has its limitations. Like other surveys depending on self-reports, some respondents might be reluctant to reveal the delinquency of their group, while others might overreport. It is also possible that some groups are wrongly categorized as street oriented or not street oriented due to the ambiguities in our measurement decisions. Third, the proportion depends on the cutting lines chosen to distinguish gangs from lightly delinquent groups. If we were to change these borders, the estimate would also change.

Despite these caveats, our results do provide a rough indication of the prevalence of gang membership. It is obvious that only a small minority belong to a gang, not the majority or even a considerable part of our youth. On the other hand, the proportion of gang members is clearly not negligible. Groups that can be called gangs, according to the Eurogang definition, are present. Moreover, although the delinquency scores of these groups vary, seriously delinquent gangs are also present. American gang researchers often warn against "moral panic" as well as against "denial." Both warnings seem valid for the prevalence of gangs among Dutch youth; it should not be exaggerated, nor should it be trivialized.

This study further shows that youths usually do not have a name for their informal groups. Those who do often choose names that sound dangerous or heavy. Some group names are clearly inspired by American gang culture. This is consistent with reports that parts of Dutch youth are very attracted to gangsta rap and gang literature (van Gemert 2001). This also matches our own observations of respondents visiting gang websites after finishing the questionnaire. It is no surprise that respondents identified as gang members most often use gang-inspired and other "heavy" names, but such names are clearly not restricted to them. The results suggest that some youths in non- or lightly delinquent groups also like to use gang-inspired names and to present themselves as dangerous.

The results also reveal that the use of the Dutch translation of the term *gang* (*jeugdbende*) is not restricted to respondents identified as gang members. Many of the respondents in lightly delinquent and even nondelinquent groups said they belonged to a jeugdbende. On the other hand, many identified as gang members said they were not in a jeugdbende. We can conclude that self-identification by respondents does not correspond well with identifications based on the Eurogang procedure. One explanation for the fact that members often called relatively innocent groups jeugdbendes could be that we misidentified these groups in our procedure as non- or lightly delinquent. This would be the case if group members were involved in other types of offenses than those we asked about. That possibility, however, is not very probable since we asked about very common and broad categories of offenses. Another explanation is more plausible. We have already noticed that the young people in this study liked to play with dangerous and heavy names for their groups. More generally, young adolescents are typically occupied with impression management, and boys, especially, want to look daring, tough, and masculine. We can expect many of them to be eager to believe they are part of a group that represents these desirable properties or at least to make that impression on others. Thus, it is understandable that youths in quite innocent groups may want to see themselves as belonging to gangs.

There are also two possible explanations for the fact that almost half of the respondents identified as gang members did not identify their groups as such themselves. Again, we may have misidentified them as gangs when they were quite innocent in reality. A more important explanation, however, would be that the word *jeugdbende* (and, in other countries, the word *gang*) did not have a clear meaning for the respondents. Since the definition issue is such a long-standing problem in criminology (see Maxson 2001; Ball and Curry 1995), why should we expect young adolescents to have a clear idea of the concept? It is quite probable that many respondents had stereotypic images in mind and compared their own troublesome youth groups to traditional American gangs. It is also possible that they thought of a jeugdbende as a large and fixed offending group, and therefore denied being in a jeugdbende because they tended to offend in small, changing groups. In either case, respondents that were clearly members of what we would call a gang did not see themselves as such. As already mentioned in the introduction, this might be especially true in the European situation, where people are not as familiar with the term *gang* as they are in the United States.

The partial divergence between identification based on the funneling method and respondents' self-identification as members of jeugdbendes suggests that studies of gangs that are based on self-identification may have measurement problems. This would certainly be the case in the Dutch situation. Had we used only self-identification, the proportion of gangs would have been overestimated, and we would have missed groups that were really gangs. In my view, studies based on objective identification of gang membership are more reliable. That is not to say that this method does not have its own problems. This chapter offers some clear examples of difficulties that still need to be solved. However, the funneling method based on the Eurogang definition is clearly promising. Subsequent studies are needed to further develop the method and explore its possibilities.

NOTES

1. One school in this category is located just outside the city borders, but the students mainly live in The Hague.

2. This question was omitted in a first pretest (before the pilot study). We soon found out that the introductory question was absolutely necessary; respondents thought about their sports team when they read the question about youth groups.

3. 61 percent of the respondents belonged to formal youth groups like sport clubs.

4. $\chi^2 = 26.3 \ p < 0.01$.

5. This is 10 percent of the total sample.

6. $\chi^2 = 48.2 \ p < 0.01$.

REFERENCES

Ball, R. A., and G. D. Curry. 1995. The logic of definition in criminology: Purposes and methods for defining "gangs." *Criminology* 33: 225–45.

Battin, S. R., K. G. Hill, R. D. Abbott, R. F. Catalano, and J. D. Hawkins. 1998. The contribution of gang membership to delinquency beyond delinquent friends. *Criminology* 36: 93–115.

Bradshaw, P. 2002. How different are Scottish youth gangs? Findings from the Edinburgh Study of Youth Transition and Crime. Paper presented at the Annual Meeting of the European Society of Criminology, Toledo, Spain, September 4–7.

Curry, G. D. 2000. Self-reported gang involvement and officially recorded delinquency. *Criminology* 38: 1253–74.

Decker, S. H., and B. Van Winkle. 1996. *Life in the gang: Family, friends, and violence.* Cambridge: Cambridge University Press.

Esbensen, F.-A., and D. Huizinga. 1993. Gangs, drugs, and delinquency in a survey of urban youth. *Criminology* 31: 565–89.

Esbensen, F.-A., and D. Peterson Lynskey. 2001. Young gang members in a school survey. In *The Eurogang Paradox: Street gangs and youth groups in the U.S. and Europe,* ed. M. W. Klein, H.-J. Kerner, C. L. Maxson, and E. G. M. Weitekamp, 93–114. Dordrecht, Netherlands: Kluwer.

Fleisher, M. S. 1998. *Dead end kids: Gang girls and the boys they know.* Madison: University of Wisconsin Press.

van Gemert, F. 2001. Crips in orange: Gangs and groups in the Netherlands. In *The Eurogang Paradox: Street gangs and youth groups in the U.S. and Europe,* ed. M. W. Klein, H.-J. Kerner, C. L. Maxson, and E. G. M. Weitekamp, 145–52. Dordrecht, Netherlands: Kluwer.

Gruter, P., and P. Versteegh. 2001. Towards a problem-oriented approach to youth groups in The Hague. In *The Eurogang Paradox: Street gangs and youth groups in the U.S. and Europe,* ed. M. W. Klein, H.-J. Kerner, C. L. Maxson, and E. G. M. Weitekamp, 137–44. Dordrecht, Netherlands: Kluwer.

Haaland, T. 2000. Safety and violence in youth environments. Paper presented at the Fourth Eurogang Meeting, Egmond, Netherlands, September 6–10.

Hagedorn, J. M. 1998. *People and folks: Gangs, crime and the underclass in a rustbelt city.* Chicago: Lake View Press.

Hill, K. G., J. D. Hawkins, R. F. Catalano, R. Kosterman, and R. D. Abbott. 1996. The longitudinal dynamics of gang membership and problem behavior. Paper presented at the Annual Meeting of the American Society of Criminology, Chicago, IL, November 20–23.

Huizinga, D., and K. F. Schumann. 2001. Gang membership in Bremen and Denver: Comparative longitudinal data. In *The Eurogang Paradox: Street gangs and youth groups in the U.S. and Europe,* ed. M. W. Klein, H.-J. Kerner, C. L. Maxson, and E. G. M. Weitekamp, 231–46. Dordrecht, Netherlands: Kluwer.

Klein, M. W., and L. Y. Crawford. 1967. Groups, gangs and cohesiveness. *Journal of Research in Crime and Delinquency* 4: 63–75.

Maxson, C. L. 2001. A proposal for multi-site study of European gangs and youth groups. In *The Eurogang Paradox: Street gangs and youth groups in the U.S. and Europe,* ed. M. W. Klein, H.-J. Kerner, C. L. Maxson, and E. G. M. Weitekamp, 299–308. Dordrecht, Netherlands: Kluwer.

Miller, J. 2001. *One of the guys: Girls, gangs and gender.* New York: Oxford University Press.

Moore, J. W. 1991. *Going down to the barrio. Homeboys and homegirls in change.* Philadelphia: Temple University Press.

Patrick, J. 1979. *A Glasgow gang observed.* London: Eyre Methuen.

Short, J. F., Jr., and F. L. Strodtbeck. 1965. *Group process and delinquency.* Chicago: University of Chicago Press.

Tertilt, H. 1995. *Turkish power boys: Ethnographie einer Jugenbande* [An ethnography of a youth gang]. Frankfurt, Germany: Suhrkamp.

Thornberry, T. P. 1998. Membership in youth gangs and involvement in serious and violent offending. In *Serious and violent offenders: Risk factors and successful interventions*, ed. R. Loeber and D. P. Farrington, 147–66. Thousand Oaks, CA: Sage Publications.

Thornberry, T. P., M. D. Krohn, A. J. Lizotte, and D. Chard-Wierschem. 1993. The role of juvenile gangs in facilitating delinquent behavior. *Journal of Research in Crime and Delinquency* 30: 55–87.

Thornberry, T. P., M. D. Krohn, A. J. Lizotte, C. A. Smith, and K. Tobin. 2003. *Gangs and delinquency in developmental perspective.* Cambridge: Cambridge University Press.

Thrasher, F. M. 1927. *The gang: A study of 1,313 gangs in Chicago.* Chicago: University of Chicago Press.

Vigil, J. D. 1988. *Barrio gangs.* Austin: University of Texas Press.

7

Youth Groups and Gangs in Amsterdam: A Pretest of the Eurogang Expert Survey

Frank van Gemert

Youth groups are a growing problem in Dutch cities. Groups hanging out on the streets are not new, and it is certainly not self-evident that they indulge in crime. Still, in some places, nuisance or illegal activity draws attention to their presence. Newspapers nowadays regularly report on youth groups getting into conflicts with shopkeepers or people who live in the neighborhoods where they meet. As a result, in addition to those directly involved, institutions like the police or city council have an interest in knowing what goes on in these groups.

From January to May 2003, a team of eight students of the Free University of Amsterdam conducted research under my supervision to shed light on the phenomenon of youth groups in the city of Amsterdam.[1] The team focused on groups in public spaces using the following questions as guidelines:

- How many youth groups are in Amsterdam?
- Where in the city can they be found?
- What is the composition of these youth groups?
- What is their behavior?
- How serious is this phenomenon?
- Which of these youth groups are gangs?

While some of the youth groups in Amsterdam would probably be intuitively considered street gangs, a definition is needed to distinguish street gangs from other youth groups. This is especially important because when it comes to youth groups and gangs, America is almost always used as a point of reference, whether implicitly or explicitly. This can lead to confusion because gangs like the Crips and the Bloods are seen as general representatives when, in fact, they are eccentric stereotypes. As has been argued repeatedly, most American gangs scarcely resemble these stereotypes. Thus, when Dutch youngsters talk about their own group and say, "No, we are not a gang," one cannot be sure what they mean. Due to films and videoclips on music channels popular among youth, these youngsters probably have in mind West Coast African American gangsters with gold chains and sexy women (van Gemert 2001). Therefore, in order to distinguish youth groups from gangs objectively, this chapter uses the Eurogang definition of a street gang, which is as follows: "A street gang is any durable street-oriented youth group whose involvement in illegal activity is part of their group identity."

- *Durability* means the gang has existed several months or more and refers to the group that continues despite the turnover of its members.
- *Street oriented* means the group spends a lot of time outside home, work, and school, and often on streets, in malls, in parks, in cars, and so on.
- *Youth* means that members' *average* age is in the teens or early twenties.
- *Illegal activity* generally means delinquent or criminal behavior, not just bothersome activity.
- *Identity* refers to the group's, not individual members', self-image.

One of the instruments of Eurogang is the Expert Survey, a questionnaire that can be used to make an inventory of youth groups or gangs in a certain area by polling people who know about these groups due to their profession or for other reasons. For example, policemen, teachers, or youth workers can be respondents. In order to build a foundation of internationally comparative research, Eurogang's primary goal, instruments like this have to be used in many different cities and countries.

In this research, the Eurogang Expert Survey was used to ask policemen on the beat about youth groups or gangs that they were aware of in the neighborhood in which they worked. The version of the survey used in this research was not the final edition (several changes have been made to this instrument since this research was conducted). Consequently, this chapter offers the results of a pretest of the instrument. At the same time, it presents an overview of youth groups and street gangs in the Dutch capital.

METHODS

Regiopolitie Amsterdam-Amstelland is the police corps that operates in the area of the Dutch capital. This corps is divided into nine districts, two of which are of no interest here because they encompass the water and harbor area (District 2) or a few smaller, separate towns southwest of the city (District 9). For a few years now, the Amsterdam police have been making a serious effort to engage in community policing and have begun working with *buurtregisseurs* ("neighborhood directors"). These police officers, who work on the beat, are well trained and not of low rank. They are expected to play an active role in the social networks of their neighborhood. As a consequence, these police officers can reasonably be expected to have a good understanding of what happens in the streets. This understanding is based on what they see themselves as well as on what they hear from citizens and shopkeepers. For this reason, these buurtregisseurs seemed like good respondents for this research.

The research team asked the corps for cooperation and offered to share the outcome in return. Once the offer was accepted, preparations for the research could begin. The police produced a list with the names, phone numbers, and addresses of all 192 buurtregisseurs. The students could then make contact with these police officers, who were all informed about the research beforehand. In a letter from the chief of police, they were told that cooperation was encouraged but not obligatory.

Because the original instrument was in English, a Dutch translation was necessary. The eight students were split into four pairs. Each pair translated part of the text. The outcome was discussed in the team and revisions were made, resulting in a first Dutch version. This version was tested in interviews with four buurtregisseurs, each of whom was interviewed by one pair of the students. The experiences were discussed, and the instrument was found to be missing a question that shed light on the seriousness or impact of youth groups. The team decided to add a question to the original list. It was also found that respondents related badly to an American typology of gangs. They were confused by the wording and by the characteristics, which they did not deem reflective of reality as they knew it. As such, the final question that addressed this typology was left out after the test interviews. Finally, some open-ended questions were added because after reading the gang literature the students became interested in such themes as the role of girls, hierarchy, and violence. It was decided that these questions were extra and could be used in face-to-face interviews when respondents were willing to invest a little more time. The material derived from these open-ended questions was not used for this chapter.

The next step was to divide the list of buurtregisseurs into equal portions so that the student pairs could start gathering data. Each pair was made responsible for two districts, except for one pair tasked with covering the biggest district, Amsterdam-West (District 6). Students tried, as much as possible, to make appointments for face-to-face interviews so that instructions could be given orally and buurtregisseurs' questions and concerns could be addressed immediately. This way, a high return rate could be expected. When respondents would not or could not go along with this proposition, they were asked to fill out the form themselves and return it to the research team, either by post or by e-mail. All the police districts in Amsterdam are split into smaller units. At the unit level, buurtregisseurs from several neighborhoods meet on a weekly basis or twice every month. The students tried to make appointments to be present on these occasions so that they could address as many as ten or even twenty buurtregisseurs at one time. In the end, 137 buurtregisseurs, more than 71 percent, responded. About half of these buurtregisseurs responded in a face-to-face settings.

The students also tried to contact youth workers for the study. Obviously, it would be interesting to learn how their views might differ from those of the buurtregisseurs. However, there is no citywide network of youth workers, and endless telephone sessions seemed necessary in order to find them. Unlike with the police, students could not present a letter of recommendation and were left with trying to convince each potential respondent, which did not work out well. Even when a youth worker was traced, cooperation was seldom established. Youth workers, in general, were not interested in research, often stating that it would do no good. Youth workers usually feel loyal to the youngsters they work with. In their eyes, criminological research focuses on the bad features of their clientele and can have a stigmatizing effect. In this research, no more than seven youth workers were interviewed. The breakdown of buurtregisseurs and interviewed youth workers by district is displayed in table 7.1.

Table 7.1. The Sample of Buurtregisseurs (Neighborhood Directors)

	District 1 North	District 3 Downtown	District 4 East	District 5 South	District 6 West	District 7 Southeast	District 8 Old West	Citywide
Number of buurtregisseurs in district	21	23	26	32	41	27	22	**192**
Number of buurtregisseur respondents	15	23	19	19	25	27	9	**137**
Number of youth-worker respondents	2	0	0	0	4	0	1	7

Table 7.2. Number of Youth Groups and Gangs in Districts and in Amsterdam

	District 1 North	District 3 Downtown	District 4 East	District 5 South	District 6 West	District 7 Southeast	District 8 Old West	Citywide
Total number of youth groups per district	16	3	14	14	17	15	6	**85**
Street gangs per district	8	1	5	8	8	7	2	**39**
Neighborhoods with no info	3	—	10	12	8	5	14	**52**

The Eurogang Expert Survey can be used to estimate how many youth groups exist in a certain area and their general characteristics. Furthermore, the instrument has specific questions that relate to aspects of the Eurogang definition of a street gang and work as gang identifiers. The answers to questions about size (at least three people), durability (at least three months), age (on average, in adolescence), street orientation (time spent together in public areas), and the association of group identity with illegal activities (as accepted by or okay with the group) can be used together to decide whether a youth group is a gang. According to our survey results, as shown in table 7.2, the city of Amsterdam has eighty-five youth groups, thirty-nine of which are street gangs. Due to problems of nonresponse, it seems safe to say that the number of both youth groups and gangs is higher in reality.

AMSTERDAM IN DISTRICTS

The city of Amsterdam has a central core; its famous canals surround this core in the shape of horseshoes. The horseshoe opens to the river Het IJ, which divides the city into two parts. The smaller northern part has a rural atmosphere and is a secluded part of the city. No fast transportation, such as a metro, connects the two parts. The part on the other side of the river is much bigger. People look upon North as a separate village. It constitutes Police District 1. The center of town, Downtown, with its many historical buildings, is District 3. Downtown has many shops but no high-rises like in other big cities. Around the center, there are three districts that belong to the older parts of the city. Old West (District 8) and East (District 4) are somewhat alike in the sense that original housing is not of high quality and older buildings are being replaced with new ones in many places. South, District 5, is about as old as the other two, but it is more diverse. It also has neighborhoods that are being renewed, but at the same time, this part of town is rich, and the famous museums lie here. West (District 6) and Southeast (District 7) are big, just like North, and they were built in the 1950s and 1960s when Amsterdam was growing rapidly. Southeast was, in its time, a very modern project that now has to deal with serious architectural problems. As mentioned above, District 9 is not included because the towns in this area do not belong to the city of Amsterdam. District 2 covers the river and the harbor and is thus not interesting to look at when it comes to youth groups. Figure 7.1 provides an illustration of the districts studied, and tables 7.3 and 7.4 present district demographic data.

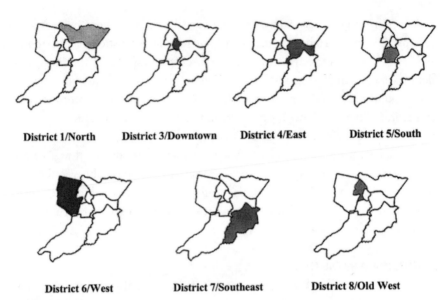

District 1/North   District 3/Downtown   District 4/East   District 5/South

District 6/West   District 7/Southeast   District 8/Old West

FIGURE 7.1
The districts of Amsterdam

Composition

In order to find out more about the composition of the groups in Amsterdam, the survey has questions about the age, sex, and ethnicity of group members. It also includes questions about the size of the group and the existence of subgroups. The paragraphs to follow will present data under the headings

Table 7.3.   General Characteristics of Districts North (1), Downtown (3), East (4), and South (5)

	North	Downtown	South	East
Number of inhabitants	86,910	78,946	128,938	96,358
Younger than 12 years old (%)	16.5	8.7	10.2	15
13 to 17 years old (%)	5.7	2.4	3.1	4.3
18 to 24 years old (%)	17.8	8.1	7.5	8.6
Ethnic minorities (%)	33.2	19	21.7	41.3
Surinamese (%)	8.7	3.1	4.3	10.1
Moroccans (%)	6.9	1.7	3.7	11.1
Turks (%)	4.6	1	1.7	6.4
Antilleans	1.2	1	0.9	1.1
Total housing supply	39,544	45,609	74,176	47,918
Private housing (%)	14.9	21.9	13.2	15.9
Social housing (%)	81.4	36.1	33.3	61.4
Private rent (%)	3.7	42	49.3	22.7
Average income (in euros)	20,511	20,647	22,000	18,968

Table 7.4. General Characteristics of Districts West (6), Southeast (7), and Old West (8)

	West	Southeast	Old West
Number of inhabitants	162,493	84,811	96,499
Younger than 12 years old (%)	16.9	18.5	13.3
13 to 17 years old (%)	5.5	7.3	3.8
18 to 24 years old (%)	8.9	10.2	9.2
Ethnic minorities (%)	44.1	64	26.5
Surinamese (%)	7.9	31.3	7
Moroccans (%)	14.4	1.6	11.9
Turks (%)	9.3	1	7
Antillean (%)	1	6.5	1
Total housing supply	74,962	37,802	52,633
Private housing (%)	18.8	13.3	10.6
Social housing (%)	59.6	78	53.7
Private rent (%)	21.6	8.7	35.7
Average income (in euros)	20,000	19,311	17,600

of size, age, sex, subgroups, and ethnicity. Organizationally, the findings relating to youth groups in general will constitute the bulk of the discussion, with any pertinent differences found for those groups identified as gangs set off in a few sentences below the main paragraph.

Size

One of the first survey questions asked respondents to record the total number of people who belonged to the group during the past twelve months. A simple question turned out not to be so simple to answer. Youngsters may come and go, and it was not always clear who belonged to the group and who did not. The answers to the question were very diverse. Groups with 5 members were reported; others were reported to have as many as 120. Sometimes respondents did not give a clear number but recorded a range instead, such as "from twenty to thirty members." Often, groups seemed to have a number of stable hardcore members. The vast majority of groups were reported to consist of from 11 to 25 people. A few groups had 60 to 120 members, which would make them especially large by Dutch standards. Three of these large groups were found in District 5, three of them mainly consisted of Moroccan boys, and one was of mixed ethnicity. Table 7.5 displays reported group sizes by district and gang status.

Age

The respondents were asked to circle one category that best described the age of most people in the group. Categories were younger than twelve, twelve

Table 7.5. Group Size Per District

Number of Members	District 1 North	District 3 Downtown	District 4 East	District 5 South	District 6 West	District 7 Southeast	District 8 Old West	Citywide	Gangs
3 to 10	4	0	5	4	4	5	5	27	7
11 to 25	7	3	7	7	11	9	1	45	25
26 to 50	5	0	1	0	2	1	0	9	5
51 to 99	0	0	0	2	0	0	0	2	1
More than 100	0	0	1	1	0	0	0	2	1
Total	**16**	**3**	**14**	**14**	**17**	**15**	**6**	**85**	**39**

to eighteen, nineteen to twenty-five, and older than twenty-five. Many groups had oldest and youngest members who did not fit into the category that best described the age of most group members. In one case, a forty-five-year-old man was mentioned; in another neighborhood, a man of no less than sixty-five had contacts with the group. These "members" were exceptional. By far, most groups fell into the category of twelve to eighteen years (sixty-five groups). This was true for all districts, underscoring the fact that street groups are an adolescent phenomenon. Only one group in Southeast had members who were mostly older than twenty-five. This group was said to have existed for a long time, during which time its members aged. Eight groups included members who were mostly twelve years old or younger. Five of those eight groups were found in District 6, West.

Gangs were not found equally in all age categories. Of the older groups, a higher percentage were considered gangs, which would seem to indicate that if members do not mature out and the group stays together, it is likely to become involved in more serious activities. See table 7.6.

Sex

Almost half of the reported groups had only male members (forty-two out of eighty-five) and more than 43 percent had mostly male members (thirty-seven out of eighty-five). The number of female members was equal to or larger than that of male members in only six groups (7 percent). Only one group in all of Amsterdam was reported to have a "mainly female" composition and was found in District 4. Its members were students at a school in the neighborhood, and while they caused some nuisance, they were not considered a serious group. These findings lead to the conclusion that youth groups in Amsterdam are a male phenomenon.

Respondents linked the fact that groups were predominantly male to the Moroccan signature of many groups. This makes sense, especially for Districts 4, 5, and 6, where a relatively large number of Moroccan citizens live and where most of these groups were found. Because Islam stresses separation of the sexes, Muslim girls are seldom seen hanging out with boys on the streets. When these groups did include girls, the girls came from non-Islamic backgrounds. Social control, particularly in the form of gossip, severely limits the presence of Moroccan, Somalian, and Turkish girls. For Muslim boys, on the other hand, it does not seem to matter if they are seen in public with girls. In this respect, gender equality still has a long way to go.

Table 7.6. Age Distribution of Groups within District

Age of Members	District 1 North	District 3 Downtown	District 4 East	District 5 South	District 6 West	District 7 Southeast	District 8 Old West	Citywide	Gangs
Under 12 years old	1	0	2	0	5	0	0	8	1
12 to 18 years old	12	2	11	12	10	13	5	65	30
19 to 25 years old	3	1	1	2	2	1	1	11	7
More than 25 years old	0	0	0	0	0	1	0	1	1
Total	**16**	**3**	**14**	**14**	**17**	**15**	**6**	**85**	**39**

Comparing the sex composition of all youth groups to that of gangs leads to the conclusion that gangs in Amsterdam are an even more exclusively male phenomenon than are youth groups in general. See table 7.7.

Subgroups

Respondents had some difficulty with determining group size, but identifying subgroups proved even harder. One reason for this was the absence of a definition for subgroup; the respondents did not know what to look for. Another reason was that possessing the knowledge to answer this question requires being able to approach the group. Buurtregisseurs are not typically in a position to do that. Some respondents reported that hardcore members and looser affiliates belonged to different subgroups, while others pointed to parts of a group hanging in different places. Many subgroups were reported in North (ten out of sixteen) and in Southeast (twelve out of fifteen). This could, however, be the result of extra explanation given by the student who did the face-to-face interviewing in those districts. Other districts reported fewer subgroups.

Ethnicity

Respondents were asked about the ethnic composition of the groups in their neighborhood. They could split the group into ethnic categories and record the approximate percentage of each category within the group. It was possible to calculate the ethnic composition of all groups per district by looking at absolute numbers. As a basis for this calculation, size and ethnicity percentages per group were used. In some cases, an estimated number had to be made exact. For example, when a respondent recorded a group as having fifteen to twenty-five members, the number twenty was used to come to an absolute figure. In order to make comparisons based on ethnicity, results for youth groups and gangs are reported in separate tables, with youth group results reported in table 7.8 and gang results in table 7.9.

The main ethnic categories within the city of Amsterdam were also found in the youth groups, but their prevalence differed. Looking at the ethnic population of the city, one would expect more Dutch and more Turkish youngsters to be part of these groups. Some ethnicities seem to find their way into youth groups more easily than others. Antilleans and Surinamese youngsters are found all over the city, but only in Southeast, where their numbers are

Table 7.7. Sex Composition of Groups within Districts

Gender of Members	District 1 North	District 3 Downtown	District 4 East	District 5 South	District 6 West	District 7 Southeast	District 8 Old West	Citywide	Gangs
Male	5	2	9	8	9	5	4	42	26
+ male	9	1	4	5	8	8	2	37	11
½ male/½ female	2	0	0	1	0	2	0	5	2
+ female	0	0	1	0	0	0	0	1	0
Female	0	0	0	0	0	0	0	0	0
Total	**16**	**3**	**14**	**14**	**17**	**15**	**6**	**85**	**39**

Table 7.8. Group Member Ethnicity by Districts and City

Ethnicity	District 1 North	District 3 Downtown	District 4 East	District 5 South	District 6 West	District 7 Southeast	District 8 Old West	Citywide	Percent age of Group Members
Dutch	153	20	26	60	19	71	1	350	21.1
Moroccan	135	20	188	306	233	3	39	924	55.8
Turkish	2	0	17	3	15	0	5	42	2.5
Surinamese/ Antillean*	41	15	58	22	20	119	7	282	17
Other**	6	5	5	2	7	32	1	58	3.5
All ethnicities	**337**	**60**	**294**	**393**	**294**	**225**	**53**	**1656**	**100**

*Surinamese and Antillean ethnic groups are listed as one category because respondents often cannot tell them apart.
**"Other" consists of groups that are not specified by respondents and of ethnicities that are not common, such as Ghanese, Yugoslavian, Iraqi, Algerian, and Ethiopian.

Table 7.9. Gang Member Ethnicity by Districts and City

Ethnicity	District 1 North	District 3 Downtown	District 4 East	District 5 South	District 6 West	District 7 Southeast	District 8 Old West	Citywide	Percentage of Group Members
Dutch	96	0	7	10	7	11	0	131	15.4
Moroccan	77	15	37	236	150	2	19	536	63.1
Turkish	0	0	0	0	12	0	0	12	1.4
Surinamese/ Antillean*	37	0	26	10	7	75	0	155	18.2
Other**	5	0	5	0	2	4	0	16	1.9
All ethnicities	**215**	**15**	**75**	**256**	**178**	**92**	**19**	**850**	**100**

*Surinamese and Antillean ethnic groups are listed as one category because respondents often cannot tell them apart.
**"Other" consists of groups that are not specified by respondents and of ethnicities that are not common, such as Ghanese, Yugoslavian, Iraqi, Algerian, and Ethiopian.

Table 7.10.   The Role of Ethnicity in Youth Groups and Gangs

	Percentage in Youth Groups	Percentage in Gangs
Dutch	21.1	15.4
Moroccan	55.8	63.1
Turkish	2.5	1.4
Surinamese/Antillean	17	18.2
Other	3.5	1.9
All ethnicities	**100**	**100**

larger, do they play an important role in youth groups. The most striking thing, however, is the level of Moroccan participation. Even though Moroccans are not the largest ethnic minority in the city (there are more people of Surinamese descent), they play an important role when it comes to youth groups. Indeed, they seem to dominate the picture in many neighborhoods, especially in the districts East, West, and Old West. In the Netherlands, this comes as no surprise. Moroccan boys have been overrepresented in police statistics for the past fifteen years, and they are frequently mentioned in the Dutch media in relation to delinquent behavior (Junger and Zeilstra 1989; Werdmölder 1990; van Gemert 1998).

The comparison of groups and gangs, shown in table 7.10, leads to an interesting point. Moroccan membership is even more prevalent in gangs compared to youth groups (to a lesser extent, this is also true for Surinamese/Antillean membership). Thus, it appears that Moroccan boys are not only disproportionately found in youth groups, but, within these youth groups, they also form gangs more often than youngsters with other ethnic backgrounds.

BEHAVIOR, SERIOUSNESS

Based on answers to questions on delinquency and criminal activities, youth groups were found mainly to indulge in nuisance behavior and in light *vermogensdelicten* ("property offenses"). In East, Southeast, and Old West, groups also committed more serious vermogensdelicten, which was rarer in other districts. Simple assaults (*lichte geweldsdelicten*) were mainly committed by groups in Downtown and Southeast. No more than seven out of the eighty-five groups were involved in dealing drugs. Two groups in South were known to have been involved in *zedendelicten* ("sexual offenses").

When looking at data on alcohol and drug use, it is striking to find that more groups were known to use drugs than alcohol on a regular basis. This was reported for twenty-eight groups. This drug use mostly concerned smoking marijuana, a drug that can easily be purchased in Dutch coffee shops by those over eighteen. Eight of these twenty-eight groups also used hard drugs. Nineteen groups were said to use alcohol regularly, sometimes excessively. Groups in Downtown seemed to use the most alcohol and drugs, while groups in Old West were believed to use these substances the least.

Of course, delinquency and substance abuse can cause problems. However, not all groups are the same, and it would be interesting to learn which groups are the most serious (i.e., problematic). In the test phase, the research team was dissatisfied because in face-to-face interviews it became clear that although groups differed in this respect, the instrument would not register this difference. For this reason, a question was added to the survey to measure substance abuse.

Obviously, asking about seriousness leads to subjective answers; therefore, some sort of standard was required. Making the questionnaire longer or asking for other material such as police data was not possible, mainly for practical reasons. The extra question asked each respondent to note, on a scale of 1 to 10, what score, according to his or her best estimate, described the seriousness of the group (10 being very serious). The question was placed in the survey after three questions about the criminal activities of the group, and it started with the phrase, *Keeping in mind the last questions. . . .* Although this clearly did not guarantee fully objective answers, the respondents did make links between behaviors and what they thought was serious. Buurtregisseurs know what goes on in their neighborhoods, and they talk with colleagues and hear what happens "next door" on a daily basis. Surveys regularly show how different neighborhoods score on crime rates and the population's feeling of safety, and buurtregisseurs are aware of these survey findings. Therefore, respondents have a kind of implicit standard that allows them to make comparisons between neighborhoods and between youth groups.

The outcome of our extra survey question was that the average score on the 1-to-10 scale was 5.9. The average score of groups in District 3 was highest (7.0), but the most serious youth groups were found in West. Some of them were given a sore of 9 or even 10. However, since other groups in this part of town were not that serious, the average number in the West district was 6.3. South and Southeast both had the lowest average score (5.4) and lowest group scores (a Southeast group had a score of 1 and two South groups had scores of 2).

When the scores of all youth groups and those of gangs were compared, we found that gangs mostly had higher scores. So, not surprisingly, gangs are among the more serious youth groups in Amsterdam.

GANG CHARACTERISTICS

American gangs have particular characteristics. Certain symbols and aspects of gang life are mentioned over and over again in the American gang literature. Are these characteristics related only to American gangs, or can one also find them in Dutch youth groups?

American gangs use symbols such as names, colors, tattoos, hand signs, and graffiti as identifiers, which makes it possible to distinguish one gang from the other. Members of Dutch youth groups sometimes use the same kind of symbols but for different reasons. Within international youth culture, American gang symbols are part of the latest fashion. Dutch youngsters copy American gangsters and become look-alikes, yet they stay different. Focusing on gang symbols, as do many American law-enforcement agencies such as gang squads, would be very confusing in the Dutch context (van Gemert 2002, 163–65). When Dutch youth groups have names, the names often turn out to have been given by others, especially by the police. One group was called the Tupac Group, but most other group names refer to the streets or squares where the groups hang out.

American gangs are also known to defend their territory. They get into conflicts with other gangs, and the gang wars that may result can be very violent. Often, firearms are used. None of this was reported during our research in Amsterdam. Dutch youth groups are not turf gangs. They seldom fight with other groups. Guns are generally absent; as a consequence, violence seems to occur at a different level than in America.

The stereotypical American gang is hierarchical and has clear leadership. Sometimes ranks are explicit, cumulating in the role of "original gangster." New members go through initiation, although members seem to leave the gang through a less clear-cut route. In some of the face-to-face interviews, respondents took the time to give their impressions of life in the Amsterdam youth groups. This led to a totally different picture from that which emerges in some of the American gang literature and popular stereotypes. Some of the boys are older, stronger, or verbally better equipped than others, and they seem to play leading roles. Those who are most involved in crime seem to be able to impress younger ones with less experience. However, this difference in position hardly ever leads to a situation where one boy can tell another what to do (see van Gemert and Fleisher, chapter 1 in this volume). Ranks were not reported, nor were initiation rituals. Boys were not "beaten in," according to the buurtregisseurs.

CONCLUSION

How Many Youth Groups Are There in Amsterdam?

This research reported eighty-five youth groups within the city of Amsterdam, comprising an estimated 1,650 youngsters. In reality, more groups can be found in this city because data from fifty-five neighborhoods was not accessible. This is especially true for the districts West, East, South, and Southeast, which have eight, ten, twelve, and fourteen neighborhoods, respectively, that were not reported on in this survey. Furthermore, although respondents were told that they could report on more than one group by using more question forms, only a very small number (two) did so. Other sources have made it known that several neighborhoods have more than one group. Thus, underreporting is evident.

Where in the City Can These Groups Be Found?

Youth groups are not found in equal numbers in all districts. In districts Downtown and Old West, the fewest groups were reported. The other districts did not show big differences in the number of youth groups reported.

What Is the Composition of These Youth Groups?

Many of the eighty-five youth groups had a majority of members in the age category twelve to eighteen years old (sixty-six groups). This research indicates that youth groups are primarily a male phenomenon; girls were not vastly outnumbered by boys in only six groups. Looking at ethnicity, it becomes clear that Moroccan boys play an important role in youth groups in the streets of Amsterdam. This research indicates that Turks, on the other hand, an ethnic minority that resembles Moroccans to a certain degree (migration history, Mediterranean Islamic background), are virtually absent.

What Is Their Behavior?

In general, youth groups in Amsterdam are mainly involved in light nuisance and minor property crime (*vermogensdelicten*). In East, Southeast, and Old West, groups were also involved in serious property crime (*zware vermogensdelicten*). Data on alcohol and drug use indicate that drugs play a more important role than alcohol. The fact that marijuana and hashish are easily accessible in Dutch coffee shops offers at least a partial explanation for this finding.

How Serious Is This Phenomenon?

The respondents scored groups on a 1-to-10 scale of seriousness based on their professional judgment. The average score for all gangs was 5.9. Of all recorded scores, 64 percent were above 5.5 (an acceptable level in the Netherlands); 20 percent of the groups were given a score of 8 or higher. These groups, according to the respondents, were really serious.

Which of These Youth Groups Are Gangs?

In Amsterdam, eighty-five youth groups were reported. By looking at the outcome of identifying questions in the Eurogang Expert Survey, it was possible to determine whether each reported group was a street gang. Thirty-nine of the eighty-five reported groups were street gangs according to the Eurogang definition.

NOTE

1. The team comprises Wybo van Biemen, Idske Boon, Milan van Diermen, Daniel de Jong, Leonie Kuperus, Christina Mulder, Martje de Roos, and Jacquelien Struik. It is important to add that while this chapter is based on data they collected from the Expert Survey, it is not a straightforward translation, in whole or in part, of the unpublished research report (van Biemen et al. 2003).

REFERENCES

van Biemen, W., I. Boon, M. van Diermen, D. de Jong, L. Kuperus, C. Mulder, M. de Roos, and J. Struik. 2003. Jeugdgroepen in Amsterdam: Een inventarisatie in 2003 op basis van Eurogang Expert Survey. Unpublished manuscript, Vrije Universiteit, Amsterdam.

van Gemert, F. 1998. *Ieder voor zich; Kansen, cultuur en criminaliteit van Marok-kaanse jongens.* Amsterdam: Het Spinhuis.

————. 2001. Crips in orange: Gangs and groups in the Netherlands. In *The Eurogang Paradox: Street gangs and youth groups in the U.S. and Europe*, ed. M. W. Klein, H.-J. Kerner, C. L. Maxson, and E. G. M. Weitekamp. Dordrecht, Netherlands: Kluwer.

————. 2002. Botsen met de buurt; overlast en de wisselwerking tussen jeugdgroepen en de buitenwereld. *Tijdschrift voor Criminologie* 44 (2): 162–71.

Werdmölder, H. 1990. Een generatie op drift; de geschiedenis van een Marokkaanse randgroep. Arnhem, Netherlands: Gouda Quint.

Junger, M., and M. Zeilstra. 1989. *Deviant gedrag en slachtofferschap onder jongens uit etnische minderheden I*. Arnhem, Netherlands: Gouda Quint.

8

Contemporary Russian Gangs: History, Membership, and Crime Involvement

ALEXANDER SALAGAEV, ALEXANDER SHASHKIN,
IRINA SHERBAKOVA, AND ELIAS TOURIYANSKIY

GANG RESEARCH IN RUSSIA

Unlike the United States, Russia has a very short history of gang research. Organized or criminal youth groups were not mentioned in Russian literature on juvenile delinquency before 1980; nor were they considered "informal groups." An early local study of juvenile gangs in the Soviet Union was conducted in the 1980s in Lyubertsy (a small town in the suburbs of Moscow) by the Institute for Scientific Research of the Russian Ministry of the Interior (Ovchinskiy 1990; Kashelkin 1990). The first major Russian study on juvenile gangs was conducted in Kazan by a group of sociologists working in the Laboratory of Sociology at Kazan State Technological University led by Alexander Salagaev from 1983 to 1989 (see Salagaev 1989, 1997).[1] Due to journalists' "special attention" to the results of this study, the phenomenon of organized youth groups became known as the "Kazan Phenomenon." A series of articles on gangs in the popular media provoked moral panic among the citizens of the Soviet Union. The Kazan Phenomenon label is still used in Russian and foreign literature to define delinquent gangs in many cities and towns of the former Soviet Union.

The beginning of the 1990s was characterized by a series of research studies of youth criminal activity in groups (e.g., Ageeva 1991; Bulatov and Shesler 1994; Petelin 1990; Prozumentov 1993; Sibiryakov 1990). However, these studies did

not deal with a whole range of theoretical questions, including methodological issues involved in studying juvenile gangs and definitions of the terms *gang*
and *gang membership*. Recent studies are mostly focused on topics adjacent to
gangs, such as prison culture in Russia (Oleynik 2001) or organized crime and
violent entrepreneurship (Volkov 2002a, 2002b).

Only the group of researchers organized by Salagaev has studied Russian
gangs for more than fifteen years. During the period of research, a great
amount of ethnographic material on Russian gangs was collected (see Salagaev 2001; Salagaev and Shashkin 2001, 2002a, 2002b). This chapter builds on
that tradition and presents the results of pretests of the Expert and School surveys conducted in two Russian cities, Moscow and Kazan. The instruments
developed by the Eurogang Program of Research were used during the research, making the data comparable internationally. This chapter addresses
the following issues:

- The history, overall description, and comparison of the gangs in Moscow
  and Kazan, based on previously conducted ethnographic studies and the
  pretests of the Eurogang Expert and School surveys
- The approximate scope of gang involvement among students of secondary
  school in the two cities, based on the self-identification and funneling models for defining gang membership used in the Eurogang School Survey
- The illegal activities performed by young people in informal groups in
  Moscow and Kazan

Gangs in the Russian Context: A Brief History and Description of the Contemporary Situation

Gang problems have been reported in numerous Russian cities, including
Aznakaevo, Volgograd, Kazan, Lyubertsy, Moscow, Naberezhnye Chelny,
Tomsk, and Ulyanovsk, among others. Russian gangs have substantial peculiarities in comparison with American and European gangs. Based on the results of our ethnographic study, we believe gangs in Russia can be
distinguished easily from other youth groups by their greater participation in
criminal activities in particular territories. Russian gangs, in contrast to the
majority of Western gangs, are ethnically heterogeneous, and their existence is
not connected with interregional migration. On the contrary, the main body
of these groups consists of the native population of the districts where they

operate, and these young people are well acquainted with local community members. *Traditional* Russian gangs (this term refers to the gangs of the Kazan type) hold prison norms and values. They are intolerant of members of other youth microcultures, are very sexist, and generally do not sell or use drugs themselves (they may, however, control drug sales). Russian gangs exhibit a strong distribution of functions and age stratification. Regular and self-reproductive social ties are maintained by recruiting new members. They also carry out negotiations for conflict resolution and collect money from members for the gang's common fund.

Our expert survey in Moscow found substantial differences between youth gangs in Moscow and Kazan. By the end of the pretest, we had found at least five types of groups that fit the definition of *street gang* in Moscow: gangs of the Kazan type, skinheads, football fans, punks, and groups of young prostitutes who occupy a particular territory and fight for the turf. In contrast, the situation remains stable in Kazan; all respondents talked about only one type of group, Kazan gangs.

As no research was conducted on "new" gangs in Moscow, we focus our attention on gangs of the Kazan type, which we have been researching for more than fifteen years. To better understand these gangs, it is important to provide an overall description of the social and economic conditions at the time they emerged. We begin with one of the most crucial preconditions of gang formation, the Russian economic reform of 1965. This reform gave a certain level of independence from the state to a substantial number of enterprises, which then led to the appearance of unregistered goods production in illegal (and even legal) shops from 1970 to 1975. Such activity became a substantial profit source in many regions of the country. A special social group called *cekhoviki* ("illegal shop managers") was formed. These criminals had a broad economic network, connections in the state power structures, and special security groups, for which they needed well-trained young people in good physical shape. Our hypothesis is that the social demand created by these groups led to the formation of juvenile gangs. By the end of the 1980s, this situation had been replicated in approximately forty cities of the former Soviet Union.

Our explanation for the emergence of Russian gangs in specific cities also focuses on the rapid industrialization processes that occurred in Russia between 1950 and 1970 (see also Salagaev 2001; Klein 1995). In Kazan, Naberezhnye Chelny, Lyubertsy, Ulyanovsk, and many other cities and towns, huge plants and factories were constructed during these times (e.g., KAMAZ truck plant in Naberezhnye Chelny and a number of military plants in Kazan and Ulyanovsk).[2] These processes were characterized by massive migration of people from rural areas to the big cities in order to fill the demand for labor. The rural population that participated in the great industrial booms of the twentieth century preserved their norms, values, and traditions and brought them into the urban environment. Among these traditions were village-to-village fights in which the majority of the male population took part (see Schepanskaya 2001). The second generation of newcomers transformed this tradition into fights for turf between groups from the different quarters and streets of the cities. These fights peaked in the beginning of the 1980s. Every young man who lived in the big blockhouses was pressured to participate. Those who did not participate were symbolically excluded from the local youth community, as had been the case in the rural areas, where those who were unable or unwilling to fight were considered weak and nonmasculine.

The second half of 1980s was the period of economic liberalization, which also influenced the development of gangs. The aim of liberalization was to foster business initiatives on part of the Russian people, broaden possibilities for improving people's well-being, and ultimately stimulate economic growth in the country. The period of economic liberalization in Russia coincided with the rapid growth in crime rates: in 1989 to 1990 the rates of all crimes increased by 20 to 25 percent annually. The rise in crimes continued until 1996, although at a lower rate of growth, which leveled off after that. On a cultural level, the process of transition in Russia has been characterized by the contradictory values of different social groups. On one side, the values of democracy and the market economy were popular, especially among youth. On the other, however, a lot of young people chose criminal careers. Gangs were and remain not only economically effective illegal groups but cultural arenas as well, where young Russian men are socialized and transmit their attitudes to others.

Russian gangs have moved through several stages of development. Before the 1980s, there were only isolated cases of such youth groups. Then, from the early 1980s until the mid 1990s, there was massive youth participation in gang activities, characterized by high levels of street violence and numerous group fights for territory. During this period a lot of gang members were imprisoned for short terms for carrying weapons or for hooliganism. The next stage started in the mid 1990s, when former gang members returned from prison, having gained prestige among their friends, and introduced prison norms and values into the community. This parallels the American situation, where some gangs were organized in prison and brought prison gang ideology and practices with them back to their communities after their release (Curry and Decker 2003, 15). The economic situation shifted gang activities from territorial fighting to gaining money and control of various businesses. They became organized and formed small brigades. Those youth groups not involved in organized crime preserved the majority of the norms of the first gangs but also started getting money by racketeering in the districts where their members lived. At the same time, the new gangs served as a reserve for organized crime, and the most gifted gangsters become professional criminals or even Mafia members.

As already mentioned, the culture of street gangs of the Kazan type is rooted in prison or criminal culture. This culture in Russia does not have a clear-cut class demarcation; it is closely incorporated into the activities of many legal social institutions (for instance, government administration at all levels), presented in public media discourses, and is widespread among different social groups, not only among young people. This culture includes a variety of cultural representations: a well-defined system of norms and values; specific lifestyle and life goals; standards for how the bearer walks, looks, and dresses and what kind of music he or she likes, among others. In terms of social structure, the acceptance of criminal culture gives its bearers new possibilities for social mobility. In terms of gender, accepting criminal culture provides the ability to construct a specific type of masculinity that is dominant in different social contexts. Finally, in terms of style, it provides broad possibilities for self-actualization and finding "cultural allies." Moreover, criminal culture is not only an urban phenomenon; it has spread its influence among the rural population. At the same time, members of youth delinquent communities (*gruppirovki*, or "gangs") have transformed the norms of criminal culture. As a consequence, the dynamics of gangs' cultural representations are rather flexible and can be altered to meet the situation.

Defining Gangs and Measuring Gang Involvement in our Former and Current Research

The question What is a gang? still remains an open one, both for social scientists and practical workers. Uncertainty on this issue leads to difficulties for police and other organizations, including the state, that deal with concrete youth groups. Scientific discussions accept various points of view on this matter, but practical work requires certainty and coordination of efforts to gain success in anticriminal youth policy. The search for common definitions and conceptualizations of gangs is also important for research purposes, and definitional issues are broadly discussed in the American gang literature (e.g., Esbensen et al. 2001; Klein 1995). The question becomes even more complicated when we try to find similar characteristics of troublesome youth groups in different cultural and national contexts. Nevertheless, considerable progress in providing an answer to this question has been made over the last several years. Since 1997, the Eurogang Research Network has been organizing internationally comparative, multimethod research on gangs and troublesome youth groups.

Before explicating the definition, typology, and operationalization of gangs developed by the Eurogang network, we would like to discuss our own attempt to conceptualize the gang phenomenon, which is based on more than fifteen years' study of troublesome youth groups in the cities and towns of the Volga region of Russia. The main limitations of the typology we propose are connected to the fact that it was derived from the result of our local study. Nevertheless, as the main features of the group behavior of young people may be found in any class and cultural context (Bloch and Niederhoffer 1958, 6), we have tried to offer general concepts that are broadly applicable.

We began with the assumption that it is not possible to define the attributive characteristics of juvenile delinquent gangs. Therefore, a general concept should be introduced, so we proposed the concept of *youth territorial community*, which includes territorial gangs and troublesome youth groups, as well as neighborhood youth groups (or "corner groups"). The attributive characteristics of youth territorial community include specific territory, similar age, incomplete socialization, situational activities, and temporary existence.

In our definition, juvenile gangs and neighborhood youth groups have different functional and structural characteristics. The functional characteristic of a neighborhood youth group is a tendency to engage in joint leisure activities; the comparable characteristic of juvenile gangs is a proclivity for illegal activities. The neighborhood youth group has a spontaneous and situational structure. The typical gang, in contrast, has a strict, formal structure based on age stratification, distribution of roles, obligatory meetings, money collection for a common gang fund, and association with a particular territory (according to the results of our study in Russia). The structural characteristics of gangs, however, can vary in different cultural contexts. Figure 8.1 illustrates our typology groups.

This definition and typology is based on the characteristics of youth territorial communities and helps us to exclude those youth groups from our study that do not have all of the features of gangs or troublesome youth groups. First, we do not consider as gangs play-groups and neighborhood youth groups with nondelinquent activities, even if they are attached to specific territory. Second, we exclude groups created and financed by adults.

Characteristics / Youth community and its types	Attributive	Functional	Structural
• Youth territorial community:	Specific territory, similar age, incomplete socialization, situational activities, and temporary existence		
• Neighborhood youth group or 'corner group'		Leisure activities	Spontaneous and situational structure and leadership
• Juvenile gang/ troublesome youth group		Illegal and violent activities	Strict formal structure based on age stratification, distribution of roles, obligatory meetings, money collection for a common gang fund, association with particular territory

FIGURE 8.1.
A conceptualization of youth territorial communities

Third, we do not include various subcultural youth groups that do not have territorial associations (such as bikers and rollers) (Klein 1995).

The Eurogang network determined that in the majority of cultural contexts, in order for a group to be defined as a gang, it must consist of young people (with average ages in the teens or early twenties), be durable (in existence for several months or more), be street oriented (spend a lot of group time outside the home, work, and school), and be involved in illegal activity (delinquent or criminal behavior). The last, involvement in crime, must be a part of the group's identity. It should be noted here that the issue of territory, or turf, is not included in the definition as that omission makes the definition more broadly applicable to youth groups across Europe.

Another important issue concerns the types of gangs that can be distinguished. Many typologies of gangs exist in the literature, for instance, delinquent, violent, and social gangs (Yablonsky 1962); scavenger, territorial, and corporate gangs (Taylor 1990); protective, aggressive, and unstable gangs (Omelchenko 1996). We use the typology suggested by Malcolm Klein and Cheryl Maxson (Klein et al. 2001), which distinguishes five types of gangs based on group size, age range, presence of subgroups, territorial attachment, and criminal activities: classical, neoclassical, compressed, collective, and specialty.

In the majority of cases, both in the United States and in Europe, juvenile gangs have been studied through ethnographic methods. While ethnographic studies provide information about the cultural context of gangs, particularly the meanings of activities, such information lacks comparative basis. It is also insufficient to define the scope of gang membership in different sites and to compare gang and nongang youths. Quantitative methods, especially general youth surveys, can fill these gaps and become a significant source of information on gang involvement (Esbensen and Huizinga 1993; Thornberry et al. 1993).

METHODOLOGICAL ISSUES

The Eurogang School and Expert surveys were implemented in two cities of the Russian Federation, Moscow and Kazan. Moscow, the federation's capital, has a large variety of youth groups with different cultural representations, including those identified with crime and violence. Kazan was one of the first cities in Russia where delinquent gangs appeared at the end of 1960s. Kazan gangs were later found in Moscow and St. Petersburg. They have spread their cultural influence and become a symbol of delinquent groups in Russian urban areas. Thus, the middle Volga region has been not only an area where gangs are widely found but a powerful center of gang formation that influences the rest of the country.

During the implementation of the Expert Survey, a total of eighteen experts were interviewed. Eight were interviewed in Moscow, including two policemen, four heads of the regional offices of the Department of Minors' Affairs attached to the Ministry of Interior, one community member, and one head of the research institution dealing with the problems of young people. In Kazan, the ten interviewees consisted of two representatives of youth clubs, one department head of the Office of the Public Prosecutor of Tatarstan Republic, two inspectors from the Inspection on Minors' Affairs, two school teachers, and three community members who were parents of young people.

The first problem we encountered was that a mail survey scheme does not work in Russia;[3] after receiving a questionnaire by mail, experts will most likely not answer it. Thus, the expert questionnaire was usually administered by the researcher. This procedure has a lot of advantages, especially for pretest purposes. For instance, we were able to ask our experts what they could suggest about the questionnaire and the research in general and explain everything that was unclear. This gave us confidence that experts understood the questionnaire.

Experts were asked to report the presence and characteristics of youth groups that fit the formal definition of a gang. Some experts had difficulty understanding the definition. For example, it was rather hard to translate the phrase *illegal activity as part of their group identity*. The term *identity* is used among social scientists in Russia without translation and has no colloquial equivalent, so we decided to leave it as *identity*. Yet, for many of our respondents, it was unclear, and some additional comments were needed to explain this issue. Another term that some of our respondents found unclear was the term *delinquent*. In the Russian scientific (sociological and criminological) tradition, this term is *delinkventniy*. As such, we included it literally in the questionnaire. However, about a half of our respondents were not acquainted with the term (some were used to the term *deviant* instead of *delinquent*), so there was a need to explain it.

During the expert survey, we asked respondents to find a category for every gang they described from the classification developed by the Eurogang Research

Network. Generally, the experts did not show uniformity in their classification. For instance, the gangs of the Kazan type were described by different respondents as classical, neoclassical, specialty, and even collective. In Moscow, the variations in attributing different kinds of gangs to the various categories were more consistent. Groups of the Kazan type and football fans were described as compressed or specialty; skinheads as specialty, neoclassical, or compressed; punks as collective; and prostitutes as specialty.

It was not easy for our respondents to provide a definite number of gangs in operation in the area or the number of participants in these groups. In fact, the responses were highly variable. Groups appear, merge, disappear, recruit new members, remain static, or get rid of the "ballast of wannabes" to become tougher and stronger. Usually, the experts had no idea about these group processes. Even the most informed experts (policemen and the representatives of the Department of Minors' Affairs) did not want to give such information or set the figures too low. On the other hand, expert interviews provided useful information about the variety of street gangs and troublesome youth groups in Moscow and Kazan. However, due to the relatively small number of experts that were interviewed, it is difficult to offer any generalizations. In the analysis that follows, we concentrate on the results of the School Survey and use expert data only to supplement the School Survey findings.

The pretest of the School Survey was carried out in six schools (three in each city). We tried to include different kinds of schools in the sample, starting from ordinary secondary schools and ending with specialized lyceums and gymnasiums. The schools were selected from geographically diverse areas of Moscow and Kazan. Some were located in the central districts of the cities and some in suburbs and the most deprived areas. Typical Russian schools have three to four classes in every grade, so we chose three classes from grades seven, nine, and eleven in every school; seventh grade students include twelve- to thirteen-year-olds, ninth grade fourteen- to fifteen-year-olds, and eleventh grade sixteen- to seventeen-year-olds. Finally, we surveyed eighteen classes with approximately 20 students in every class, making the total sample 371 students. Of course, the sample is neither large nor randomly selected and thus cannot be fully representative of the general youth population in Moscow or Kazan. That said, the results in table 8.1 provide the first objective study of gangs in a comparative context in Russia.

Table 8.1. Characteristics of the Moscow and
Kazan Samples

Variable	Percentage (number)
Total sample size	100 (371)
City	
Moscow	40 (147)
Kazan	60 (224)
Gender	
Male	51 (191)
Female	49 (180)
Age	
12	9 (33)
13	25 (93)
14	14 (53)
15	20 (72)
16	16 (60)
17	14 (52)
Refused to answer	2 (8)
Grade	
7th	34 (126)
9th	34 (125)
11th	30 (112)
Refused to answer	2 (8)

Before starting the pretest, we established contacts with school administrators (either the head master or the head of the teaching department) and asked them to give us a class period to conduct the research and introduce us to the students in the class. After that, we asked school officials or teachers to leave the class because their presence could affect the responses of our respondents as well as their willingness to comment on the questionnaire. Our experience has shown that without the researcher's supervision, students tend to fill out the questionnaire with their desk neighbors and to comment on and laugh at questions, which totally disturbs the whole process. Thus, the presence of researchers was useful for avoiding "collective" administration of the questionnaire, as well as for maintaining a quiet and peaceful environment for completing it. Before the study, students were notified about the anonymity of the study and were assured that neither their teachers nor their parents would have access to the individual questionnaires.

We used the self-administered questionnaire designed by the Eurogang Research Program for the definition of gangs and gang membership. Both the self-identification and funneling models of defining attachment to the gang were used. The funneling model consists of questions that progressively identify more involved levels of gang membership, moving from group to identification to criminal involvement. This taps the different aspects of the group in which a respondent is involved, aiming to verify if this group could be considered a gang. During the self-identification procedure, respondents were asked simply to state if their group was a gang. The main difficulty here was connected with the translation of the term *gang*. We thought that it might be a problem if we translated it as *gruppirovka*. This Russian term refers to the Kazan Phenomenon. While conducting the survey in Kazan, this would not cause any problems and every respondent would know what groups were meant. However, in Moscow, where there is a greater variety of troublesome youth groups, it might be misunderstood. Thus, we decided to translate the terms using a slash (as in the English variant of the questionnaire): street gangs/troublesome youth groups. At the same time, the English term *gang* is the closest translation of our Russian word *gruppirovka*, so we used it in this study to identify the youth groups that were the objects of our research.

Defining Gang Membership: Funneling Model and Self-identification

While the majority of survey studies conducted in the United States have defined gang membership on the basis of young people's self-identification (see Fagan 1989; Esbensen et al. 1993; Esbensen and Winfree 1998), the Eurogang Research Network has developed an alternative procedure for measuring gang involvement, the so-called funneling model, which asks young people a set of follow-up questions about the informal groups they belong to regarding durability, street orientation, and identification with illegal behavior. Based on the results, we can decide whether the respondent's informal group fits the gang definition and can be considered a gang. Table 8.2 illustrates the scope of gang involvement as determined by the funneling model.

Table 8.2 shows that 8 percent of all respondents were members of groups that could be regarded as juvenile gangs. Consistent with the differences between cities in the types of the gangs we observed in the pretest of the Expert Survey, the levels of youth involvement in gangs also differed by city quite clearly. The ratio of gang involvement in Moscow and Kazan was 1:0.67. About 12 percent of the respondents from Moscow were involved in troublesome youth groups. This proportion was about two times higher than that

Table 8.2.   The Application of the Funneling Model to Gang Definition

Characteristic	Percentage of Informal Youth Groups	Percentage of Total Sample	Absolute Numbers N = 371
Total in informal groups	100	78	288
Moscow	100	81	119
Kazan	100	75	169
Male	100	70	134
Female	100	86	154
Street oriented	75	59	217
Moscow	78	63	93
Kazan	73	55	124
Male	77	54	103
Female	74	63	114
Durable (existing more than three months)	89	69	255
Moscow	83	67	99
Kazan	92	70	156
Male	90	63	121
Female	87	74	134
Illegal activities are seen as normal	15	12	43
Moscow	22	12	26
Kazan	10	8	17
Male	14	10	19
Female	16	13	24
Perform illegal activities	14	11	41
Moscow	24	19	28
Kazan	8	6	13
Male	16	12	22
Female	12	11	19
Total in gangs/troublesome youth groups according to the definition (funneling model)	11	8	31
Moscow	15	12	18
Kazan	8	6	13
Male	11	8	15
Female	10	9	16

found in other European countries and the United States (Klein et al. 2001) and suggests that the problem of youth participation in juvenile delinquent gangs in Russia should be taken very seriously.

Surprisingly, female respondents showed almost the same level of gang involvement as males (8 and 9 percent, respectively). Ethnographic work with Kazan gangs indicated that these gangs had a very strict regime that did not allow the participation of girls in the gang. One explanation of this finding is that girls are broadly involved in the activities of Moscow gangs in different ways than they are in Kazan gangs. For example, girls involved in gangs might differ from those described by experts in important structural ways. Alternatively, it may be that girls claim participation in ganglike groups even when they have a marginal role, such as being the girlfriend of a male gang member. At the same time, as Ann Campbell (1984) shows in her study of female gangs in New York City, girls are not necessarily satellites of male gangs. Rather, they often create gangs of their own or play an important role in the predominantly male troublesome youth groups. F.-A. Esbensen and D. Huizinga's (1993) work has demonstrated that, as compared to official and ethnographic work, girls are much more likely to be reported as gang members in school-based surveys. The parallels between methodologies and results in the Russian and U.S. contexts are most interesting.

Examining informal groups more broadly, the findings indicate that the differences between the levels of informal group involvement in Moscow and Kazan are statistically insignificant (more than three-fourths of all respondents belonged to informal groups). At the same time, girls were more likely to participate in informal groups than boys (86 percent for girls as compared to 70 percent for the whole sample). As we can see from table 8.2, about 75 percent of all group members reported that they usually spent a lot of time together in public places like parks, the streets, or the neighborhood. This parallels the American scene, where most gang members report that "hanging out" is their major activity (Klein 1995; Decker and Van Winkle 1996).

We also measured the attachment of informal groups to a particular territory with the question "Does this group have an area that it calls its own?" The pretest showed that youth groups in Moscow were more likely than those in Kazan to be attached to a particular territory (ratio of 1:0.69). In addition, girls claimed territorial attachment more than boys (ratio of 1:0.76). The most popular public places where members of informal groups spent their time and that they called their own were as follows: parks (10 percent), street or square (9 percent), house or apartment (9 percent), street corner (5 percent), cafe (4 percent), pub (4 percent), and other places (13 percent). About one-fourth of all informal groups defended their territory against other groups, but Moscow groups were more likely to do so than those in Kazan (ratio of 1:0.58).

Generally, informal youth groups in Russia are quite durable; more than half of them exist for over a year. Respondents from the Kazan and Moscow samples reported similar levels of durability, a measure that was true for both males and females. Respondents from the Moscow sample were twice as likely to view criminal activity as normative in the informal group, and delinquency was seen as normal by almost the same percentage of boys and girls. The differences became more visible when we asked about criminal activities actually performed in the informal groups. For instance, the ratio of criminal activities reported by the Moscow and Kazan samples was 1:0.3. These differences suggest that that there is diversity in gangs in Moscow and Kazan and that the cultural and institutional factors in these cities are somewhat different.

For the purpose of comparison, we also employed the self-identification model of defining gang involvement. The results are displayed in table 8.3, which shows that the differences between the levels of self-identified gang involvement and those obtained by employing the funneling model are insignificant. This suggests that both models work adequately in the Russian context. In addition, these findings also indicate that the definition of troublesome youth group is similar both for the researchers and the survey participants. The table also shows differences in the proportions of gang members in Moscow and Kazan.

Indirect evidence of gang presence can be provided by the awareness of young people of the troublesome youth groups in their neighborhoods or cities. Table 8.4 provides answers to the question, "Are you aware of any gangs in your neighborhood or city?" Surprisingly, the level of awareness of gangs was almost the same in Moscow and in Kazan, despite the differences in actual

Table 8.3. The Role of Self-identification in Defining Gang Membership

	No	*Yes*	*N/A*	*Total (in Informal Groups)*
Moscow	95	20	4	**119**
	80%	17%	3%	**100%**
Kazan	143	16	10	**169**
	85%	10%	5%	**100%**
Male	107	19	8	**134**
	80%	14%	6%	**100%**
Female	131	17	6	**154**
	85%	11%	4%	**100%**
Total	**238**	**36**	**14**	**288**
	83%	**13%**	**4%**	**100%**

Table 8.4.   Awareness of Gangs in Your Neighborhood or City

	No	Yes	N/A	Total
Moscow	50	66	3	119
	42%	55.5%	2.5%	100%
Kazan	60	101	8	169
	35.5%	59.8%	4.7%	100%
Male	52	75	7	134
	38.8%	56%	5.2%	100%
Female	58	92	4	154
	37.7%	59.7%	2.6%	100%
Total	**110**	**167**	**11**	**288**
	38.2%	**58%**	**3.8%**	**100%**

gang involvement in the two cities. Generally, about one-half of the respondents reported that they knew about gangs operating in their neighborhoods. Female respondents showed a higher level of gang awareness than their male counterparts, a finding that the researchers did not expect.

Informal Groups and Delinquency

One of the important tasks for the researchers was to measure the level of group involvement in illegal activities as well as the types of illegal activities that are performed most often. While the format of the pretest does not allow us to make generalizations and compare the levels of crime involvement for gang and nongang youths, we can trace the general trends in criminal activities committed by the members of informal youth groups. We asked students, "How often are the following things done by your group?" The results are presented in table 8.5. We listed only those illegal activities that were performed by more than 5 percent of the informal youth groups. It is also important to note that crime involvement was measured by the self-report method, a method with known limitations. Moreover, it is possible that the most delinquent students were not present in the classroom when the survey was conducted, as skipping classes without an excuse seems to be quite popular in Russia. According to the results of the pretest, about one-fifth of all respondents skipped classes more than ten times during the past year. The ratio of students who skipped classes more than ten times reported by Moscow and Kazan samples was 1:0.5.

Among the most prevalent illegal activities performed by the members of informal groups were using alcohol, fighting, and writing graffiti (30 percent, 21 percent, and 14 percent, respectively). Generally, informal groups in

Table 8.5.   Group Involvement in Illegal Activities

Types of Illegal Activities Performed Sometimes or Often	Percentage of Informal Youth Groups	Percentage of Total Sample	Absolute Numbers N = 371
Total in informal groups	100	78	288
Threaten people	8	6	22
Moscow	13	11	16
Kazan	4	3	6
Male	6	4	8
Female	9	8	14
Fight	21	16	61
Moscow	29	24	35
Kazan	15	11	26
Male	22	15	29
Female	21	18	32
Damage or destroy property	7	6	21
Moscow	11	9	13
Kazan	5	4	8
Male	6	4	8
Female	8	7	13
Beat someone up	8	7	24
Moscow	11	9	13
Kazan	7	5	11
Male	8	5	10
Female	9	8	14
Write graffiti	14	11	40
Moscow	23	18	27
Kazan	8	6	13
Male	14	10	19
Female	14	12	21
Use drugs	5	4	13
Moscow	8	7	10
Kazan	2	1	3
Male	2	2	3
Female	7	6	10
Use alcohol	30	23	85
Moscow	45	36	53
Kazan	19	14	32
Male	27	19	36
Female	32	27	49

Moscow were more frequently involved in illegal activities. The ratios reported by the Moscow and Kazan samples were 1:0.3 for threatening people, 1:0.5 for fighting, 1:0.5 for damaging or destroying property, 1:0.6 for beating someone up, 1:0.3 for writing graffiti, 1:0.25 for using drugs, and 1:0.4 for using alcohol. The researchers did not predict that the level of girls' involvement in illegal activities would be higher than or equal to that of boys. For instance, in both cities, the ratios reported for girls versus boys committing illegal activities were 1:0.7 for threatening people, 1:0.3 for using drugs, and 1:0.8 for using alcohol. The high level of involvement in gang activity by females and their substantial involvement in criminal and delinquent activity remains one of the most important findings of the study.

CONCLUSION

This chapter presents the results of the first tests of the Eurogang School and Expert surveys in Russia. The general trends discovered and the possibilities for future research are quite interesting. The high levels of gang involvement obtained by using the funneling and self-identification models provide strong evidence of the existence of gangs in Moscow and Kazan. Furthermore, our experiences provide support for the use of these instruments in cross-cultural contexts.

A number of sources assert that delinquency is a characteristic of the period of becoming adult. Indeed, the United Nations' "Riyadh Guides" urge us to consider "that youthful behavior or conduct that does not conform to overall social norms and values is often part of the maturation and growth process and tends to disappear spontaneously in most individuals with the transition to adulthood; a great majority of young people commit some kind of petty offence at some point during their adolescence without this turning into a criminal career in the long term."[4] Nevertheless, it is very important to note that juveniles often create stable criminal groups with a corresponding subculture and start to engage in the activities of adult criminal groups, wittingly choosing delinquent careers.

Statistical data in many countries shows that delinquency is a group phenomenon; two-thirds to three-fourths of all juvenile offenses are committed by various groups. Even if a juvenile commits an offense alone, he or she, nevertheless, may associate with a group. At the same time, the Expert Survey has shown that the group characteristic of youth delinquency is often neglected. Interestingly, professionals who work at the local offices of the Department of Minors' Affairs (Inspections on Minors' Affairs) attached to the Ministry of the Interior of the Russian Federation usually register and focus their activities only on individual delinquents. Our findings indicate that they would be well advised to focus their attention on the group context of such activity.

Practical workers dealing with the illegal activities performed by youths in groups often underestimate the cultural aspect of juvenile delinquency. Different juvenile groups reproduce heterogeneous values predetermined by both the structural (e.g., class, social status) and individual (e.g., family, neighborhood) conditions of their lives. Youth culture forms the patterns of behavior that have substantial symbolic value for the involved individuals. The participants in the Expert Survey reported the presence of a number of youth cultures in which deviant behavior and violence is a part of group identity. These groups include juvenile gangs of the Kazan type, skinheads, football fans, groups of young prostitutes, punks, charismatic religious cults and sects, and extreme right-wing youth groups, among others. The lack of ethnographic information about the gangs existing in Moscow proves the need for further scientific research.

While the methods for defining gang involvement developed by the Eurogang project worked quite well in the Russian context, the classification of gangs developed by Klein and Maxson showed less promising results. Experts participating in our study did not show consistency in assigning different gangs to the defined categories. While it is possible that similar groups display variations in their formation and group dynamic, another explanation could be that the experts did not understand the subtle differences between the group types described in the typology. In any case, it was hard for the researchers to generalize information provided by the experts and to connect different youth groups with the particular ideal types from the typology.

The results of the School Survey showed that young people in Moscow were two times more likely to be involved in gangs than those in Kazan. In addition, girls reported the same level of involvement in gangs as boys. At first glance, troublesome youth groups in Moscow seemed to be more dangerous than Kazan gangs. The former were more likely to normalize and perform different types of criminal activities such as fighting, writing graffiti, damaging or destroying property, and threatening and beating people. They also used alcohol and drugs more often. However, if we look at the findings from an ethnographic point of view, the Kazan gangs clearly caused substantial trouble. The activities of gangs of the Kazan type were much more hidden and very much aimed at getting money. For example, their typical crime was taking protection money from individuals and small businesses operating in their neighborhoods. At the same time, gang members did not respect the application of direct physical force. They preferred to establish power re-lations on the discursive level, with the help of words. They also tried to be-have properly at school and not to get involved in additional trouble with adults (e.g., teachers, police). Finally, gangs of the Kazan type usually did not permit members to use drugs or alcohol because addicts are considered un-reliable. These differences prove the importance of combining different re-search methods when studying such a complicated field as gangs and juvenile delinquency.

Girls were as involved in gangs as their male counterparts and participated in the whole range of illegal activities, especially in Moscow. However, anti-criminal youth policy, according to our interviews with experts, has never fo-cused on girls. These results illustrate the importance of focusing on the delinquency and gang involvement of girls, an issue that official policy has heretofore overlooked.

The researchers got the general impression that some issues relating to cross-cultural and comparative study need more attention. Specifically, im-portant issues to consider include the classification of gangs, particular ques-tions on the questionnaires and the difficulties involved in translating several terms, building an expert database for the survey, and the possibility of com-bining different context-sensitive quantitative and qualitative research meth-ods. However, we believe the Eurogang project has developed an adequate theoretical background, methodology, and set of instruments for multicity, multimethod, comparative research on troublesome youth groups in Europe and the United States.

NOTES

1. The order for this research study was given by the Ideological Department of the Tatarstan Regional Committee of the Communist Party and the Ministry of Interior of the Tatarstan Republic.

2. The same situation occurred in America in the late 1800s, when such cities as New York, Philadelphia, Boston, Chicago, St. Louis, and Pittsburgh experienced im-migration and industrial development, which increased the origins of organized ado-lescent groups involved in crime that can be identified as gangs (see Curry and Decker 2003: 14).

3. Our previous attempts to carry out expert surveys via mail failed due to very low response rates, so we then conducted face-to-face interviews. This was especially true for the officials working in the institutions attached to the Russian Ministry of Inte-

rior, where the information is released only through special departments for communication with the media, which filter it according to ideological standards. Information concerning youth groups, juvenile delinquency, and violence is usually stamped "for internal use only," which means that it is closed to the general public. The response rate can be raised after obtaining a special order from the minister to support a particular research study, but this procedure is even more complicated because the researchers then have to sign a paper indicating that they will ask for the ministry's permission every time they publish the research findings. These difficulties can be avoided when communication is based on informal, personal connections with experts, which substantially limits research possibilities as well.

4. United Nations Guidelines for the Prevention of Juvenile Delinquency (The Riyadh Guidelines) adopted and proclaimed by General Assembly Resolution 45/112 of December 14, 1990.

REFERENCES

Ageeva, L. V. 1991. Kazanskiy fenomen: Myth and reality [Kazan phenomenon: Myth and reality]. Kazan, Russia: Tatknigoizdat.

Bloch, H. A., and A. Niederhoffer. 1958. The gang: A study in adolescent behaviour. New York: Greenwood Press Reprint.

Bulatov, L. M., and A. V. Shesler. 1994. *Kriminogennye gorodskie territorialnie podrostkovo-molodezhnie gruppirovki (ugolovno-pravovye i kriminologicheskie aspekty)* [Urban criminal territorial youth gangs (penal and criminological aspects)]. Kazan, Russia: Knigoizdat.

Campbell, A. 1984. *The girls in the gang.* Cambridge, MA: Basil Blackwood.

Curry, G. D., and S. H. Decker. 2003. *Confronting gangs: Crime and community.* 2nd ed. Los Angeles: Roxbury Publishing.

Decker, S. H., and B. Van Winkle. 1996. *Life in the gang: Family, friends, and violence.* Cambridge: Cambridge University Press.

Esbensen, F.-A., and D. Huizinga. 1993. Gang and non-gang youth in a survey of urban youth. *Criminology* 31: 565–87.

Esbensen, F.-A., D. Huizinga, and A. W. Weiher. 1993. Gang and nongang youth: Differences in explanatory factors. *Journal of Contemporary Criminal Justice* 9: 94–116.

Esbensen, F.-A., and L. T. Winfree. 1998. Race and gender differences between gang and nongang youth: Results of a multisite survey. *Justice Quarterly* 15: 505–26.

Esbensen, F.-A., L. T. Winfree, N. He, and T. J. Taylor. 2001. Youth gangs and definitional issues: When is a gang a gang and why does it matter? *Crime and Delinquency* 47: 105–30.

Fagan, J. 1989. The social organization of drug use and drug dealing among urban gangs. *Criminology* 27 (4): 633–69.

Kashelkin, A. B. 1990. Mezhregionalniy kriminologicheskiy analiz podrostkovo-molodezhnikh gruppirovok s antiobshestvennoy napravlennostyu [Cross-regional criminological analysis of antisocial juvenile delinquent gangs]. In *Sociologicheskie aspekty gosudarstvenno-pravovoy raboty v usloviyakh perestroyki* [Sociological aspects of the legal governmental work in conditions of perestroika], 19–20. Kazan, Russia: Kazan University Press.

Klein, M. W. 1995. *The American street gang*. New York: Oxford University Press.

Klein, M. W., H.-J. Kerner, C. L. Maxson, and E. G. M. Weitekamp. 2001. *The Eurogang Paradox: Street gangs and youth groups in the U.S. and Europe*. Dordrecht, Netherlands: Kluwer.

Oleynik, A. N. 2001. *Tyuremnaya subkultura v Rossii: Ot povsednevnoy zhizni do gosudarstvennoyvlasti* [Prison subculture in Russia: From everyday life to the state power]. Moscow: INFRA-M.

Omelchenko, E. L. 1996. Young women in provincial gang culture: Case study of Ul'anovsk. In *Gender, generation and identity in contemporary Russia*, ed. H. Pilkington, 218–20. London: Routledge.

Ovchinskiy, V. S. 1990. "Gastrolniye" poezdki antiobshestvennikhgruppirovok podrostkov I molodezhi—noviy phenomen ["Tours" of antisocial groups of teenagers and youth—new phenomenon]. In *Kriminologi o neformalnikh molodezhnikh obyedineniyakh* [Criminologists on informal youth units], ed. I. Karpetz, 192–96. Moscow: Juridical Literature.

Petelin, B. Y. 1990. Organizovannaya prestupnost nesovershennoletnikh [Organized crime of minors]. *Sociologicheskie Issledovaniya* [Sociological research] 9: 92–98.

Prozumentov, L. M. 1993. *Gruppovaya prestupnost nessovershennoletnikh I eepreduprezhdenie* [Group juvenile delinquency and its prevention]. Tomsk, Russia: Tomsk State University Publishing House.

Salagaev, A. 1989. Podrostkovaya kompaniya i predkriminalnaya gruppirovka kak usloviyasocializacii [Socialization in youth company and precriminal gang]. *Proceedings of the International Conference 'Actual Problems of the Regional Social Development.'* Barnaul, Russia: Barnaul University Press.

———. 1997. *Molodezhnie pravonarusheniya i delinkventnie soobshestva skvoz prizmuamerikanskikh sociologicheskikh teoriy* [Studying youth delinquency and delinquent communities using American sociological theories]. Kazan, Russia: Ekocentr.

———. 2001. Evolution of delinquent gangs in Russia. In *The Eurogang Paradox: Street gangs and youth groups in the U.S. and Europe*, ed. M. W. Klein, H.-J. Kerner, C. L. Maxson, and E. G. M. Weitekamp. Dordrecht, Netherlands: Kluwer.

Salagaev, A., and A. Shashkin. 2001. Peace or war: Scenarios of behavior before a fight. In *Youth on the threshold of 3rd millennium*, ed. V. Puuronen, 89–93. Joensuu, Finland: University of Joensuu, Karelian Institute.

———. 2002a. Gang violence and masculinity construction. *Journal of Sociology and Social Anthropology* 5 (1): 151–60.

———. 2002b. Russian delinquent gangs: Gender regime and masculinities construction. In *Kön och våld i Norden* [Gender and violence in the Nordic countries], ed. Maria Eriksson, Aili Nenola, and Muhonen Nilsen, 399–409, report from a conference in Køge, Denmark, November 23–24, 2001. Copenhagen: Nordisk Ministerråd, available at www.norfa.no/_img/3._Masculinity=Culture.pdf (accessed February 1, 2004).

Schepanskaya, T. B. 2001. Zony nasiliya (po materialam russkoy selskoy isovremennykh subkulturnikh tradiciy) [The zones of violence (on the materials from Russian rural and contemporary subcultural traditions)]. In *Antropologiyanasiliya* [Anthropology of violence], ed. V. Bocharov and V. Tishkov. St. Petersburg, Russia: Nauka.

Sibiryakov, S. L. 1990. Ulichnie gruppirovki molodezhi v g. Volgograde [Street juvenile gangs in Volgograd city]. In *Kriminologi o neformalnikh molodezhnikh obyedineniyakh* [Criminologists on informal youth units], ed. I. Karpetz, 168–76. Moscow: Juridical Literature.

Taylor, C. S. 1990. Gang imperialism. In *Gangs in America*, ed. R. C. Huff. Newbury Park, CA: Sage Publications.

Thornberry, T. P., M. D. Krohn, A. J. Lizotte, and D. Chard-Wierschem. 1993. The role of juvenile gangs in facilitating delinquent behavior. *Journal of Research in Crime and Delinquency* 30: 5–87.

Volkov, V. 2002a. *Violent entrepreneurs: The use of force in the making of Russian capitalism.* Ithaca, NY: Cornell University Press.

———. 2002b. Who is strong when the state is weak: Violent entrepreneurship in Russia's emerging markets. In *Beyond the state crisis: Postcolonial Africa and post-Soviet Eurasia in comparative perspective*, ed. M. Beissinger and C. Young, 81–104. Washington, D.C.: Woodrow Wilson Center Press.

Yablonsky, L. 1962. *The violent gang.* New York: MacMillan.

9

Terrors and Young Teams: Youth Gangs and Delinquency in Edinburgh

Paul Bradshaw

The United States has a long history of gang-related research stretching back to the work of F. M. Thrasher (1936) and H. Ashbury (1928), who published studies of gangs in the early part of the twentieth century. Gang research in the United States continued throughout the century and closely mirrored the development of criminology as a distinct discipline. While the majority of this research is observational or ethnographic in nature, there have also been several recent examples of survey research on gangs within the particular context of longitudinal research projects, which are reviewed below. Perhaps the most significant finding to have emerged from gang research in the United States is that, irrespective of the historical period, research methodology, study design, and sample, gang members commit more crimes than nonmembers (Howell 1997).

The result of such a voluminous research output on juvenile street gangs in North America is that until recently many considered these gangs to be a strictly American phenomenon not replicated anywhere else in the world. Movements such as the Eurogang network, however, have helped to increase gang awareness internationally. Research is now being undertaken outside of the United States to examine the prevalence of juvenile gangs and the effects of gang membership on juvenile delinquency.

Unfortunately, in the past century, the volumes of gang research produced
in the United States have not been produced elsewhere, certainly not in the
United Kingdom. When D. Downes failed to find any evidence of the structured gang in England, he concluded that "research into gang delinquency in
this country is in my view a fair reflection of its absence" (1966, 116). Furthermore, A. Campbell and S. Muncer (1989) have claimed that Britain plays
host to subcultures rather than gangs. Consequently, there remains an igno-
rance of the existence of youth gangs in British criminological research. However, this is not to say that the annals of social research in the United Kingdom
are completely devoid of exploration of the gang phenomenon; neither is it to
argue that the United Kingdom has not witnessed a proliferation of juvenile
street gangs, albeit in certain geographical areas at certain periods in history
(see, for example, Davies 1998, 1999; Mares 2001; McCallum 1994; Patrick
1973). What is true is that a large proportion of British studies on ganglike
youth groups, such as the teddy boys of the 1950s, the mods and rockers of the
1960s, the skinheads of the 1970s, and the football hooligans of the 1980s, are
influenced more by a youth culture or subculture approach, in line with the
thinking of Campbell and Muncer (1989). This approach has tended to involve qualitative study of the values and ideology of subcultures rather than
examination and explanation of any offending behavior in which they may
have been involved. As such, specifically criminological studies of juvenile
street gangs in Britain are relatively scarce.

However, a small number of British social research studies have identified
peer groups that could be identified as youth gangs. James Patrick (1973) provides perhaps the most notable example in his ethnographic research, which
identified numerous, territorial, ganglike groups in Glasgow in the late 1960s.
These gangs, Patrick argued, were primarily organized for emotional gratification, and all activities in which they took part were centered on violence
(1973, 176). The earlier existence of gangs similar to those Patrick studied is
currently being researched by Andrew Davies (1998, 1999), a social historian
at Liverpool University who is producing historical insights into patterns of
gang activity in Britain. Through parallel case studies of Manchester, Salford,
and Glasgow in the late nineteenth and early twentieth centuries, his research
has uncovered the early existence of urban youth gangs and is examining the
origins, nature, and extent of street violence among those gangs. D. Mares
(2001) has provided a more contemporary insight into the gang situation in

Manchester and Salford, identifying a number of newly emergent, neotraditional, and compressed gangs in these areas.[1] K. Bullock and N. Tilley (2002) have also documented this situation in their examination of the Manchester gang situation with specific reference to gun violence perpetrated by gang members and policing strategies aimed at reducing it. The publication of results from the first detailed quantitative study of gangs in the United Kingdom in 2004 represents a significant step forward for British gang research. Using data from the New English and Welsh Drug Abuse Monitoring (NEW-ADAM) program, the researchers have provided a comprehensive descriptive account of gang membership and gang-member characteristics among arrestees across fourteen cities in England (Bennett and Holloway 2004).

In these pieces of largely ethnographic and qualitative work, we find some of the clearest references in British research to the existence of street gangs similar to those in North America. To date, however, apart from the work of T. Bennett and K. Holloway (2004), little survey research has been undertaken on the prevalence of gangs in the United Kingdom and gang membership among British youth, despite the prevailing media suggestion of the existence of such gangs. This chapter aims to combat this dearth of survey research on British youth gangs by exploring the prevalence of gang membership, the characteristics of gangs and gang members, and the effects of gang membership on delinquency among a large cohort of British, or more specifically Scottish, young people within the context of the Edinburgh Study of Youth Transitions and Crime. This chapter is consistent with the Eurogang definition of gangs and Eurogang measurement tools, although not explicitly based upon them. I will draw on the comparable gang-survey work of several American researchers, and by replicating as closely as possible certain aspects of the analysis carried out in each of those papers, I will explore the similarities between youth gangs in Scotland and America.

GANG MEMBERSHIP AND GANG MEMBERS—AN AMERICAN PICTURE

In order to make comparisons between gangs in Scotland and North America, it is first useful to set out, in brief, some of the key findings from survey-based gang research in the United States. Notable studies that have produced important gang-related data include the Seattle Social Development Project (Battin et al. 1998), the Denver Youth Study (Esbensen and Huizinga 1993), and the Rochester Youth Study (Thornberry 1998; Thornberry et al. 1993; Thornberry et al. 1994). Furthermore, some significant, large-scale, quantitative research on gangs has also been carried out using data from the National Evaluation of Gang Resistance Education and Training (GREAT) program (Esbensen et al. 2001). This section illustrates some of the key results from these studies.

Prevalence of Gang Membership

Each of the American research studies being considered uses a self-report measure of gang membership. Data from the Denver Youth Study indicate that, between 1988 and 1992, 14 percent of the sample were gang members (Esbensen and Huizinga 1993). In the Seattle Social Development Study, membership levels differed only slightly, with 15 percent of the cohort identifying themselves as having been gang members at one point between the ages of thirteen and eighteen (Hill et al. 1999). These proportions are very similar to that found by Esbensen et al. (2001) in their analysis of data from the National Evaluation of GREAT. In this instance, a little under 17 percent of the sample, who were predominantly between thirteen and fifteen years old, indicated that they had at one time or another been a gang member. Findings from the Rochester study, however, set prevalence a little higher, with 30 percent of the cohort reporting street-gang membership prior to the end of high school (Thornberry 1998).

Gang-Member Demographics

American research over the years has shown gang membership to be a predominantly, in some cases almost exclusively, male pursuit. However, more recent data has shown a quite different picture and suggests that females may account for more than one-third of youth gang members in some cases (Esbensen and Osgood 1997). Another dominant demographic among gang youths is that they are very often reported to be members of a racial or ethnic minority group, although there is some indication that this may be due to overrepresentation of minority groups within the samples selected. In the Denver Youth Study gang subsample, for instance, African American and Hispanic youths dominated, with majorities ranging from 85 to 94 percent in the various years of the research (Esbensen and Huizinga 1993, 573).

Risk Factors for Gang Membership

The various longitudinal studies have identified a considerable number of risk factors that are associated with gang formation, gang membership, and the attraction of gangs for young people. These risk factors can be categorized under five broad headings: family, individual, peer group, school, and community.

Family

Gang members' family situations vary widely; they are found both in intact two-parent families and in single-parent families. Nor do they come solely from homes in which parents have low incomes or low educational attainment. However, findings from the Rochester study indicate that young people growing up in low-income families or in families without both biological parents are at an increased risk for gang membership. The same research also identifies low parental attachment and low parental supervision as risk factors leading to gang membership (Thornberry 1998, 155).

Individual

Researchers have measured a full range of individual and personality characteristics in a bid to predict gang membership. Esbensen et al. (2001) have found gang members to be more impulsive and engaged in more risk-seeking behavior than nongang youths. They also found that gang members could more easily justify fighting in certain situations. In addition, a number of studies link the probability of gang membership to alcohol and drug use (Bjerregaard and Smith 1993; Thornberry et al. 1993).

Peer Group

Peer influence has been found to have a major effect on adolescent behavior, and this influence stretches to gang membership. Gang members have been shown to have a lower commitment to positive peers than nongang youths (Esbensen et al. 1993; Esbensen et al. 2001). Furthermore, a higher level of exposure, attachment, and commitment to delinquent peers has been identified as a predictor of gang membership in a number of studies (Bjerregaard and Smith 1993; Esbensen and Huizinga 1993; Thornberry 1998).

School

School factors, although less commonly explored, have also been shown to be important. Gang members, for example, show less commitment and a lower attachment to school than nongang youths (Hill et al. 1999).

Community

A number of studies have examined the importance of community factors in determining both gang prevalence and gang membership. For example, using data from the Seattle Social Development Project, Hill et al. (1999) found that youths from neighborhoods with a high number of delinquent young people and those from neighborhoods where drugs were more readily available were more likely to join a gang than youths from other neighborhoods.

Gang Membership and Delinquency

Undoubtedly, the most significant finding to emerge from gang research in the United States is that gang members report involvement in significantly higher levels of delinquency than nonmembers. Comparison of data from the Rochester, Denver, and Seattle studies shows that gang members were responsible for 50 to 86 percent of the delinquent acts reported by the various cohorts. This is despite, as we have seen above, the fact that gang members constituted only a minority of the sample in each study (Thornberry 1998). Furthermore, S. R. Battin et al. (1998, 101) found that gang members committed twice as much delinquency as nongang youths with delinquent friends and over five times as much as nongang youths with nondelinquent friends. Similarly, using data from the Denver study, Esbensen and Huizinga (1993, 573) found that gang males reported involvement in around five times as many street offenses as nongang males, with an even more marked gap between gang and nongang females. Importantly, Esbensen and Huizinga's (1993) longitudinal analysis also found that delinquent activity among the same individuals increased during periods of gang membership and decreased dramatically following their departure from the gang.

Summary

This review has set out some of the key findings from survey-based gang research conducted in the United States. The lack of similar research in the United Kingdom, and indeed in many other countries outside of the United States, has meant that until now, there has been no indication as to whether the characteristics detailed are unique to American gang youths or whether they are more generally representative of the type of young person who joins a gang anywhere in the world. This chapter attempts to resolve this gap by measuring the prevalence of gang membership and the characteristics of gang members within a large cohort of British adolescents.

METHODS

This research presents data from the Edinburgh Study of Youth Transitions and Crime, a prospective longitudinal study of criminal offending among a cohort of forty-three hundred young people in the city of Edinburgh (see Smith and McVie 2003). The main aim of this study is to further our understanding of criminal offending in young people and find out why some young people become serious or persistent offenders as they get older, while many others either desist from offending or do not offend at all. The study began in August 1998, when the cohort was, on average, twelve years old. The study was not selective in any way, and there was no sampling. It aimed to cover a complete one-year cohort as far as possible. Children in all types of school were included (mainstream, special, and independent), although a few independent schools refused to participate, with the result that 92 percent of eligible children in Edinburgh attended participating schools.

Data was obtained on an annual basis from multiple sources, including the young people, children's hearing records, social work records, police records, and school records. Surveys of parents and teachers were also undertaken (at sweeps 4 and 2, respectively). This chapter mainly uses data collected at sweep 2, when respondents were asked about their involvement in gangs. The analysis is based on self-completion data from 4,299 young people aged approximately thirteen at the time of data collection and representing 95.6 percent of all pupils attending participating schools within the city of Edinburgh.

Measures

Gang Definition and Membership

The exact attributes that combine to constitute a gang and the criteria necessary to classify someone as a gang member have been subject to considerable debate for some time, and various definitions and techniques of identification have been applied in research. As with the comparable American studies, gang definition in the Edinburgh study data relied on self-nomination. That is, if a respondent claimed to be a gang member, this was considered adequate grounds for his or her classification as such. The self-definition technique has been positively supported by M. Klein (1995) and was recently tested as a definition technique by Esbensen et al. (2001), using data from the National Evaluation of the GREAT Program. Importantly, in that study, the researchers concluded that "the self-nomination technique is a particularly robust measure of gang membership capable of distinguishing gang from non-gang youth" (2001, 124).

Edinburgh study respondents were first asked, "How many friends do you usually go about with at once?" Possible responses included "one or two," "a group of between three and five," and "a group of six or more." Those who gave either of the last two responses were then asked, "Would you call the group of friends you usually go about with a gang?" A positive response to this question provided our baseline level of gang membership. Two more descriptive questions on whether the gang had a name and whether it had any special signs or sayings were then asked. Respondents were not asked whether the gang was involved in any delinquent activities; thus, the gang definition employed in this study is not that of a strictly "delinquent" gang.

In an attempt to replicate the work of Esbensen et al. (2001), who applied five increasingly restrictive gang-membership definitions to their cohort, we created four group types, each with a more restrictive definition based on factors different from those used by Esbensen et al. The first group includes non-gang members. The second includes members of any gang that had neither a name nor a special sign or saying, identified here as gang type 1. The third group comprises members of any gang that had either a name or a special sign or saying, identified as gang type 2. The fourth group includes members of any gang that had both a name and a special saying or sign, identified as gang type 3. We hypothesize that each consecutive gang type represents a higher degree of gang identification and organization so that the final grouping, gang type 3, signifies a well-established group whose members readily identify themselves with a specific gang name and sign or symbol.

Demographic, Attitudinal, and Delinquency Measures

Again, drawing on the American research, a range of demographic, attitudinal, and delinquency measures were extracted from the self-report data and analyzed with the gang membership variables. The demographic characteristics of our cohort are described through their gender, race, family structure, and social class. The attitudinal measures employed in this chapter (all of which are described in more detail in appendix 9.A) are representative of social-learning (Akers et al. 1979) and self-control theories (Gottfredson and Hirschi 1990), which are frequently used in attempts to explain or predict gang membership. Some additional measures are also included. Social-learning theory, which emphasizes the importance of adopting the behavior and attitudes exhibited by one's friendship group in its explanation of deviant behavior, is represented by indicators measuring peer delinquency, negative peer influence, and strength of conventional moral beliefs. Self-control theory, which posits that inadequate socialization, stemming in part from poor childrearing, leads to low self-control and subsequently crime, is represented by measures of parental supervision, impulsivity, and risk taking. Variables measuring conflict with parents, parental punishment, and attachment to school are also included. Note that these indicators are included for comparison purposes. Theory testing will not be undertaken at this stage.

To measure delinquency, cohort members were asked about their involvement in a range of sixteen different delinquent activities over the course of the previous year (see appendix 9.A). Respondents were also asked how many times they had engaged in each type of delinquent act. The results from these questions have been used to compute both a *variety score*, based on the number of different delinquency types the respondent had been involved in, and a *volume score*, based on the total number of delinquent acts reported. From these two overall delinquency measures, we created two subindexes: serious delinquency (including joyriding, housebreaking, robbery, fire setting, theft from a car, assault, and carrying a weapon) and offenses against the person (including robbery, assault, and carrying a weapon).

RESULTS

Prevalence of Gang Membership

Almost exactly one-fifth (19.9 percent) of the entire cohort considered the group of friends that they went about with to be a gang; these are referred to as "any" gang members. More descriptive definitions of the gang reduce the proportions dramatically. As table 9.1 clearly demonstrates, the vast majority of gang youths fall into the gang type 1 category; 66 percent of

Table 9.1. Prevalence of Gang Membership

Gang Type	Percentage of Gang Members	Percentage of Cohort
Nongang n = 3,389	—	80.1
Gang type 1 n = 555	66.6	13.1
Gang type 2 n = 150	17.8	3.5
Gang type 3 n = 139	16.5	3.3

gang members are in this type of gang, representing 13.1 percent of the entire cohort. The remaining gang members are split almost evenly between
gang types 2 and 3, although a slightly higher proportion of gang members
fall within the gang type 2 description. Indeed, only 3.3 percent of the whole
cohort reported being a member of our most organized gang type. Overall,
the prevalence of gang membership among the Edinburgh study and the
various American studies cohorts is very similar. In Edinburgh, the 'any'
gang prevalence figure is only slightly higher than that reported at Denver
and Seattle and in the National Evaluation of GREAT (14 percent, 15 percent, and 17 percent respectively), but is still lower than that reported in the
Rochester cohort (30 percent).

Gang Characteristics

The limited information on gang names and symbols collected in the questionnaire does not allow for particularly detailed descriptions of specific gangs,
which would demand a qualitative approach. However, some inferences can be
drawn from the data. One clearly identifiable characteristic of youth gangs in
Edinburgh is that, for the most part, they appear to be fiercely territorial. This
is borne out through analysis of gang names, especially names of those gangs
that meet the type 3 definition. The gang names follow a common convention.
The vast majority of groups refer to themselves as *young teams* and, in most
cases, make reference to the particular area of the city in which they live or
hang around. For example, one of the most prominent gangs evident originates from Leith, a densely populated, historic port area to the northeast of the
city; the gang is thus named the Young Leith Team. There are a small number
of variations to this standard, usually involving the replacement of *team* with a
symbolic phrase indicating the danger that the gang represents. These variations still contain an obvious territorial reference. Examples include the group
Young Niddrie Terror, which originates from the socially disadvantaged and
somewhat notorious Niddrie housing estates in the southeast of the city, and
the Young Mental Drylaw group from the Drylaw estate in the northwest.

Interestingly, the territorial naming trait and the widespread use of the term
young team are not restricted to Edinburgh gangs but are evident elsewhere in
Scotland. Patrick (1973, 21) commented on these characteristics in his ethnographic study of a Glasgow gang in the 1960s. Furthermore, in compiling a
comprehensive list of Glasgow gang names stretching from 1840 to 1994, R. G.
McCallum provides a vast number of further examples (1994, 136–43).

The importance of territory for Edinburgh youth gangs is also reflected in local media reports, which suggest that it often appears to be the basis for gang fights (Davidson 1998; Lyst 2000; Gardner 1999a, 1999b). These fights, however, are not disputes over territorial boundaries but rather are running battles between gangs from contiguous areas. The purpose of these battles is either to establish which gang is the "hardest" or, in some cases, simply to provide a brief diversion from the common and normally mundane pursuits of hanging around.

The location of gang territories throughout Edinburgh is reflective of the city's particular social geography. The most deprived areas, and those that are most often gang territories, are away from the city center and, in some cases, close to the city periphery. Thus, the model of inner-city deprivation does not apply to Edinburgh. In this respect, as in others, Edinburgh is more like continental European cities than English or American ones.[2] Note that this particular social geography does not correspond to a lack of the social problems and marginalization associated with inner-city deprivation. Instead, these problems have developed more intensely in the densely populated housing estates toward the outskirts of the city, such as those mentioned above, and it is in these estates that gang membership is concentrated in Edinburgh.

No specific information detailing the size and age range of youth gangs in Edinburgh has been collected. Looking at the characteristics of gang members' friendship groups, however, shows that gang members were more likely than nongang youths to have a large group of friends. For example, just over 66 percent of gang type 3 members reported regularly socializing with a group of six or more friends, compared to only 34 percent of nongang youths. Gang members were also more likely to socialize with older youths or with a mixed-age friendship group than nongang members, who were most likely to socialize with others of the same age. Around 28 percent of gang type 3 members reported that most of their friends were a year or more older, and 35 percent had a similar number of friends both younger and older, compared to 6.1 percent and 19.1 percent for nongang members, respectively.

Gang Member Demographics

Demographic analysis produced some interesting distinctions between gang members and nongang youths (see table 9.2). These findings are categorized and discussed under four broad headings: gender, family structure, social class, and ethnic group.

Table 9.2. Demographic Characteristics of Gang and Nongang Youths

	Percentage of Total Sample	Percentage of Nongang Youths	Percentage of Any Gang Members	Percentage of Gang Type 1 Members	Percentage of Gang Type 2 Members	Percentage of Gang Type 3 Members
Gender*						
Male	50.7	51.5	47.4	42.7	51.3	61.9
Female	49.3	48.5	52.6	57.3	48.7	38.1
Family structure**						
Two birth parents	69.7	71.4	63.2	67.6	56.7	52.5
Parent and step parent	11.2	9.9	16.3	14.6	21.3	18.0
Single parent	17.6	17.4	18.5	16.9	20.0	24.5
In care/not with parents	1.4	1.3	2.0	0.9	2.0	5.0
Social class**						
1 and 2	36.1	38.9	24.4	27.9	16.1	18.7
3: nonmanual	9.2	9.3	8.7	10.5	6.8	3.7
3: manual	24.0	22.4	30.6	31.1	33.1	25.2
4 and 5	13.7	13.0	16.7	15.2	21.2	18.7
Unemployed	10.2	9.7	12.6	10.1	12.7	23.4
Not living with parents	6.8	6.8	7.0	5.2	10.2	10.3
Race						
White	94.3	93.7	96.5	96.6	95.9	97.1
Black	0.7	0.7	0.7	0.8	1.4	—
Indian subcontinent	2.5	2.7	1.6	1.5	2.2	2.2
Chinese	1.1	1.3	0.4	0.4	—	2.1
Other	1.4	1.6	0.8	0.9	1.4	—

Note: All chi-square tests comparing gang youths with nongang youths are statistically significant at $p > 0.001$ where indicated (**) and at $p > 0.005$ where indicated (*).

Gender

First, the gender of gang members was clearly split almost evenly between boys and girls. However, and rather surprisingly, girls represented the majority of any gang members and, although only slight (52.6 percent girls versus 47.4 percent boys), the difference was statistically significant. As the gang definition became more restrictive, the gender balance changed so that males dominated the membership of the more organized and recognized gangs. In gang type 3, over 60 percent (61.9 percent) of members were male.

These findings are interesting given that female involvement in gangs has been recorded at a minimum in previous youth-gang research and especially in recent British research. S. Batchelor, for example, reports in a study of young female violence in Scotland that "not one of 800 teenage girls that took part in the research claimed to be in a girl gang" (2001, 26). Furthermore, research from the NEW-ADAM program in England and Wales found that only 5 percent of all gang members were female, and 4 percent of current gang members were female (Bennett and Holloway 2004). This is perhaps not surprising. F.-A. Esbensen and D. P. Lynskey's (2001) review of gang literature suggests that the proportion of female gang members reported in gang research tends to vary by the age of the sample and the methodology. The gang definition that Batchelor (2001) questioned teenage girls about differed considerably from the definition used by the Edinburgh study in that her definition required gangs to be gender-specific (female-only gangs) and of a particular organized nature, involving not just a name or a sign but a formal authority structure and endurance over time. The sample Bennett and Holloway (2004) used in their research was not only several years older than the Edinburgh study cohort at the time this data was collected but also comprised solely individuals who had been arrested by the police.

However, the proportions of female gang youths evident within our data do reflect the findings of some of the most recent American studies, which adopt a more similar methodology and have a sample more comparable to the Edinburgh study. These studies suggest that females may account for more than one-third of youth gang members in some cases (Esbensen and Osgood 1997).

Family Structure

Both the vast majority of nongang youths (71.4 percent) and the majority of any gang youths (63.2 percent) lived with both of their birth parents, which is perhaps not surprising given that this family status was true for almost 70 percent of the total cohort. While youths from two-parent families continued to dominate each gang definition, it is notable that their majority decreased as the definition became more restrictive, so that while 67.6 percent of gang type 1 members were from two-birth-parent families, only 52.5 percent of gang type 3 members said the same. The opposite trend was true for those gang members who fell within nonconventional family categories. For example, the proportions of single-parent youths and of youths in care increased as the gang definitions grew more restrictive.

Social Class

In order to assign social-class status, respondents were asked to describe their parents' occupations, which were then coded using the Registrar General Social Classification (RGSC) scheme. Nongang members were most likely to be from social classes 1 and 2, whereas the largest proportion of any gang members was from class 3—manual (30.6 percent). Moving through the gang definitions, youths from lower-class and unemployed households assumed higher positions. In the most restrictive gang type, although the largest proportion of members was still from class 3—manual (25.2 percent), almost one-quarter (23.4 percent) of members of this gang type came from households with unemployed parents, despite this class group constituting only one-tenth (10.2 percent) of the cohort as a whole.

Ethnic Group

In contrast to the cities in which many American gang studies are carried out, or more specifically, the areas within these cities in which youth gang research is undertaken, the population of Edinburgh and Scotland as a whole is overwhelmingly white, with only a very small proportion of ethnic groups. Indeed, 94.3 percent of study respondents described themselves as white. It is hardly surprising, therefore, to discover that the majority of gang members in the study were white. Thus, analysis by ethnic group is of little interest. The chi-square statistic comparing nongang with gang youths across ethnic groups is not significant. This reflects Esbensen and Lynskey's (2001) suggestion that the composition of youth gangs indicates community-level demographics. For example, gang members are white in predominantly white communities and are Asian in predominantly Asian communities.

Gang Membership and Attitudinal Variables

Table 9.3 reports the mean scores for both gang and nongang youths on the self-control, social-learning, and additional attitudinal measures. The data in table 9.3 clearly illustrates that gang members reported lower levels of parental supervision than nongang youths. This trend between gang and nongang youths was repeated in all of the parental variables. Gang youths had more frequent arguments with and were subject to more punishment by their parents, indicating that their overall experience of the parent-child relationship was more turbulent.

Indeed, for each measure tested, gang members were presented as more antisocial than their nongang peers. Gang members were more impulsive, took more risks, were more influenced by negative peers, had more delinquent friends, found it easier to justify delinquent behavior, and had a lower attachment to school. Furthermore, the increase in both the influence of negative peers and peer delinquency evident when moving through the more restrictive gang definitions was statistically significant, suggesting that gang type 3 youths were less committed to positive peers and had more delinquent friends than both gang type 1 and 2 youths.

These results are found to be very favorable when compared to attitudinal data on gang youths in American studies. Esbensen et al. (2001), for example, found that the expressed attitudes of gang members were significantly different from those of nongang members. They also found that gang youths represented a distinctly more antisocial character than their nongang peers.

Gang Membership and Delinquency

The overriding conclusion from the vast amount of gang research in the United States is that gang members are involved in significantly more delinquent acts than their nongang peers. The results of this study are consistent with this conclusion. Table 9.4 reports the mean scores for both gang and nongang youths on each of the six delinquency measures calculated for this study. An immediate and significant distinction is detectable on each delinquency measure between gang and nongang youths. On both the general measures of delinquency, the mean score for any gang members is at least double that of nongang members. In terms of more serious delinquency, the difference between the two groups increases by up to eightfold. For offenses against the person, the pattern is similar to general delinquency, with gang members

Table 9.3. Mean Scores on Attitudinal Variables among Gang and Nongang Youths

	Total Sample	Nongang Youths	Any Gang Members	Gang Type 1 Members	Gang Type 2 Members	Gang Type 3 Members
Parental						
Supervision	6.72	6.95	5.85	5.99	5.60	5.57
Punishment	2.86	2.76	3.27	3.21	3.22	3.51
Conflict	2.84	2.72	3.34	3.13	3.33**	4.43
Personality						
Impulsivity	13.24	12.87	14.76	14.49	14.25*	16.27
Risk taking	7.0	6.60	8.62	8.18	8.98	10.1
Negative peer influence	5.00	4.59	6.57	6.23	6.70**	7.85
Peer delinquency	3.52	2.94	5.88	4.87*	7.06*	8.56
Strength of conventional moral beliefs	8.37	7.96	10.03	9.65	10.39	11.23
Attachment to school	12.60	12.86	11.59	11.75	11.25	11.28

Note: All t tests of the attitudinal variables between gang and nongang youths are statistically significant at the 0.01 level. Tests of the scores between gang types 1 and 2 and 2 and 3 are significant at the 0.01 level where indicated (*) and at the 0.05 level where indicated (**).

Table 9.4. Mean Delinquency Scores across Different Gang Definitions

	Total Sample	Nongang Youths	Any Gang Members	Gang Type 1 Members	Gang Type 2 Members	Gang Type 3 Members
Variety of delinquency	2.83	2.25	5.20	4.43	6.06**	7.31
Volume of delinquency	9.64	7.07	19.92	15.5	24.95*	31.76
Variety of serious delinquency	0.55	0.36	1.31	0.96	1.69**	2.30
Volume of serious delinquency	1.66	1.04	4.15	2.73	5.68**	8.13
Variety of offenses against the person	0.63	0.52	1.09	0.91	1.37	1.5
Volume of offenses against the person	2.11	1.56	4.29	3.19	5.69**	7.13

Note: All *t* tests of the delinquency scores between gang and nongang youths, gang type 1 and gang type 2 youths and gang type 1 and gang type 3 youths are statistically significant at the 0.01 level. Tests of the scores between gang types 2 and 3 are significant at the 0.01 level where indicated (**) and at the 0.05 level where indicated (*).

having an average score at least double that of nongang members. In each instance, the delinquency scores for gang members were significantly different from those of nongang youths.

With each progressively more restrictive definition of gang membership, the gang members reported greater participation in delinquent activity. For example, whereas the mean variety of serious delinquency for those respondents who were not in a gang was 0.36, those young people in gang type 3 reported committing an average of 2.30 acts of delinquency, an increase of around sixfold. Interestingly, while differences between the different gang types were not significant on many of the demographic and attitudinal measures, in the case of delinquency, the difference in scores between each gang type and its subsequent stricter definition was significant to at least the 95 percent level (99 percent between gang types 1 and 2). This suggests not only that membership in a gang affects the respondent's delinquency but that the more organized and easily identified the gang is, the greater its effect on its members' delinquency.

The Comparable Effects of Gang Membership and Delinquent Peers

The data presented so far has demonstrated that gang members are significantly different demographically and attitudinally from nongang members. It has also shown that delinquency is considerably higher among gang members than nongang youths and also that delinquency levels increase as the gang definition grows more restrictive and the gang takes on a more organized manifestation. Furthermore, the difference in delinquency scores is significant between the gang definitions.

A large number of researchers have sought to determine exactly why being a gang member influences delinquency. One particular strand of this inquiry surrounds the attempt to disentangle the influence of gang membership from the effects of delinquent friends on subsequent delinquency. Peer delinquency is a well-proven influence on individual offending. Numerous research studies have examined the relationship between delinquent peers and individual delinquent behavior (see Rutter et al. 1998, 193–99), and many of these studies have found peer delinquency to be one of the strongest predictors of individual delinquency (Akers et al. 1979; Elliot and Menard 1996).

Given that, as gang members, individuals are likely to be in contact with delinquent peers, to what extent can gang members' delinquency be attributed to the effect of their delinquent friends rather than the fact that they are gang members? Battin et al. (1998) undertook an examination of this question recently using data from the Seattle Social Development Project, which compared involvement in delinquency for gang members, nongang youths with delinquent friends, and nongang youths without delinquent friends. They found that gang members, compared to the other groups, had a higher rate of offending in the previous year. Gang membership was found to predict independently both self-report and officially recorded delinquency *beyond the effects of having delinquent friends.*

Again, to test the similarity between American and British gang youths, relevant but more simplified analysis was carried out on the data to allow comparison between juvenile gangs in Edinburgh and Seattle. First, the cohort was separated into three groups: self-reported gang members, individuals involved with delinquent peers but who were not gang members, and individuals who were not gang members and had nondelinquent peers. To validate gang membership, Battin et al. (1998) asked follow-up questions on the gang's name and characteristics. Thus, for this analysis, only those youths who fell within the gang type 2 and 3 definitions were designated as gang members.

Delinquent friends were measured using items that asked respondents to report whether any of their friends had been involved in any of fifteen types of delinquency. Nongang youths with delinquent friends were those respondents who were not members of a gang from the above definition and whose friends had committed two or more acts of delinquency in the past year. Nongang youths with nondelinquent friends were respondents who were not members of a gang from the above definition and whose friends had committed fewer than two acts of delinquency in the past year.

Table 9.5 lists the mean scores on each of the delinquency measures for the three defined status groups. A consistent pattern was found across the groups for all six measures of delinquency. On each measure, offending rates were lowest for youths with nondelinquent peers, higher for youths with delinquent peers, and highest for gang members. For example, the figures in table 9.4 show that overall, youths with nondelinquent peers committed an average of 1.58 acts of self-reported delinquency in the past year, while those young people with delinquent peers committed an average of 11.34 acts, and gang members committed just over 28 acts. T-tests were carried out on these figures to determine whether observed differences in offending between gang

Table 9.5. Mean Delinquency Scores by Group Status

	Youths with Nondelinquent Friends	Youths with Delinquent Friends	Gang Members
Variety of delinquency	0.68	3.47	6.65
Volume of delinquency	1.58	11.34	28.19
Variety of serious delinquency	0.006	0.59	1.98
Volume of serious delinquency	0.15	1.73	6.84
Variety of offenses against the person	0.21	0.75	1.43
Volume of offenses against the person	0.54	2.35	6.39

Note: All t tests of the delinquency scores between gang and nongang youth, both with and without delinquent friends, are statistically significant at the 0.01 level.

members and nongang youths with delinquent peers were statistically different. These tests proved that gang members had statistically higher offense rates in each of the six measures of delinquency used.

It would thus appear that the data from the Edinburgh study, like that of Battin et al. (1998), supports the conjecture that gang membership contributes to delinquency over and above associating with delinquent peers. However, in this analysis, it is also possible that delinquency rates are higher among gang members because they also associate with delinquent peers. Therefore, the observed effect of gang membership may actually derive from the simple fact that gang members have a lot of delinquent friends rather than from the particular symbolic meanings attached to gang membership. At this stage, the analysis in which the impact of gang membership can be measured after controlling for the effect of delinquent peers has not been undertaken; thus, further conclusions cannot be drawn.

CONCLUSION

This chapter began by reviewing the rich history of gang research in the United States. In recent years, results from a number of survey-based gang research studies in the United States have provided large-scale information on the prevalence of gang membership, as well as detailed data on the individual and family characteristics of gang members. The dominant finding from this research, and indeed from the vast volumes of U.S. gang research, is that gang members are more heavily involved in delinquency than nongang youths. Until recently, the lack of similar research in the United Kingdom, and indeed in many other countries outside of the United States, has meant that youth gangs and the problems associated with gang membership have been considered unique to American social life. Furthermore, there has been no indication as to whether the characteristics of gang members detailed are exclusive to research conducted in the United States or whether they are more generally representative of the type of young person who joins a gang anywhere in the world.

Data from the Edinburgh study has identified the existence of youth gangs in Edinburgh. Some fundamental similarities in terms of names, territories, and territorial battles between these gangs and the Glasgow gangs identified by Patrick (1973) and McCallum (1994) suggest that the youth gang type that emerges from the Edinburgh study data is a type mirrored across Scotland or at least the densely populated central belt. This data and the preceding analysis further suggest that youth gangs and gang members in Scotland are not that different from their comparable American counterparts. The prevalence of gang membership is similar, and Scottish gang members are similar both demographically and attitudinally to gang youths in the United States. Perhaps the most important finding, however, is that gang membership in Scotland clearly has the same relationship to the delinquency of the youths concerned as it does across the Atlantic: in both countries, gang members are involved in significantly higher levels of delinquent behavior than their nongang peers.

The independent influence of gang membership on offending may be explained in a number of ways. The first explanation is based on the idea of *social selection*. Results from the above analysis show how gang members differ significantly in terms of personality and attitudes toward nongang members. It may be, therefore, that the gang specifically attracts individuals predisposed to risky behavior and unconventional moral values, who in turn commit delinquent acts. A second explanation suggests that the gang facilitates offending by the individual (Thornberry et al. 1993). In other words, if the norms and group processes within the gang are favorable toward offending behavior, members would be expected to commit to those norms and participate in delinquent acts while part of the group. A third explanation is that both processes are operating concurrently. Individuals of a particular disposition are attracted to and accepted by gangs with similar characteristics. The group processes within the gang that are favorable to delinquency subsequently encourage participation in offending behavior. While the results of the preceding analysis do not go far enough to promote conclusively one of these explanations above the other, the data does clearly suggest that preventing youths from joining gangs holds promise for preventing and reducing their delinquent behavior.

Evidently, it is necessary to develop this analysis further by both examining in more depth why joining a gang affects young people in this respect and by investigating the predictive factors related to gang membership, thereby providing a fuller picture of youth gangs in Scotland. However, this research has shown that contrary to Downes' (1966) comments and despite Campbell and Muncer's (1989, 274) dismissal of Patrick's gangs as unstable and unstructured youth groups, membership in the young teams is closely related to the delinquency of many Scottish adolescents.

NOTES

1. Neotraditional gangs are usually medium to large in size, have a duration of ten years or less, have distinct subgroups, and are strongly territorial. Compressed gangs are usually small in size and have a short history, no subgroups, and a narrow age range. For a fuller discussion, see Maxson and Klein (1995).

2. See Smith et al. (2001) and Smith and McVie (2003) for more on social geography within the Edinburgh Study.

REFERENCES

Akers, R. L., M. D. Krohn, L. Lanza-Kaduce, and M. Radosevich. 1979. Social learning and deviant behavior: A specific test of a general theory. *American Sociological Review* 44: 636–55.

Ashbury, H. 1928. *The gangs of New York: An informal history of the underworld*. New York: A. A. Knopf.

Batchelor, S. 2001. The myth of girl gangs. *Criminal Justice Matters* 43: 26–27

Battin, S. R., K. G. Hill, R. D. Abbott, R. F. Catalano, and J. D. Hawkins. 1998. The contribution of gang delinquency beyond delinquent friends. *Criminology* 36: 93–115.

Bennett, T., and K. Holloway. 2004. Gang membership, drugs and crime in the U.K. *British Journal of Criminology* 44: 305–23.

Bjerregaard, B., and C. Smith. 1993. Gender differences in gang participation, delinquency and substance use. *Journal of Quantitative Criminology* 9: 329–55.

Bullock, K., and N. Tilley. 2002. *Shootings, gangs and violent incidents in Manchester: Developing a crime reduction strategy*. Crime Reduction Research Series Paper 13. London: Home Office.

Campbell, A., and S. Muncer. 1989. Them and us: A comparison of the cultural context of American gangs and British subcultures. *Deviant Behavior* 10: 271–88.

Davies, A. 1998. Street gangs, crime and policing in Glasgow during the 1930s: The case of the Beehive Boys. *Social History* 23: 251–67.

———. 1999. These viragoes are no less cruel than the lads: Young women, gangs and violence in late Victorian Manchester and Salford. *British Journal of Criminology* 39: 72–89.

Davidson, G. 1998. It's café society as gangs try to live with the enemy. *Evening News* (Edinburgh), October 15.

Downes, D. 1966. *The delinquent solution: A study in subcultural theory.* London: Routledge and Kegan-Paul.

Elliot, D. S., and S. Menard. 1996. Delinquent friends and delinquent behavior: Temporal and developmental patterns. In *Delinquency and crime: Current theories*, ed. J. D. Hawkins. Cambridge: Cambridge University Press.

Esbensen, F.-A., and D. Huizinga. 1993. Gangs, drugs and delinquency in a survey of urban youth. *Criminology* 31: 565–87.

Esbensen, F.-A., D. Huizinga, and A. W. Weiher. 1993. Gang and non-gang youth: Differences in explanatory variables. *Journal of Contemporary Criminal Justice* 9: 94–116.

Esbensen, F.-A., and D. P. Lynskey. 2001. Youth gang members in a school survey. In *The Eurogang Paradox: Street gangs and youth groups in the U.S. and Europe*, ed. M. W. Klein, H.-J. Kerner, C. L. Maxson, and E. G. M. Weitekamp. Dordrecht, Netherlands: Kluwer.

Esbensen, F.-A., and D. W. Osgood. 1997. *National evaluation of G.R.E.A.T., research in brief.* Washington D.C.: U.S. Department of Justice, Office of Justice Programs, National Institute of Justice.

Esbensen, F.-A., L. T. Winfree Jr., N. He, and T. J. Taylor. 2001. Youth gangs and definitional issues: When is a gang a gang and why does it matter? *Crime and Delinquency* 47: 105–30.

Eysenck, S. B. J., G. Easting, and P. R. Pearson. 1984. Age-norms for impulsiveness, venturesomeness and empathy in children. *Personality and Individual Differences* 5: 315–21.

Gardner, C. 1999a. Gang terror on streets. *Evening News* (Edinburgh), September 28.

———. 1999b. Meet "normal teenagers" who smoke dope and fight with machetes. *Evening News* (Edinburgh), October 4.

Gottfredson, M. R., and T. Hirschi. 1990. *A general theory of crime.* Palo Alto, CA: Stanford University Press.

Grasmick, H. G., C. R. Tittle, R. J. Bursik Jr., and B. J. Arnekle. 1993. Testing the core assumptions of Gottfredson and Hirschi's general theory of crime. *Journal of Research in Crime and Delinquency* 30: 5–29.

Hill, K. G., J. C. Howell, J. D. Hawkins, and S. R. Battin-Pearson. 1999. Childhood risk factors for adolescent gang membership: Results from the Seattle Social Development Project. *Journal of Research in Crime and Delinquency* 36: 300–322.

Howell, J. C. 1997. Promising approaches for youth gang violence prevention and intervention. In *Report of the study group on serious, violent, and chronic juvenile offenders*, ed. R. Loeber and D. P. Farrington. Washington, D.C.: U.S. Department of Justice, Office of Justice Programs, Office of Juvenile Justice and Delinquency Prevention.

Klein, M. W. 1995. *The American street gang: Its nature, prevalence and control.* New York: Oxford University Press.

Lyst, C. 2000. Children bring terror to streets in gang riot. *Evening News* (Edinburgh), July 13.

Mares, D. 2001. Gangstas or lager louts? Working class street gangs in Manchester. In *The Eurogang Paradox: Street gangs and youth groups in the U.S. and Europe*, ed. M. W. Klein, H.-J. Kerner, C. L. Maxson, and E. G. M. Weitekamp. Dordrecht, Netherlands: Kluwer.

Maxson, C., and M. W. Klein. 1995. Investigating gang structures. *Journal of Gang Research* 3: 33–40.

McCallum, R. G. 1994. *Tongs Ya Bas: A history of the Glasgow gangs, part 1: 1850–1940.* Glasgow, Scotland: New Glasgow Library.

Patrick, J. 1973. *A Glasgow gang observed.* London: Eyre Methuen.

Rutter, M., H. Giller, and A. Hagell. 1998. *Antisocial behavior by young people.* Cambridge: Cambridge University Press

Smith, D., and S. McVie. 2003. Theory and method in the Edinburgh Study of Youth Transitions and Crime. *British Journal of Criminology* 43: 169–65.

Smith, D., S. McVie, R. Woodward, J. Shute, J. Flint, and L. McAra. 2001. *The Edinburgh Study of Youth Transitions and Crime: Key findings at ages 12 and 13.* Edinburgh: ESYTC, available at www.law.ed.ac.uk/cls/esytc/findingsreport.htm (accessed February 1, 2004).

Thornberry, T. P. 1998. Membership in youth gangs and involvement in serious and violent offending. In *Serious and violent juvenile offenders: Risk factors and successful interventions*, ed. R. Loeber and D. P. Farrington. Thousand Oaks, CA: Sage Publications.

Thornberry, T. P., M. D. Krohn, A. J. Lizotte, and D. Chard-Wierschem. 1993. The role of juvenile gangs in facilitating delinquent behaviour. *Journal of Research in Crime and Delinquency* 30: 55–87.

Thornberry, T. P., A. J. Lizotte, M. D. Krohn, M. Farnworth, and S. J. Jang. 1994. Delinquent peers, beliefs and delinquent behaviour: A longitudinal test of interactional theory. *Criminology* 32: 47–83.

Thrasher, F. M. 1936. *The gang: A study of 1,313 gangs in Chicago*, 2nd rev. ed. Chicago: University of Chicago Press.

APPENDIX 9.A: ATTITUDINAL MEASURES AND SUMMARY SCALES

Peer delinquency: Sixteen items asking about delinquent activities in which friends may have been involved. The delinquency items mirror those included in the self-report delinquency scale.

Negative peer influence: Five questions such as "How likely is it that you would still hang around with your friends if they were getting you into trouble at school?" and "How likely is it that you would do what your friends said if they told you to do something that you thought was wrong?"

Strength of conventional moral beliefs: Twelve items examining the extent to which respondents support conventional moral beliefs. Questions were divided into three groups. The first group concerned lying ("It's okay to tell a lie if it doesn't hurt anybody"), the second, stealing ("It's okay to take little things from a shop without paying for them because shops make a lot of money"), and the third fighting ("It's okay to fight with someone if they hit you first").

Impulsivity: Six items measuring impulsive behavior using a modified version of the Eysenck Impulsivity Scale (Eysenck et al. 1984). Respondents were asked whether they agreed or disagreed, on a five-point scale, with statements such as "Having to plan things makes them less fun to do" and "I get into trouble because I do things without thinking."

Risk-taking: Four items about risk-seeking behavior taken from the self-control scale in H. G. Grasmick et al. (1993). Respondents were asked whether they agreed or disagreed, on a five-point scale, with statements including "I like to test myself every now and then by doing something a bit risky" and "Sometimes I will take a risk just for the fun of it."

Parental supervision: Three items measuring the extent to which parents are aware of where their child is, what they are doing, and whom they are with, such as "When you went out during the last year, how often did your parents know where you were going?"

Conflict with parents: Six items measuring the frequency and subject of parent-child arguments, including questions like, "How often do you disagree or argue with your parents about each of these things: homework, friends, how tidy my room is, etc."

Parental punishment: Five items measuring the types and frequency of punishment given to respondents by their parents, including questions like, "How often do your parents punish you in these ways: tell you off or give you a row, stop you from seeing your friends," and so forth.

Attachment to school: Four items measuring attitudes toward school. Respondents were asked whether they agreed or disagreed, on a five-point scale, with statements such as, "School is a waste of time" and "Working hard at school is important."

SELF-REPORTED DELINQUENCY
During the last year did you . . .

- Travel on a bus or train without paying enough money or using someone else's bus pass?
- Take something from a shop or store without paying for it?
- Act noisy or cheeky in a public place so that people complained or you got into trouble?
- Ride in a stolen car or van or on a stolen motorbike?
- Break into a car or van to try and steal something out of it?
- Steal money or something else from school?
- Steal money or something else from home?
- Go into or break into a house or building to try to steal something?
- Write or spray paint on property that did not belong to you?
- Damage or destroy property that did not belong to you on purpose?
- Carry a knife or other weapon with you for protection or in case it was needed in a fight?
- Hit, kick, or punch someone on purpose?
- Use force, threats, or a weapon to steal money or something else from somebody?
- Set fire or try to set fire to something on purpose?
- Hurt or injure any animals or birds on purpose?
- Skip or skive school?

Note that the full content of all Edinburgh study youth questionnaires can be accessed via our website at www.law.ed.ac.uk/cls/esytc.

10

A Cross-National Comparison of Youth Gangs: The United States and the Netherlands

FRANK M. WEERMAN AND FINN-AAGE ESBENSEN

Gang research in the United States has a long history, one that experienced a resurgence of interest in the 1990s. No comparable history of gang research exists elsewhere, although assessments of youth gangs outside the United States have appeared periodically (see, for example, Klein 2001, 2002; Covey et al. 1997). With but one exception (Huizinga and Schumann 2001), gang research has been quite parochial, focusing on one gang (sometimes case studies of only a few gang members), gangs in one city, or at best, gangs in several cities. Thus, much of what is known about youth gangs is piecemeal and relies primarily upon information gleaned from the almost one hundred years of gang research in the United States. As the world becomes increasingly "one world," cultures, languages, economies, and religions as well as criminal activities transcend national boundaries. While youth gangs have traditionally been viewed as an American phenomenon, the past decade has witnessed the emergence of considerable ganglike behavior in Europe, Australia, South and Central America, Africa, and Asia (for a review of this literature, consult Covey et al. 1997; Klein 2002). To what extent are these "emerging" youth gangs around the world similar to those found in the United States? While this is a simple question, it is nonetheless an interesting and intriguing one. Oddly enough, though, it is also virtually impossible to answer due to the simple paucity of data with which to address it. There is even an absence of data within the United States to address adequately the issue of the nature and extent of youth gangs within that country. The National Youth Gang Center's annual surveys of law-enforcement agencies provide the closest thing to a national assessment of youth gangs in the United States.

Our goal in this chapter is to continue the work of D. Huizinga and K. F. Schumann (2001) in assessing the extent to which youth gangs in the United States are similar to troublesome youth groups found in other nations. We draw upon data from two school-based surveys of young adolescents—one in the United States and the other in the Netherlands. Between 2001 and 2003, the Eurogang Program of Research developed instruments for use in the comparative study of youth groups. The research reported here preceded the Eurogang program and, as such, informed some of the decisions of that group. This research was not conceived as a collaborative effort; therefore, we do not have identical measures for a number of our core concepts, but the two studies do share similar measures and procedures that allow for cross-national comparisons. Our objectives are modest yet groundbreaking. We add to the growing knowledge of youth gangs by addressing the following six questions:

1. How prevalent is gang membership?
2. What are the demographic characteristics of gang members?
3. What risk factors are associated with gang membership?
4. Which of these risk factors predict gang membership in a multivariate analysis?
5. Are the illegal activities of Dutch and American gang-involved youths similar?
6. To what extent are Dutch and American youth gangs similar?

Prior to discussion of the research and results, however, we provide a cursory overview of the key issues that we explore.

DEFINITIONAL ISSUES

The term *gang* evokes considerable reaction regardless of locale or audience. Movies, music (especially rap), and other forms of the mass media have dispersed gang culture and concern about gangs throughout much of the industrialized world. *Drive-by, wannabe,* and *colors* are but some of the terms that have been part of this dispersion of gang culture. With the dispersion has come a moral panic in some areas (McCorkle and Miethe 1998; St. Cyr 2003) and concern about formally acknowledging a gang presence in others (Huff 1990). In spite of the apparent dispersion of gangs during the last fifteen years, there is still considerable debate about what constitutes a gang, with different agencies and different researchers using different criteria. (For further discussion of definitional issues, consult Ball and Curry 1995; Curry and Decker 2003; Esbensen et al. 2001; Klein 1995). A common understanding of the meaning of what constitutes a gang is even more complicated within a cross-national perspective. One reason for this is that wordings and terms used for gangs have different meanings and emotional weight in different languages. Another reason is that many non-Americans compare their troublesome youth groups to stereotypes or ideal types of a highly organized Chicago-style gang or the Bloods and Crips of Los Angeles. Within this framework, they usually conclude that no such gangs exist in their country. Interestingly, research by C. L. Maxson and M. W. Klein (1995), among others, has documented that the majority of American youth gangs do not match this stereotypical picture. Klein (2001) has referred to this false impression as the Eurogang Paradox. To resolve this paradox, members of the Eurogang program engaged in numerous discussions and ultimately developed the following definition that allows for classification of youth groups as youth gangs: a *gang*, or *troublesome youth group*, is "any durable, street-oriented youth group whose involvement in illegal activity is part of their group identity." Because in some languages or national contexts, the word *gang* either cannot be translated or carries with it such an emotionally charged meaning that it cannot be used meaningfully, consensus was reached to describe such groups as troublesome youth groups. The research reported in this chapter examines similarities and differences between gang and nongang youths in the Netherlands and the United States.

SOURCES OF INFORMATION AND GANG MEMBER CHARACTERISTICS

Varying definitions of youth gangs are not the only reason for divergent estimates of the magnitude of the "gang problem" or for the different descriptions of gang youth that permeate the gang literature. Different sources of information (i.e., police reports, field studies, general surveys of youth) provide different pictures of gang-member characteristics. A clear example of this type of "methods effect" is drawn from the American study included in this chapter.

An official with a gang task force reported in an interview that in his jurisdiction, there were no girls in gangs. Survey results from the school sample in that same city, however, indicated that almost half of the gang members in the city were female and that they were involved in a variety of violent crimes.

Within the American experience, it is well known that varying definitions and sources of information produce different pictures of gangs and gang members. In general, law-enforcement data paints a picture of gang members as inner-city, minority males, generally from single-parent households (Moore and Cook 1999). Ethnographic studies of older and more homogeneous samples tend to confirm this picture. Surveys involving younger samples, however, call into question the extent to which these stereotypes accurately depict youth gang members. A similar picture of gang members appears to be evolving in Europe, based largely on police accounts and on relatively recent ethnographic studies (van Gemert 2001; Lien 2001; Tertilt 2001). To what extent, however, are these findings based upon stereotyping or on limited information? In the United States, as survey findings have raised questions about the validity of the stereotypical gang member image, findings based on law-enforcement data have begun to reveal a slightly different picture of gangs in America. Results from the *National Youth Gang Center (NYGC) Survey* (Moore and Cook 1999) have revealed the emergence of youth gangs in small towns and rural areas. One consequence of the previous concentration in large urban areas is that police estimates may have overestimated minority gang-member representation; the 1998 NYGC survey revealed that the race or ethnicity of gang members is closely tied to the size of the community. While white youths made up only 11 percent of gang members in large cities (where most gang research has taken place), they accounted for approximately 30 percent of gang members in small cities and rural counties.

Most ethnographic studies of gangs have been conducted in socially disorganized communities in Los Angeles and New York—in other words, in urban areas characterized by high concentrations of minority residents. The general surveys of youths conducted in the 1990s examined youth gangs in smaller cities lacking a long tradition of gangs; nonetheless, several of these studies were concentrated in high-risk neighborhoods that (by definition) included disproportionate representations of racial and ethnic minorities (e.g., Esbensen and Huizinga 1993; Thornberry et al. 2003). The same appears to be the case with European ethnographers; those studies are based on gangs in

Frankfurt, Oslo, Amsterdam, Manchester, and other major cities. To date, studies of gang-involved youths in small American and European cities and towns are lacking. Thus, it is difficult to ascertain not only the prevalence but also the characteristics of gang youths.

As research expands to include more representative samples of the general population, a redefinition of the racial and ethnic composition of gang members is likely. F.-A. Esbensen and D. P. Lynskey (2001) report that the composition of youth gangs reflects community-level demographics; that is, gang members are white in primarily white communities and African American in predominantly African American communities.

Family characteristics of gang members, such as family structure, parental education, and income, also have been revised because the traditional stereotype is too restrictive—gang youths are found in two-parent, single-parent, and recombined families. In addition, gang youths are not limited to homes in which parents have low educational achievement or low incomes.

RISK FACTORS ASSOCIATED WITH GANG MEMBERSHIP

The use of youth surveys to study gangs is a relatively new phenomenon. It is only since the beginning of the 1990s that general youth surveys became a significant source of information on gangs and gang members (see, especially, Esbensen and Huizinga 1993; Thornberry et al. 1993). In Europe, there is still no established use of surveys to study gangs or troublesome youth groups, although a few recent survey studies have included items about gangs or youth groups (e.g., Bradshaw 2002; Haaland 2000; Huizinga and Schumann 2001; and Weerman, chapter 6 of this volume). While ethnographic studies offer rich and descriptive accounts of gang members or particular gangs, youth surveys provide information about the proportion of a population involved in youth gangs and enable comparisons and generalizations. They inform us about the organizational characteristics of gangs at different sites (Esbensen and Lynskey 2001), about risk factors for gang membership (Thornberry 1998; Esbensen and Deschenes 1998), and about the longitudinal development of gang members and nongang members (Esbensen and Huizinga 1993; Hill et al. 1999; Thornberry et al. 2003). They also provide information about the unique contribution of gang membership to delinquent behavior, apart from the influence of delinquent friends (Thornberry et al. 1994; Battin et al. 1998). The following discussion of risk factors associated with gang membership draws upon this emerging field of knowledge, based on more general youth surveys.

It is important to keep several methodological distinctions in mind as risk factors associated with gang membership are reviewed. These surveys are usually based on samples of middle and high school students. This implies that the results are primarily valid for the youth population. Ethnographies and law-enforcement statistics generally include older gang members. Moreover, ethnographic studies often rely on key informants who are core members of gangs, and law-enforcement statistics likely reflect the most delinquent of gang members. School surveys include more respondents from the periphery of gangs, including wannabes. Surveys cover the less serious, but also more common, part of youth involvement in gangs and troublesome youth groups (see also Curry 2000).

Some researchers (e.g., Yablonsky 1962) claim that compared with nongang youths, gang members are more socially inept, have lower self-esteem, and in general have sociopathic characteristics. T. Moffitt (1993) has stated that youth gang members are likely to be "life-course persistent offenders." To what extent are such depictions accurate? Are gang youths substantively different from nongang youths? Comparisons between gang and nongang youths have been reported from Denver (Esbensen et al. 1993), Rochester (Bjerregaard and Smith 1993), Seattle (Hill et al. 1999), San Diego (Maxson et al. 1998), and in an eleven-city study (Esbensen and Deschenes 1998; Esbensen et al. 2001).

The authors of these different studies used different questions and different sampling methods that resulted in slightly different findings. In the Seattle study, Hill et al. (1999) found that gang youths held more antisocial beliefs, while Maxson, M. L. Whitlock, and M. W. Klein (1998), among other authors, found that gang members had more delinquent self-concepts, tended more to resolve conflicts with threats, and had experienced more critical stressful events. On a more generic level, both the Seattle and San Diego studies found significant differences between gang and nongang youths within multiple contexts, namely, regarding individual, school, peer, family, and community characteristics.

In an attempt to examine the unique relationship of gang membership to attitudinal and behavioral characteristics, Esbensen, Huizinga, and A. W. Weiher (1993) examined gang youths, serious youthful offenders who were not gang members, and nondelinquent youth. They found that the nondelinquent youths were different from the delinquent and gang youths in that nondelinquent youths reported lower levels of commitment to delinquent peers, lower levels of social isolation, lower tolerance for deviance, and higher levels of commitment to positive peers.

Using a somewhat different approach, Esbensen et al. (2001) examined differences between gang members. They classified gang members on a continuum, beginning with a broad definition of gang members and steadily restricting the definition until only those youths who claimed to be core members of a delinquent gang that had a certain level of organizational structure were classified as gang members. They found significant attitudinal and behavioral differences between core gang members and those classified as gang members using the broad definition. They did not find any demographic differences among the different gang definitions.

In another report from the Seattle study, S. R. Battin-Pearson et al. (1998) compared nongang youths, transient gang youths (members for one year or less), and stable gang youths (members for two or more years). Both the transient and stable gang members differed significantly from the nongang youths on a variety of attitudinal and behavioral measures. However, few distinctions between the transient and stable gang members were found. The measures on which differences occurred tended to represent individual and peer-level measures (e.g., personal attitudes and delinquency of friends).

One consistent finding from research on gangs, as is the case with research on delinquency in general, is the importance of peers during adolescence (Battin-Pearson et al. 1998; Elliott and Menard 1996; Warr 2002; Warr and Stafford 1991). In their comparison of stable and transient gang youths, Battin-Pearson et al. reported that the strongest predictors of sustained gang affiliation were a high level of interaction with antisocial peers and a low level of interaction with prosocial peers. Researchers have examined the influence of peers through a variety of measures, including exposure to delinquent peers, attachment to delinquent peers, and commitment to delinquent peers. Regardless of how this peer affiliation is measured, the results are the same: association with delinquent peers is one of the strongest predictors (i.e., risk factors) of gang membership.

Gang researchers examine school factors less frequently than other factors; however, they have found that these issues are consistently associated with the risk of joining gangs. Research indicates that gang youths are less committed to school than nongang youths (Bjerregaard and Smith 1993; Esbensen and Deschenes 1998; Hill et al. 1999; Maxson et al. 1998). Some gender differences have been reported with regard to this issue. In the Rochester study, expectations for educational attainment were predictive of gang membership for girls but not for boys. In a similar vein, Esbensen and E. P. Deschenes (1998) found that commitment to school was lower among gang girls than nongang girls. No such differences were found for boys. Studies that examine juveniles' cultures and ethnic backgrounds also attest to the role of school factors in explaining gang membership (Campbell 1991; Fleisher 1998).

The community is the domain examined most frequently with regard to both the emergence of gangs and the factors associated with joining gangs. Numerous studies indicate that poverty, unemployment, the absence of meaningful jobs, and social disorganization contribute to the presence of gangs (Curry and Thomas 1992; Fagan 1990; Hagedorn 1988; Huff 1990; Vigil 1988). There is little debate that gangs are more prominent in urban areas and that they are more likely to emerge in economically distressed neighborhoods. However, as previously stated, surveys conducted by NYGC during the 1990s have identified the proliferation of youth gangs in rural and suburban communities. Except for law-enforcement identification of this phenomenon, few systematic studies have explored these rural and suburban youth gangs. L. T. Winfree, T. Vigil-Backsrom, and G. L. Mays (1994) studied youth gang members in Las Cruces, New Mexico, and Esbensen and Lynskey (2001) reported on gang youths in rural areas and small cities that were included in an eleven-site study. While neither report addressed environmental characteristics, they did indicate that these gang members were engaged in a substantial level of violence.

The traditional image of American youth gangs, however, is characterized by urban social disorganization and economic marginalization; the housing projects, or barrios, of Los Angeles, Chicago, and New York are viewed as the stereotypical homes of youth gang members. The publication of W. J. Wilson's (1987) account of the underclass—those members of society who are truly disadvantaged and affected by changes in social and economic conditions—has renewed interest in the social disorganization perspective advanced by F. M. Thrasher (1963) and C. R. Shaw and H. D. McKay (1942). Los Angeles barrio gangs, according to J. D. Vigil (1988) and J. Moore (1991), are a product of economic restructuring and street socialization. Vigil refers to the multiple marginality (i.e., the combined disadvantages of low socioeconomic status, street socialization, and segregation) of both male and female gang members who live in these socially disorganized areas (1988, 9). In addition to the pressures of marginal economics, these gang members experience the added burden of having marginal ethnic and personal identities. These juveniles look for identity and stability in the gang and gang subculture. Social structural conditions alone, however, cannot account for the presence of gangs. J. Fagan comments that "inner-city youths . . . live in areas where social controls have weakened and opportunities for success in legitimate activities are limited. Nevertheless, participation in gangs is selective, and most youths avoid gang life" (1990, 207).

In the research reported here, we use school-based surveys of youths to examine the similarities and differences between gang and nongang youths in the United States and the Netherlands. Our research seeks to address the six questions posed at the beginning of this chapter. Conceived somewhat differently, our interests are the examination of individual-level issues (i.e., demographic characteristics of gang and nongang youths, risk factors associated with gang membership, and levels of involvement in illegal activity) and group-level factors (i.e., the prevalence of gang membership in a general youth sample and the characteristics of youth gangs in two different national and cultural settings).

RESEARCH DESIGN

The U.S. Sample

During the spring of 1995, eighth-grade students in eleven cities—Las Cruces, New Mexico; Omaha, Nebraska; Phoenix, Arizona; Philadelphia, Pennsylvania; Kansas City, Missouri; Milwaukee, Wisconsin; Orlando, Florida; Will County, Illinois; Providence, Rhode Island; Pocatello, Idaho; and Torrance, California—completed self-administered questionnaires as part of the National Evaluation of the Gang Resistance Education and Training (GREAT) program (Esbensen and Osgood 1999). The final sample consisted of 5,935 eighth-grade public school students, representing 42 schools and 315 classrooms. Passive parental consent (excluding only those students whose parents indicated that they did not want their children to participate) was used in thirty-eight schools representing ten of the study sites. Participation rates, or the percentage of children providing answers to the questionnaires, varied between 98 and 100 percent at the passive-consent sites. At the four active-consent schools in the remaining site, the participation rates varied from a low of 53 percent to a high of 75 percent (Esbensen et al. 1996). Comparison of school-district data indicates that the study sample is representative of eighth-grade students enrolled in public schools in these eleven communities.

This public school–based sample has the standard limitations associated with school-based surveys (i.e., exclusion of private school students, truants, sick and tardy students, and the potential underrepresentation of high-risk youth). With this caveat in mind, the current sample comprises nearly all eighth grade students in attendance on the days questionnaires were administered in these eleven jurisdictions. The sample includes primarily thirteen- to fifteen-year-old students attending public schools in a broad cross-section of communities across the continental United States. This is not a random sample, and strong generalizations cannot be made to the adolescent population as a whole. However, students from these eleven jurisdictions do represent the following types of communities: large urban areas with a majority of students belonging to a racial or ethnic minority (Philadelphia, Phoenix, Milwaukee, and Kansas City), medium-sized cities (population ranges between one hundred thousand and five hundred thousand) with considerable racial or ethnic heterogeneity (Providence and Orlando), medium-sized cities with a majority of white students but a substantial minority enrollment (Omaha and Torrance), a small city (fewer than one hundred thousand inhabitants) with an ethnically diverse student population (Las Cruces), a small racially homogeneous (i.e., white) city (Pocatello), and a rural community in which more than 80 percent of the student population is white (Will County).

Students completed questionnaires (paper and pencil) in their classrooms (approximately twenty-five students per classroom). At least two researchers administered the surveys, with one person reading the questionnaire out loud as students followed along and wrote their answers in the questionnaires. A second, and sometimes a third, researcher monitored the classroom, enhancing respondent confidentiality and assisting students requiring assistance.

The Dutch Sample

The Dutch data were collected within the framework of the Netherlands Institute for the Study of Crime and Law Enforcement (NSCR) School Project, a larger longitudinal study focused on the roles of peer-network formation, personal development, and school interventions in the development of problem behavior. Data from the first wave (2002) of the longitudinal study were used in the analyses reported in this chapter. Two objectives guided the selection of respondents for the sample: obtaining a relatively high-risk sample (i.e., with a substantial proportion of youths involved in illegal activities) and maintaining adequate inclusion of lower-risk students to allow for variation in school contexts and student populations. To accomplish this, less educated students from The Hague, a city with clear inner-city problems, were overrepresented. Students from smaller cities in the vicinity, including a school for agricultural education and a reformatory school, were also recruited. This sample is not a random sample, but it is fairly representative of (less educated) Dutch youths in the southwest region of the Netherlands.

The final sample consists of 1,978 students from the first and third grades in secondary education (roughly equivalent to seventh and ninth grades in the United States; in the Netherlands, secondary school starts at about age twelve, and pupils usually turn thirteen during their first year in school) in twelve schools with a total population of 2,370 first and third graders. As was the case in the American study, passive parental consent procedures were used (only two parents refused their child's participation). Thus, virtually all students in attendance on the day of survey administration completed questionnaires. Due to some scheduling problems on the part of the school and due to some minor computer problems, a small number of students were unintentionally excluded from participation.

The questionnaire was group-administered in the classroom during normal school hours. Respondents received a small reward (a CD check of €5) to stimulate current and future participation. Two or three researchers were present during the administration of the questionnaire to monitor the situation and to answer questions. Computers were used to administer the questionnaire instead of the usual paper-and-pencil method.

Measures

It is important to state at the outset that this research compares survey responses from similarly aged school youths in the Netherlands and the United States. A similar conceptual framework guided the two independent studies, but the actual measures used were not identical. This lack of exact comparability is unfortunate, but at the same time, the inclusion of common concepts does allow for examination of general relationship patterns between risk factors and gang membership in the two samples.

Gang Definition

To establish gang membership in youth surveys can be difficult. Ethnographies are usually restricted to clear cases of gang situations and use rich and varied sources of information. Youth surveys are necessarily based on a limited number of questions. The identification of youth groups as gangs (or troublesome youth groups) is further complicated by definitional and operational problems with the gang concept. In many American surveys, researchers have relied on the self-nomination technique: respondents are simply asked, "Do you belong to a gang?" To control for overreporting or inclusion of youth groups that do not meet the criteria of being youth gangs, researchers have used follow-up questions. For instance, some researchers have relied on a gang name, whether the gang is involved in delinquent activity, or whether the gang has group characteristics such as leadership and organization. In a 2001 article, Esbensen et al. examined the effect of varying definitions and found that the self-report item was, in and of itself, a robust measure. Each additional criterion led to the classification of fewer youths as gang members, and these youths were increasingly more antisocial in their attitudes and behavior. This procedure appears to work quite well in the American situation where the concept of a gang is familiar to most respondents. In Europe, however, the use of the word *gang* or its synonyms (e.g., *jeugdbende*, *bande*) is less widespread and more ambiguous. Asking directly if a respondent belongs to a gang might result in less reliable answers than in the United States.

As reported earlier, the Eurogang Program of Research developed a consensus definition of youth gangs: "A street gang is any durable, street-oriented youth group whose involvement in illegal activity is part of their group identity." To measure gang affiliation, a funneling approach was designed. Respondents are asked a set of questions about formal and informal peer groups, the characteristics of these groups, and illegal activities within the groups. After these questions, respondents are asked if they consider their group a gang (or its synonym in their own language). This technique offers "objective" criteria for the researcher to define a group as a gang under the Eurogang definition. At the same time, it incorporates the more "subjective" criterion of respondents' self-identification as members of a gang.

The Dutch school survey discussed in this chapter used the funneling technique developed by the Eurogang network, defining gang members as those youths who indicated that their group of friends was a street-oriented youth group and that their group had a serious level of illegal activity. A serious level of illegal activity meant that some or most group members were substantially involved in damaging property, assaults, shoplifting, stealing things worth more than €5, burglary or robbery. Either most group members were involved in two or more of these offenses, or some group members were involved in four offenses or more. This was the first study to apply survey methods to the subject of gangs and troublesome youth groups in the Netherlands. In the American study, respondents were asked two filter questions: "Have you ever been a gang member?" and "Are you now in a gang?" These questions were followed by a number of questions seeking information about the gang and its members. In this chapter, we restrict our gang sample to those youths who indicated that they were currently in a gang, which was involved in at least one of the following illegal activities: getting in fights with other gangs, stealing things, robbing other people, stealing cars, selling marijuana, selling other illegal drugs, or damaging property.

Demographic, Attitudinal, and Behavioral Measures

Both studies collected information on the age, sex, and household living arrangements of the youths. In the American sample, information about race and ethnicity was collected, while in the Dutch sample, information about ethnicity and nationality was obtained. See table 10.1 for a summary of this information.

Attitudinal measures used in these analyses are representative of social control, social learning, and self-control theory. In this chapter our primary goal is description, not theory testing. We nonetheless use theoretical groupings in our discussion of the measurement and analysis results. Indicators of self-control theory include parental monitoring, impulsivity, and risk seeking. Social learning theory is represented by peer delinquency, peer pressure, and moral attitudes/ moral disengagement. Social control theory measures include attachment to parents and school commitment. As stated earlier, it is important to remember that the measures used in the following analyses tap conceptual areas with different operationalizations; that is, the Dutch and American studies used different, though similar, questions to measure respondent attitudes and behaviors. (See appendix 10.A for a description of the Dutch and American scales measuring each of these theoretical concepts.)

Table 10.1. Demographic Characteristics of Nongang and Gang Youths in the Netherlands and the United States

	Netherlands			United States		
	Total	Nongang	Gang	Total	Nongang	Gang
Sample size	1,978	1,861 (93%)	117 (6%)	5860	5,393 (92%)	467 (8%)
Average age	14.0	14.0	14.3	13.8	13.8	14.1
Sex						
Male (%)	55	55	60	48	47	63
Female (%)	45	45	40	52	53	37
Family structure						
Two-parent (%)	80	82	78	62	63	46
Single-parent (%)	16	16	20	31	30	41
Other (%)	2	2	2	7	7	13
Race/ethnicity						
Dutch (%)	62	62	61			
Moroccan (%)	5	5	3			
Turkish (%)	8	8	3			
Surinamese (%)	7	7	8			
Antillean (%)	2	2	7			
White (%)				41	42	25
African American (%)				27	26	31
Hispanic (%)				19	18	25
Other (%)	17	17	19	14	14	19

We also obtained measures of self-reported delinquency and drug use. Students were provided a list of behaviors and different drugs, then asked to indicate if they had ever committed the act or used the drug. Students who answered yes were asked to indicate how many times they had engaged in the behavior during the past twelve months or school year. In addition to a general delinquency measure, we created three subscales of behavior: minor offenses, property offenses, and crimes against persons. To facilitate discussion of the findings from these two projects, we converted all of the risk-factor and behavioral analyses into ratios of nongang-to-gang scores.

RESULTS

Table 10.1 provides an overview of sample characteristics of nongang and gang members. As can be seen, the demographic composition of the two samples was quite similar. The overall Dutch sample consisted of 1,978 students; 55 percent were boys. The American sample comprised 5,935 students; 48 percent were boys. Almost all respondents in both studies were between the ages of 12 and 16, with average ages of 14.0 and 13.8, respectively, in the Dutch and American samples. Ethnic minorities were relatively overrepresented. More than one-third of the Dutch sample consisted of respondents with a foreign background, but respondents with Dutch parents were still in the majority (62 percent). Turkish (8 percent), Surinamese (7 percent), and Moroccan (5 percent) respondents were the most common ethnic categories other than Dutch. In the American sample, whites (41 percent), African Americans (27 percent), and Hispanics (19 percent) were the dominant groups. Most of the youths in each sample also resided in a two-parent household (80 percent and 62 percent, respectively, in the Dutch and American samples).

Focusing on the breakdown by gang membership reported in table 10.1, we see that the gang youths in both samples shared common characteristics relative to the nongang youths. The gang youths tended to be older and were more likely to be male, less likely to live in two-parent families, and, especially in the U.S. sample, more likely to be a minority.

Risk Factors

Prior research in the United States has found that a number of risk factors are associated with youths who belong to gangs. Much of that research is cross-sectional, which precludes testing for causality; that is, whether the presence of these risk factors leads to joining a gang or whether being in a gang leads to the development of these attributes. Some longitudinal studies (i.e., the Denver, Rochester, and Seattle studies), however, have established that these risk factors do precede gang involvement. Thus, while we cannot address the temporal relationship of risk factors and gang membership in this study, we can examine the extent to which these established risk factors are present in two distinct samples of youths in the Netherlands and the United States.

Our primary interest in the subsequent analyses is to compare gang youths with nongang youths in these two samples. Following our analysis of individual-level comparisons of the gang and nongang youths in each country, we turn our attention to examining the characteristics of the gangs to which these individuals belong.

Self-Control

Each of the studies included three scales that measure self-control theory (Gottfredson and Hirschi 1990). Low self-control is viewed as a cause of criminal and other analogous behaviors. M. R. Gottfredson and T. Hirschi have indicated that low levels of parental monitoring contribute to low levels of self-control. Further, they suggest that individuals with low self-control tend to be more impulsive and more likely to engage in risky behavior.

The questions used in the two studies to measure parental monitoring were quite similar. For instance, the Dutch youths responded to the following question, "My parents know where I go to outside home," while the American sample was asked, "My parents know where I am when I am not at home or at school." The other Dutch questions in this scale also measured rule enforcement at home (e.g., "At home, I have to do what my parents say"), while the American scale did not include this element of parenting. Contrasting gang to nongang youths, we see that the gang youths in both samples reported lower levels of parental monitoring than the nongang youths. In the Dutch sample, a ratio of 0.88:1 indicates that the Dutch gang youths experienced 12 percent less monitoring than the nongang youths. Similarly, the gang youths in the American sample reported 18 percent less monitoring than did the nongang youths.

The indicators for impulsivity and risk seeking were more similar in content than those for parental monitoring. The American questions were based on the scale developed by H. G. Grasmick et al. (1993) to test Gottfredson and

Hirschi's self-control theory directly, and the Dutch questions were a modification of those questions. As such, both scales were quite similar as indicated by the following two questions: "I often do things without thinking first" (Dutch), and "I often act on the spur of the moment without stopping to think" (U.S.). (See appendix 10.A for a listing of all of the scale items.) As with parental monitoring, the findings with regard to impulsivity and risk seeking reveal a significant difference between the gang and nongang youths in each country. In both samples, the gang youths reported higher levels of impulsivity and risk seeking—16 and 30 percent more—than the nongang youths (see table 10.2). For instance, the ratios of impulsivity reported by the Dutch and American samples were 1.29:1 and 1.16:1, respectively. For risk seeking, the ratios were 1.30:1 and 1.25:1, respectively. Thus, while employing slightly different questions to measure three components of self-control theory, statistically significant differences between nongang and gang youths were found in each sample.

Social Learning

Each of the two studies also included three scales measuring social learning theory: peer delinquency, peer pressure, and moral attitudes. As with the self-control measures, these three indicators of social learning theory differed somewhat in their actual measurement. Peer delinquency, for instance, consisted of respondents indicating how many of their friends had committed delinquent acts during the past year. The American study listed sixteen illegal acts, while the Dutch sample included six different illegal activities. The Dutch study requested that respondents indicate whether none, some, or most of their friends had committed these acts, while the American youths could indicate if none, a few, half, most, or all of their friends were involved in these illegal activities. In spite of these differences, the results were once again quite similar. The ratios of gang to nongang reports of friends involved in these activities were 4.37:1 in the Dutch sample and 1.69:1 in the American sample. It is likely that the inclusion of some relatively minor illegal acts in the American study (i.e., "skipped school without an excuse" and "lied, disobeyed, or talked back to adults such as parents, teachers, or others") contributed to the smaller difference between gang and nongang youths in that sample.

The differences between the gang and nongang youths appear to be quite robust. Comparisons of the two remaining social learning measures, peer pressure ("My friends sometimes make me do things I actually don't want to do" and "If your group of friends was getting you into trouble at home, how likely is it that you would still hang out with them?") and moral attitudes/moral disengagement ("It's okay to steal if you need money" and "It's okay to steal something if that's the only way you could ever get it") produced ratios indicating that the gang youths felt more peer pressure to commit delinquent acts and held less conforming attitudes. The gang youths were more likely than the nongang youths, in both samples, to indicate that stealing, lying, and hitting people were okay in a variety of circumstances (i.e., ratios of 1.57:1 and 1.30:1 for the Dutch and Americans, respectively).

Social Control

Two elements of social control theory were included in the two studies, school commitment and attachment to parents, although in the American study, independent measures of attachment were obtained for mothers and fathers. As with the indicators of social learning and self-control perspectives, these risk factors associated with social control theory distinguished gang from nongang youths. The gang youths reported lower levels of both commitment to school (0.80:1 for both the Dutch and U.S. samples) and attachment to parents (0.92:1 for Dutch and 0.85:1 for both maternal and paternal attachment for the U.S. sample). The same caveat about measurement of these concepts discussed above applies here. The wording of questions was different between the two samples, but the same concept was being measured.

MULTIVARIATE ANALYSES

The preceding bivariate analyses revealed considerable similarity between the gang and nongang youths in our two samples; that is, the risk factors associated with gang membership in the Netherlands were similar to those in the U.S. sample. To summarize briefly: gang youths, relative to nongang youths, in both nations tended to be older and were more likely to be male with lower rates of parental monitoring, higher levels of impulsivity and risk seeking, more delinquent friends, more pressure from peers to commit delinquency, higher rates of moral disengagement, and lower levels of attachment to parents and commitment to school. The extent to which these risk factors predict gang membership, however, remains unanswered by these bivariate analyses. To answer this question, we tested four models using logistic regression. In model 1, we included the four demographic variables presented in table 10.1. Model 2 consisted of all of the risk factors detailed in table 10.2, with the exception of peer delinquency. Model 3 included both demographic and attitudinal risk-factor variables. Given the fact that a core criterion for classification as a gang member in both studies was some degree of group-level delinquency, one could argue that the use of peer delinquency as a predictor of gang membership was tautological. While potentially tautological, we nonetheless present results from model 4, which included peer delinquency as a predictor of gang association. Tables 10.3 (the Dutch sample) and 10.4 (the U.S. sample) present the results of these analyses.

Given the similarity between the Dutch gang and nongang youths on measures of family structure and race or ethnicity and the slight sex difference, it is not surprising that demographic variables were not predictive of gang membership in the Dutch sample. Examination of table 10.4, however, reveals that all four of the demographic variables included in model 1 for the American sample were statistically significant predictors of gang membership. For each additional year of age, the odds of being a gang member doubled, while the odds of a male being a gang member were 82 percent greater than those for a female. Similarly, white youths and those from two-parent families were less likely to be in gangs.

Models 2 and 3 in both tables 10.3 and 10.4 report the predictive power of attitudinal risk factors. Relative to the demographic variables, it is quite clear

Table 10.2. Risk Factors and Gang Membership in the Netherlands and the United States*

	Netherlands	United States
Self-control theory		
Parental monitoring	0.88**	0.82
Impulsivity	1.29	1.16
Risk seeking	1.30	1.25
Social-learning theory		
Peer delinquency	4.37	1.69
Peer pressure	1.16	1.55
Moral attitudes/moral disengagement	1.57	1.30
Social-control theory		
Parental attachment	0.92	0.85
School commitment	0.80	0.80

*All comparisons between nongang and gang youths in each sample were statistically significant at $p < 0.05$.
**Ratio of gang to nongang members.

Table 10.3. Logistic Regression Analysis for the Dutch Sample

	Model 1		Model 2		Model 3		Model 4	
	b (S.E.)	Exp(b)	b (S.E.)	Exp(b)	b (S.E.)	Exp(b)	b (S.E.)	Exp(b)
Constant	−5.00 (1.09)***	0.01	−2.53 (.93)**	0.08	−3.81 (1.63)*	0.02	−5.26 (1.84)**	0.00
Demographics								
Age	0.16 (.07)*	1.18			0.10 (.08)	1.10	−0.01 (.09)	0.99
Gender (male = 1)	0.19 (.20)	1.21			−0.25 (.23)	0.78	−0.39 (.26)	0.68
Family (two parent = 1)	−0.24 (.24)	0.78			−0.08 (.25)	0.92	−0.25 (.28)	0.78
Ethnicity (Dutch = 1)	0.02 (.20)	1.02			−0.36 (.22)	0.70	−0.07 (.25)	0.94
Attitudinal risk factors								
Parental monitoring			−0.10 (.05)	0.91	−0.10 (.05)*	0.90	−0.06 (.06)	0.94
Impulsivity			0.14 (.04)**	1.15	0.23 (.04)**	1.14	0.15 (.05)**	1.16
Risk seeking			0.13 (.04)**	1.14	0.15 (.04)***	1.16	0.09 (.04)*	1.10
Peer pressure			−0.03 (.03)	0.98	−0.01 (.03)	0.99	−0.04 (.04)	0.96
Moral attitudes			−0.12 (.03)***	0.89	−0.12 (.03)***	0.89	−0.01 (.04)	1.01
Parental attachment			−0.04 (.03)	0.96	−0.03 (.03)	0.97	−0.06 (.04)	0.95
School commitment			−0.06 (.04)	0.95	−0.06 (.04)	0.94	0.01 (.04)	1.01
Peer delinquency								
Peer delinquency							0.66 (.06)***	1.94
Chi-square	7.14 (n.s.)		139.00***		137.84**		160.31***	
Nagelkerke's R-square	0.01		0.19		0.20		0.40	

*p ≤ 0.05,
**p ≤ 0.01,
***p ≤ 0.001

Table 10.4. Logistic Regression Analysis for the U.S. Sample

	Model 1		Model 2		Model 3		Model 4	
	b (S.E.)	Exp(b)	b (S.E.)	Exp(b)	b (S.E.)	Exp(b)	b (S.E.)	Exp(b)
Constant	−12.00 (1.11)***	0.00	−5.83 (.70)**	0.80	−12.38 (1.55)***	0.00	−12.07 (1.63)***	0.00
Demographics								
Age	0.69 (.08)***	2.00			0.54 (.10)***	1.71	0.43 (.10)***	1.54
Sex (male = 1)	0.60 (.10)***	1.82			0.10 (.13)	1.11	0.04 (.14)	1.04
Family (two parent = 1)	−0.46 (.10)***	0.63			−0.45 (.13)***	0.64	−0.34 (.13)**	0.71
Ethnicity (White = 1)	−0.59 (.12)***	0.55			−0.89 (.14)***	0.41	−0.75 (.15)***	0.47
Attitudinal risk factors								
Parental monitoring			−0.33 (.08)***	0.72	−0.25 (.08)**	0.78	−0.14 (.09)	0.87
Impulsivity			0.04 (.09)	1.04	−0.02 (.10)	0.98	−0.03 (.10)	0.97
Risk seeking			0.03 (.09)	1.03	0.18 (.09)*	1.20	0.05 (.09)	1.05
Peer pressure			0.53 (.06)***	1.70	0.55 (.06)***	1.74	0.41 (.06)***	1.51
Moral attitudes			0.86 (.10)***	2.37	0.67 (.11)***	1.96	0.34 (.11)**	1.41
Maternal attachment			0.11 (.05)*	1.12	0.07 (.05)	1.08	0.07 (.05)	1.07
Parental attachment			−0.01 (.04)	0.99	0.01 (.04)	1.01	0.03 (.04)	1.03
School commitment			−0.22 (.09)*	0.80	−0.33 (.09)***	0.72	−0.22 (.10)	0.80
Peer delinquency							0.96 (.08)***	2.61
Chi-square	209.81***		613.88***		689.52***		831.11***	
Nagelkerke's R-square	0.09		0.28		0.32		0.38	

*p ≤ 0.05,
**p ≤ 0.01
***p ≤ 0.001

to see that attitudinal risk factors played a greater role in differentiating gang from nongang youths. Second, quite different factors appear to influence gang affiliation in the Netherlands and the United States. The models produce quite different coefficients and odds ratios for the two samples. Given the findings from the bivariate analyses reported above, that is somewhat surprising. While low levels of parental monitoring and low scores on moral attitudes were predictive of gang membership in both nations, the similarities end there. Whereas impulsivity and risk seeking were associated with gang membership in the Netherlands, once other variables were introduced into the multivariate analyses, only risk seeking was modestly associated with gang membership in the United States. Surprisingly, given the consistent finding that peers were influential in shaping adolescent behavior, peer pressure (as measured) did not have an effect on gang membership in the Dutch sample. In the American sample, however, peer pressure was the second most powerful discriminator of gang and nongang youths.

More specifically, in the American sample, the following variables were associated with an increased probability of gang membership: risk seeking (odds ratio of 1.20), peer pressure (odds ratio of 1.74), and moral attitudes (odds ratio of 1.96). The following attitudinal measures were negatively associated with gang membership: parental monitoring (odds ratio of 0.78) and school commitment (odds ratio of 0.72). For the Dutch sample, we see a slightly different pattern of relationships: impulsivity (1.14) and risk seeking (1.16) were associated with a higher probability of gang membership, while parental monitoring (0.90) and conventional moral attitudes (0.89)[1] had a negative effect on gang membership. Neither school commitment nor peer pressure, two factors that predicted gang membership in the American sample, played a role in the Dutch sample. We will return to a discussion of these findings in the concluding section of this chapter.

Self-reported Delinquency

One last area of investigation of nongang and gang youths is the extent to which these youths were involved in illegal activities. Relying upon self-reported measures of delinquency, both studies found that, consistent with prior American research, the gang youths were much more likely to report involvement in criminal behavior. Whether we examine minor offending, property offending, crimes against persons, drug use, or a composite measure of all

Table 10.5. Self-reported Delinquency and Gang Membership in the Netherlands and the United States*

	Netherlands	United States
Minor offending	3.56**	4.05
Property offending	6.65	4.72
Crimes against persons	4.11	4.26
Total delinquency	4.38	4.91
Drug use	5.70	4.08

* All comparisons between nongang and gang youths in each sample were statistically significant at $p < 0.05$.
** Ratio of gang to nongang members.

these subscales, gang youths report approximately four times more offending than nongang youths. The findings, as seen in table 10.5, are strikingly similar in these two samples.

Gang Characteristics

We now turn our attention to the gang as the unit of analysis. The gang-involved youths were asked a series of questions to describe their gangs. Table 10.6 presents these results. A cursory review of these findings, unlike those for the analyses focusing on individual gang youths, reveals substantial differ-

Table 10.6. Gang Characteristics: The Netherlands and United States

	Netherlands	United States
Gang size	34	61
Males	22	49
Females	11	29
Descriptors		
Constant meeting times/regular meetings	37%	58%
Rules	38%	75%
Have to do something special to join/initiation	21%	80%
Established leaders	29%	76%
Colors/symbols	24%	92%
Subgroups/age groups	44%	38%
Behaviors		
Vandalism	95%	80%
Assault	95%	
Shoplifting	86%	
Larceny	95%	70%
Burglary	43%	
Robbery	45%	61%
Gang fights		91%
Auto theft		70%

ences between the Dutch and American gangs, at least in terms of what we refer to as *gang descriptors*. The American gang youths estimated their gangs to
be larger (having approximately twice as many members as reported by the
Dutch gang youths) and to have more characteristics associated with more
formal or organized gangs. More than half of the American gang members described their gang as having colors or symbols (92 percent), some type of initiation rite (80 percent), established leaders (76 percent), specific rules or
codes (75 percent), and regular meetings (58 percent). Contrary to this picture, fewer than 40 percent of the Dutch gang members indicated that their
gangs had rules (38 percent), constant meeting times (37 percent), initiation
rites (21 percent), leaders (29 percent), or symbols (24 percent). Two other dimensions that were tapped with different questions reflected more similarity
than difference: 44 percent of the Dutch and 38 percent of the American gang
youths indicated that their gangs had subgroups, and while 56 percent of the
Dutch indicated that boys and girls did not do same things in the gang, 53 percent of the Americans said that there were specific roles for girls.

While the gangs were perceived quite differently between the two samples
of gang youths, the level of their gangs' involvement in delinquent activity
were very similar. As reflected in table 10.6, the members of these youth gangs
were involved in a variety of illegal activities. Among the Dutch gang youths,
almost all of them indicated that at least some of their members committed
vandalism (95 percent), assault (95 percent), theft (95 percent), and shoplifting (86 percent). Burglary (43 percent) and robbery (45 percent) were less
common. The American gang members revealed a similar level of "cafeteria-
style" involvement in illegal activity on the part of their gang: gang fights (91
percent), vandalism (80 percent), theft (70 percent), car theft (70 percent),
and robbery (61 percent).

CONCLUSION

At the outset of this chapter, we posed the following six questions:

1. How prevalent is gang membership?
2. What are the demographic characteristics of gang members?
3. What risk factors are associated with gang membership?
4. Which of these risk factors predict gang membership in a multivariate
   analysis?

5. Are the illegal activities of Dutch and American gang-involved youths similar?
6. To what extent are Dutch and American youth gangs similar?

Using a common definition of youth gang membership, one requiring that the group be involved in group-level delinquency, resulted in the classification of 6 percent of the Dutch and 8 percent of the American samples as gang members. A prevalence rate of 6 percent in a general sample (although this represents a slight oversampling of high-risk youth) of Dutch school children is surprisingly similar to the American prevalence rate. Denial that there are gangs in Europe (until recently, this has been the usual response to inquiries about gangs in most European cities) no longer appears valid. As defined in this chapter (a durable, street-oriented youth group whose involvement in illegal activities is part of their group identity), youth gang membership in the Netherlands is not all that dissimilar to that found in the United States. Whether these groups are referred to as gangs or troublesome youth groups may be a matter of choice, but that does not negate the fact that membership in these youth groups is substantial in both countries.

Equally interesting is the finding that the Dutch and American gang youths "look" alike, especially in terms of risk factors that have been found to be associated with a number of adolescent problem behaviors. In both samples, the gang youths tended to be older and were slightly more likely to be male. Race or ethnicity and living arrangement were not significantly different for gang and nongang youths in the Netherlands, but they were for the American youth. The finding that Dutch gang youths were not disproportionately "non-Dutch" is of considerable importance, given the tendency in Holland and elsewhere to identify troublesome youth groups as comprising foreigners or immigrants. These findings suggest that a considerable number of these troublesome youths are indeed native Dutch and are either undetected or unacknowledged.

Our analysis of risk factors revealed consistent and stable similarities between the Dutch and American samples. In all instances, the responses by the nongang youths were significantly different from those given by the gang youths. Importantly, the differences (as represented by the ratio of nongang to gang responses) were of approximately the same magnitude in both samples. Theoretical constructs from self-control, social learning, and social control theories distinguished gang from nongang youths. These findings are quite robust and provide encouragement that criminological constructs measured differently are valid indicators of risk factors for gang affiliation.

Our multivariate analyses identified differences in the extent to which the different risk factors were predictive of gang membership. These findings are difficult to understand given the similarity in the bivariate analyses. One important part of the explanation is the role of measuring similar concepts with different questions in the current research. The two studies were not conducted jointly, but the two coauthors realized that they had similar samples and employed similar measures that would allow for this exploration of gang youths in the United States and the Netherlands. Despite all similarities, however, the exact item formulations of the measurements did differ. Such dissimilarities may have led to the differences in predictive power found in the multivariate analyses we conducted.

Without identical measures, we can never be quite certain that findings are truly related to underlying similarities and differences in the subject matter and not attributable to measurement error. The research reported in this chapter provides an example of the post hoc type of analyses that can be conducted with independent cross-national studies. At the same time, it demonstrates that serious limitations are introduced in this type of post hoc research when different questions are used to measure similar conceptual areas. We therefore recommend that future cross-national researchers collaborate from the outset and employ not only comparable but identical measures and methods.

The analysis of illegal and delinquent behavior provided results that were very similar in both countries. The Dutch and American gang-involved youths were four to six times more likely than nongang youths to be involved in minor as well as serious forms of delinquency. Interestingly, however, while the individual gang members in the two countries look and act similar, the gangs were described quite differently. The Dutch gangs appeared to be smaller and more loosely organized than the American gangs. Only a minority of the Dutch gang youths indicated that their gang had features like leadership, gang rules, and symbols, while such characteristics were reported by a majority of American gang youths. In short, our results suggest that American and Dutch gangs are quite different in their appearance, while at the same time their members are remarkably similar in terms of demographics and risk factors.

The research reported in this chapter, as stated earlier, was not a planned collaborative effort. As such, methods and measurement in the two studies were not identical. Three issues could have affected the results. The first concern is the fact that the two studies, although they measured the same criminological concepts, included actual questions that differed in their formulations. As said earlier, these differences may have biased the results. Because nonidentical measures tend to produce slightly different results, it may well be that the results reported in this chapter underestimate the similarities between gang and nongang youths in the two countries. This concern highlights the importance of the recommendations of the Eurogang Program of Research to incorporate a core of identical measures for all researchers to use in the study of youth gangs.

A second concern is raised by the time differential between the two studies; the Dutch study was completed in 2002, seven years after the completion of the American study. Did the gang situation in the United States change during the course of these seven years? One recent publication reports that the number of communities reporting gang problems declined during this period and that the number of gangs and gang members also declined slightly from 1996 to 2002 (Egley et al. 2004). This suggests that the prevalence of gangs may even be more similar in the two countries than the 6 and 8 percent reported in these two studies. While the magnitude of the youth gang problem may vary across time, it is less likely that the characteristics of gangs and gang members would change dramatically in such a short period. Studies of American youth gangs report considerable stability in the risk factors associated with not only gang membership but also with delinquent activity. Thus, the seven-year difference between the studies may have underestimated rather than overstated similarities.

A third and final concern is perhaps the most important and potentially most biasing: the two studies used different definitions of gang membership. The American study used self-definition and group-level involvement in illegal activity, while the Dutch study relied on the funneling approach developed by the Eurogang program. One potential criticism is that two different types of groups were compared. To address this concern, different operationalizations of gang membership were used in additional analyses. The Dutch results were consistent with the American results, using multiple operationalizations that had been published previously (Esbensen et al. 2001). Regardless of the criteria used to identify gang youths, the risk factors distinguishing gang and nongang youths remained statistically significant in all of the analyses; only the magnitude of the differences varied. Therefore, we are quite confident that our findings are not the result of different methodologies and measurement. Nevertheless, the differences and potential biases remain, and we encourage future comparative efforts to employ not only similar but identical measures and operationalizations of gang membership.

In addition to the methodological issues discussed above, future researchers are encouraged to explore more fully our finding that while gang members appear to be quite similar in the two countries, the gangs differ considerably. These gang differences suggest that structural and cultural features of gang life are not universal and appear to vary across nations. Are the American gangs larger and more organized due to the historical tradition of youth gangs in the United States? Are the differences attributable to varying portrayals of gangs in the media in the United States and the Netherlands? One recent study found that American youths accept the social reality represented by the media (St. Cyr 2003), and as such, gang-involved youths were more likely to exaggerate the presence and problems of gangs in the community. The American media relies largely upon law-enforcement sources in its reporting on youth gangs, and law enforcement promotes a picture of organized gangs with leadership, symbols, and other structural elements. Conversely, the Dutch media and Dutch law enforcement view youth gangs mainly as loosely organized, though dangerous, groups of delinquent youths. The question thus remains: are the youths responding to the media presentations of their gangs or are the media accurately reporting the nature and structure of the youth gangs?

NOTES

An earlier version of this chapter was published as an article in the *European Journal of Criminology* (2005/1). The chapter is printed with copyright permission and is an expanded version of the article.

1. The odds ratio of moral attitudes has different signs in the two samples because these variables were operationalized in opposite directions. In the U.S. sample, this variable measures moral disengagement (the belief that it is appropriate to engage in certain behaviors), while in the Dutch sample, it measures the degree to which these behaviors are rejected as an option.

REFERENCES

Ball, R. A., and G. D. Curry. 1995. The logic of definition in criminology: Purposes and methods for defining "gangs." *Criminology* 33: 225–45.

Battin, S. R., K. G. Hill, R. Abbott, R. F. Catalano, and J. D. Hawkins. 1998. The contribution of gang membership to delinquency beyond delinquent friends. *Criminology* 36: 93–115.

Battin-Pearson, S. R., T. P. Thornberry, J. D. Hawkins, and M. D. Krohn. 1998. *Gang membership, delinquent peers, and delinquent behavior.* Juvenile Justice Bulletin. Washington, D.C.: U.S. Department of Justice.

Bjerregaard, B., and C. Smith. 1993. Gender differences in gang participation, delinquency, and substance use. *Journal of Quantitative Criminology* 4: 329–55.

Bradshaw, Paul. 2002. *How different are Scottish youth gangs? Findings from the Edinburgh Study of Youth Transition and Crime.* Paper presented at the Second Annual Conference of the European Society of Criminology in Toledo, Spain, September 4–7.

Campbell, A. 1991. *The girls in the gang*, 2nd ed. Cambridge, MA: Basil Blackwell.

Covey, H. C., S. Menard, and R. J. Franzese. 1997. *Juvenile gangs*, 2nd ed. Springfield, IL: Charles C. Thomas Publisher.

Curry, G. D. 2000. Self-reported gang involvement and officially recorded delinquency. *Criminology* 38: 1253–74.

Curry, G. D., and S. H. Decker. 2003. *Confronting gangs: Crime and community*, 2nd ed. Los Angeles: Roxbury Publishing.

Curry, G. D., and R. W. Thomas. 1992. Community organization and gang policy response. *Journal of Quantitative Criminology* 8 (4): 357–74.

Decker, S. H., and B. Van Winkle. 1996. *Life in the gang: Family, friends, and violence.* New York: Cambridge University Press.

Egley, Jr., A., J. C. Howell, and A. K. Major. 2004. Recent patterns of gang problems in the United States: Results from the 1996–2002 National Youth Gang Survey. In *American youth gangs at the millennium*, ed. F.-A. Esbensen, L. K. Gaines, and S. G. Tibbetts. Prospect Heights, IL: Waveland Press.

Elliott, D. S., and S. Menard. 1996. Delinquent friends and delinquent behavior: Temporal and developmental patterns. In *Delinquency and crime: Current theories*, ed. J. D. Hawkins. New York: Cambridge University Press.

Esbensen, F.-A., and E. P. Deschenes. 1998. A multisite examination of youth gang membership: Does gender matter? *Criminology* 36: 799–828.

Esbensen, F.-A., E. P. Deschenes, R. E. Vogel, J. West, K. Arboit, and L. Harris. 1996. Active parental consent in school-based research: An examination of ethical and methodological issues. *Evaluation Review* 20: 737–53.

Esbensen, F.-A., and D. Huizinga. 1993. Gangs, drugs, and delinquency in a survey of urban youth. *Criminology* 31: 565–89.

Esbensen, F.-A., D. Huizinga, and A. W. Weiher. 1993. Gang and nongang youth: Differences in explanatory factors. *Journal of Contemporary Criminal Justice* 9: 94–116.

Esbensen, F.-A., and D. P. Lynskey. 2001. Youth gang members in a school survey. In *The Eurogang Paradox: Street gangs and youth groups in the U.S. and Europe*, ed. M. W. Klein, H.-J. Kerner, C. L. Maxson, and E. G. M. Weitekamp. Dordrecht, Netherlands: Kluwer.

Esbensen, F.-A., and D. W. Osgood. 1999. Gang Resistance Education and Training (G.R.E.A.T.): Results from the national evaluation. *Journal of Research in Crime and Delinquency* 36: 194–225.

Esbensen, F.-A., L. T. Winfree Jr., N. He, and T. J. Taylor. 2001. Youth gangs and definitional issues: When is a gang a gang and why does it matter? *Crime and Delinquency* 47: 105–30.

Fagan, J. 1990. Social processes of delinquency and drug use among urban gangs. In *Gangs in America*, ed. C. R. Huff. Newbury Park, CA: Sage Publications.

Fleisher, M. 1998. *Dead end kids*. Madison: University of Wisconsin Press.

van Gemert, F. 2001. Crips in orange: Gangs and groups in the Netherlands. In *The Eurogang Paradox: Street gangs and youth groups in the U.S. and Europe*, ed. M. W. Klein, H.-J. Kerner, C. L. Maxson, and E. G. M. Weitekamp. Dordrecht, Netherlands: Kluwer.

Gottfredson, M. R., and T. Hirschi. 1990. *A general theory of crime*. Palo Alto, CA: Stanford University Press.

Grasmick, H. G., C. R. Tittle, R. J. Bursik, and B. J. Arneklev. 1993. Testing the core empirical implications of Gottfredson and Hirschi's general theory of crime. *Journal of Research in Crime and Delinquency* 30(1): 5–29.

Haaland, T. 2000. *Safety and violence in youth environments*. Paper presented at the Fourth Eurogang Meeting in Egmond, the Netherlands, September.

Hagedorn, J. M. 1988. *People and folks: Gangs, crime, and the underclass in a rustbelt city*. Chicago: Lakeview Press.

Hill, K. G., J. C. Howell, J. D. Hawkins, and S. R. Battin-Pearson. 1999. Childhood risk factors for adolescent gang membership: Results from the Seattle Social Development Project. *Journal of Research in Crime and Delinquency* 36: 300–322.

Huff, C. R. 1990. Denial, overreaction, and misidentification: A postscript on public policy. In *Gangs in America*, ed. C. R. Huff. Newbury Park, CA: Sage Publications.

Huizinga, D., and K. F. Schumann. 2001. Gang membership in Bremen and Denver: Comparative longitudinal data. In *The Eurogang Paradox: Street gangs and youth groups in the U.S. and Europe*, ed. M. W. Klein, H.-J. Kerner, C. L. Maxson, and E. G. M. Weitekamp. Dordrecht, Netherlands: Kluwer.

Klein, M. W. 1995. *The American street gang*. New York: Oxford University Press.

———. 2001. Gangs in the United States and Europe. In *Modern gang reader*, ed. J. Miller, C. L. Maxson, and M. W. Klein, 2nd ed. Los Angeles: Roxbury Publishing.

———. 2002. Street gangs: A cross-national perspective. In *Gangs in America III*, ed. C. R. Huff. Thousand Oaks, CA: Sage Publications.

Lien, I.-L. 2001. The concept of honor, conflict, and violent behavior among youths in Oslo. In *The Eurogang Paradox: Street gangs and youth groups in the U.S. and Europe*, ed. M. W. Klein, H.-J. Kerner, C. L. Maxson, and E. G. M. Weitekamp. Dordrecht, Netherlands: Kluwer.

Mares, D. 2001. Gangsta or lager louts? Working class street gangs in Manchester. In *The Eurogang Paradox: Street gangs and youth groups in the U.S. and Europe*, ed. M. W. Klein, H. J. Kerner, C. L. Maxson, and E. G. M. Weitekamp. Dordrecht, Netherlands: Kluwer.

Maxson, C. L., and M. W. Klein. 1995. Investigating gang structures. *Journal of Gang Research* 3: 33–40.

Maxson, C. L., M. L. Whitlock, and M. W. Klein. 1998. Vulnerability to street gang membership: Implications for prevention. *Social Services Review* 72: 70–91.

McCorkle, R. C., and T. D. Miethe. 1998. The political and organizational response to gangs: An examination of a "moral panic" in Nevada. *Justice Quarterly* 15: 41–64.

Moffitt, T. 1993. Adolescence-limited and life-course persistent-antisocial behavior: A developmental taxonomy. *Psychological Review* 100: 674–701.

Moore, J. 1991. *Going down to the barrio: Homeboys and homegirls in change*. Philadelphia: Temple University Press.

Moore, J. P., and I. L. Cook. 1999. *Highlights of the 1998 National Youth Gang Survey*. Washington, D.C.: U.S. Department of Justice, Office of Juvenile Justice and Delinquency Prevention.

Shaw, C. R., and H. D. McKay. 1942. *Juvenile delinquency and urban areas*. Chicago: University of Chicago Press.

St. Cyr, J. L. 2003. The folk devil reacts: Gangs and moral panic. *Criminal Justice Review* 28: 26–46.

Tertilt, H. 2001. Patterns of ethnic violence in a Frankfurt street gang. In *The Eurogang Paradox: Street gangs and youth groups in the U.S. and Europe*, ed. M. W. Klein, H.-J. Kerner, C. L. Maxson, and E. G. M. Weitekamp. Dordrecht, Netherlands: Kluwer.

Thornberry, T. P. 1998. Membership in youth gangs and involvement in serious and violent offending. In *Serious and violent juvenile offenders: Risk factors and successful interventions*, ed. R. Loeber and D. P. Farrington. Thousand Oaks, CA: Sage Publications.

Thornberry, T. P., M. D., Krohn, A. J. Lizotte, and D. Chard-Wierschem. 1993. The role of juvenile gangs in facilitating delinquent behavior. *Journal of Research in Crime and Delinquency* 30: 5–87.

Thornberry, T. P., M. D. Krohn, A. J. Lizotte, C. A. Smith, and K. Tobin. 2003. *Gangs and delinquency in developmental perspective*. New York: Cambridge University Press.

Thornberry, T. P., A. J. Lizotte, M. D. Krohn, M. Farnworth, and S. J. Jang. 1994. Delinquent peers, beliefs, and delinquent behavior: A longitudinal test of interactional theory. *Criminology* 32: 47–83.

Thrasher, F. M. 1963[1927]. *The gang: A study of 1,313 gangs in Chicago*. Chicago: University of Chicago Press.

Vigil, J. D. 1988. *Barrio gangs: Street life and identity in southern California*. Austin: University of Texas Press.

Warr, M. 2002. *Companions in crime. The social aspects of criminal conduct*. Cambridge: Cambridge University Press.

Warr, M., and M. Stafford. 1991. The influence of delinquent peers: What they think or what they do? *Criminology* 29: 851–65.

Wilson, W. J. 1987. *The truly disadvantaged: The inner city, the underclass, and public policy*. Chicago: University of Chicago Press.

Winfree, L. T., Jr., T. Vigil-Backsrom, and G. L. Mays. 1994. Social learning theory, self-reported delinquency, and youth gangs: A new twist on a general theory of crime and delinquency. *Youth and Society* 26: 147–77.

Yablonsky, L. 1962. *The violent gang*. New York: MacMillan.

APPENDIX 10.A: SCALE ITEMS AND RELIABILITY

Self-Control Scales

Parental Monitoring (Dutch)

At home, I have to do what my parents say.

I know what is and what is not allowed for me at home.

My parents know where I go to outside home.

Alpha = 0.40

Parental Monitoring (U.S.)

When I go someplace, I leave a note for my parents or call them to tell them where I am.

My parents know where I am when I am not at home or at school.

I know how to get in touch with my parents if they are not at home.

My parents know who I am with if I am not at home.

Alpha = 0.73

Impulsivity (Dutch)

I often do things without thinking first.
I make fun if I can, even if it leads me into trouble.
I say immediately what I think, even when that's not clever.
I often do what I feel like immediately.
Alpha = 0.64

Impulsivity (U.S.)

I often act on the spur of the moment without stopping to think.
I don't devote much thought and effort to preparing for the future.
I often do whatever brings me pleasure here and now, even at the cost of some distant goal.
I'm more concerned with what happens to me in the short run than in the long run.
Alpha = 0.63

Risk Seeking (Dutch)

I like to do exciting and adventurous things.
I like to try out scary things.
I love doing dangerous things.
I think it's stupid to do things for fun where you might get hurt.
Alpha = 0.66

Risk Seeking (U.S.)

I like to test myself every now and then by doing something a little risky.
Sometimes I will take a risk just for the fun of it.
I sometimes find it exciting to do things for which I might get in trouble.
Excitement and adventure are more important to me than security.
Alpha = 0.82

Social-Learning Scales

Peer Delinquency (Dutch)

Three possible responses (no one, some, most, or all):
Do your friends sometimes:
Vandalize stuff on the street (like bicycles, traffic signs, bus stops, etc.)?
Hit somebody so hard he or she gets wounded/hurt?

Steal small things from shops (less than 5 euro, like candy, pencils)?

Steal things worth more than 5 euro (like CD's, make-up, bags, jackets, or money)?

Break and enter to steal something?

Rob someone?

Alpha = 0.82

Peer Delinquency (U.S.)

During the last year, how many of your current friends have done the following:

Skipped school without an excuse?

Lied, disobeyed, or talked back to adults such as parents, teachers, or others?

Purposely damaged or destroyed property that did not belong to them?

Stolen something worth less than $50?

Stolen something worth more than $50?

Gone into or tried to go into a building to steal something?

Stolen or tried to steal a motor vehicle?

Hit someone with the idea of hurting them?

Attacked someone with a weapon?

Used a weapon or force to get money or things from people?

Sold marijuana?

Sold illegal drugs such as heroin, cocaine, crack, or LSD?

Used tobacco products?

Used alcohol?

Used marijuana?

Used other illegal drugs such as heroin, cocaine, crack, or LSD?

Alpha = 0.93

Peer Pressure (Dutch)

My friends sometimes make me do things I actually don't want to do.

My friends would think it's stupid when I don't dare to do something.

My friends laugh at me when I am afraid of something.

Alpha = 0.74

Negative Peer Commitment (U.S.)

If your group of friends was getting you into trouble at home, how likely is it that you would still hang out with them?

If your group of friends was getting you into trouble at school, how likely is it that you would still hang out with them?

If your group of friends was getting you into trouble with the police, how likely is it that you would still hang out with them?

Alpha = 0.84

Moral Attitudes (Dutch)

It's okay to do something illegal, as long as you don't get caught.

It's okay to lie if that brings you a lot of money.

Breaking and entering in rich peoples' houses is not so bad.

It's okay to steal if you need money.

Alpha = 0.68

Moral Disengagement (U.S.)

It's okay to lie if it will keep your friends from getting in trouble with parents, teachers, or police.

It's okay to lie to someone if it will keep you out of trouble with them.

It's okay to tell a small lie if it doesn't hurt anyone.

It's okay to steal something from someone who is rich and can easily replace it.

It's okay to take little things from a store without paying for them since stores make so much money that it won't hurt them.

It's okay to steal something if that's the only way you could ever get it.

It's okay to get into a physical fight with someone if they hit you first.

It's okay to get in a physical fight with someone if you have to stand up for or protect your rights.

It's okay to get in a physical fight with someone if they are threatening to hurt your friends or family.

Alpha = 0.86

Social-Control Scales

Attachment to Parents (Dutch)

I have nice parents.

I would like to have other parents.

I don't like being with my parents.

I feel fine when I'm with my parents

Alpha = 0.72

Warmth at Home (Dutch)

    I can tell that my parents love me.

    My parents are friendly toward me.

    My parents know the things I like.

    My parents tell me when I have done something well.

    Alpha = 0.66

Maternal and Paternal Attachment (U.S.)

    Think about your mother or mother figure (father or father figure).

Can talk about anything	7	6	5	4	3	2	1	Can't talk about anything
Always trusts me	7	6	5	4	3	2	1	Never trusts me
Knows all my friends	7	6	5	4	3	2	1	Does not know any of my friends
Always understands me	7	6	5	4	3	2	1	Never understands me
Always ask her advice	7	6	5	4	3	2	1	Never ask her advice
Always praises me when I do well	7	6	5	4	3	2	1	Never praises me when I do well

    Maternal alpha = 0.84

    Paternal alpha = 0.88

Attachment to School (Dutch)

    I go to school with pleasure.

    I get bored at school.

    I have a nice school.

    I would rather be at another school.

    At school, I feel at home.

    Alpha = 0.75

Commitment to School (Dutch)

    I pay much attention in class.

    I do as much I can for school.

    I work hard to get good grades.

    Alpha = 0.77

School Commitment (U.S.)

Homework is a waste of time.

I try hard in school.

Education is so important that it's worth it to put up with things about school that I don't like.

In general, I like school.

Grades are very important to me.

I usually finish my homework.

If you had to choose between studying to get a good grade on a test or going out with your friends, which would you do?

Alpha = 0.81

III

INTEGRATIVE APPROACHES

11

Gang and Youth Violence Prevention and Intervention: Contrasting the Experience of the Scandinavian Welfare State with the United States

YNGVE CARLSSON AND SCOTT H. DECKER

INTRODUCTION

The problem of violent groups, gangs, or *bandes*[1] is complex. There are major controversies over the definition of such "structures." What is a gang or bande in relation to a violent group, subculture, friendship network, or organized crime network? We could discuss this for not just hours but weeks and would probably not reach a common understanding of the words. The controversies over the gang concept do not make the definition of *gang prevention* any easier. Should gang prevention include all kinds of preventive efforts aimed at reducing delinquency in general? Should it also include social policies on both the national and local levels to prevent poverty, unemployment, and social marginalization? In some cases, it has been taken to cover both national and local policies to integrate new immigrants or marginalized individuals into society since many gang members obviously belong to immigrant groups living at the margins of society. Should it include broader measures to prevent or ameliorate family problems, child neglect, or lack of parental control over children? Or should such efforts include strategies to cope with individual problems, ranging from the treatment of attention deficit hyperactivity disorder to learning problems? Some have argued that gang prevention be limited to dealing with just those factors that induce young people to form a special structure—a gang structure—from which they commit criminal acts. These questions and perspectives achieve greater significance in cross-cultural and cross-national research. However, we believe that the definition offered by the Eurogang Research Program offers an appropriate solution to the definitional morass often faced by gang researchers. The Eurogang program defines *gang* as "any durable, street-oriented youth group whose involvement in illegal activity is part of their group identity." With that in mind, we return to our assessment of gang responses in two different cultural and institutional settings: Scandinavia and the United States.

This chapter reports on the responses to gangs and delinquent groups in two Scandinavian countries,[2] Norway and Denmark (with some additional information on Sweden), and provides a contrast to the American experience. This chapter focuses primarily on the nature of Scandinavian responses, responses that reflect the fundamental differences in government structure and approaches to delinquency and social services in Scandinavia and the United States. In this context, we examine the structural basis for defining and responding to problems in each context. It is important to keep the distinction between street gangs and other delinquent groups in mind. Different kinds of prevention and intervention strategies are required for each of these groups, owing to their differences in offending, persistence, identity, and structures.

M. Klein (1995) has identified the Eurogang Paradox as the relative lack of identification of youth gangs in Europe, despite many objective indicators to the contrary. For example, Klein et al. (2001) note the existence of gangs in such diverse European locations as Amsterdam, The Hague, Berlin, Paris, Manchester, Belgium, Oslo, and Stockholm, and Blanc (1995) identifies conditions related to the origin of gangs in Africa, Indonesia, South America, and Europe. Despite the objective evidence to the contrary, there continues to be a general denial of, or at least ambivalence toward, the existence of "American-style" gangs in many European quarters (Klein et al. 2001). From the American perspective, such a denial is counterproductive to formulating responses to gangs.

In Scandinavia, there has been considerable debate among researchers, professionals working with delinquent youth, and the police force over the issue of whether gangs exist. Yet, whatever label is affixed to the phenomenon of troublesome youth groups, the Scandinavian countries, on both the state and the local municipal levels, are active both in preventing youth delinquency in general and in intervening in troublesome youth groups, gangs, and criminal networks. Many of these measures are a part of the traditional welfare state response of building up permanent institutions (e.g., youth clubs, sport facilities, the child-care service, street-worker units, treatment institutions, and so on). But recently, they have come to rely on the use of specialized programs—some developed in Scandinavia, but many of them imported from the United States. While the United States, generally, has recognized its gang problems (Huff 1989), such problems have often been met with theory-based and targeted programs. The vast amount of prevention programs in the United States may reflect the lack of more lasting structural mechanisms to respond to such problems. We believe that the U.S. emphasis on special programs and the underlying institutional approach of the Scandinavian welfare state best distinguish the two approaches.

The Scandinavian countries have a lot in common. They are among the richest countries in the world and have been heavily influenced by strong social democratic parties for more than a half century. They share a similar welfare system that aims to yield social security for every citizen in all stages of life. They even share the same language. They pursue fairly similar policies against crime, which would be characterized as "soft" in the United States. There has been a widespread reluctance to put youths below the age of eighteen in prison.

Sentences are generally light compared to those in the United States, which has a major impact on the size of the prison population. While the United States has 730 prisoners for each 100,000 inhabitants, Denmark has 66, Sweden 64, and Norway 62 (Christie 2004, 70).

These three countries are now simultaneously adopting a more market-oriented approach in their welfare states, where more welfare services are produced on a market. This implies a greater freedom for public agencies to choose how they will solve their problems and challenges and a greater freedom for the citizens to choose the producers of public goods and services. But it also implies a tilting toward the American approach of providing "special" interventions rather than relying on the state foundation.

PREVENTION STRATEGIES WITHIN THE WELFARE MUNICIPALITY

Social Problems as Social Constructs

The Scandinavian welfare state is built on a solid local pillar. To a large extent, the welfare state can be seen as a *welfare municipality*, a concept that recognizes the importance of municipalities in responding to emerging social problems. The legitimacy of this welfare system is based on its giving people social security and social services and on its ability to solve defined problems. If the welfare system does not solve problems that the citizens define as real, their support will diminish and probably turn in a politically populist direction.

The great challenge for this system is that problems defined as a public responsibility to prevent or solve are steadily growing. New problems are steadily defined by both the social and medical sciences. The threshold for acceptance of old and known problems is getting lower. The drive to solve problems has grown immensely, and problem-solving capacity has grown due to economic growth and a more professional workforce. The citizens themselves, both individually and through client organizations and social movements, often put pressure on the authorities to solve their problems (Halvorsen 2001). In addition, the media hold politicians' feet to the fire, requiring them to answer why problems remain unresolved, particularly after a dramatic incident. And the politicians themselves contribute to this pressure, especially the political opposition, which steadily criticizes those in power for not doing enough (Brunsson 1989). There is hardly any problem or form of human suffering that is not made a public obligation, and as such, the demand for public prevention and intervention grows. Such problems include not only all kinds of criminal activity but also loneliness, hyperactivity among children, social incompetence, learning difficulties and dyslexia, obesity, anorexia and bulimia, passive smoking, parents who do not stimulate their children, and so on and so forth.

The Scandinavian countries have also undergone changes that have produced new problems and challenges. Immigration has brought with it female circumcision, forced marriage, children with war experience and post-traumatic stress disorder, parents who do not understand the language and who have problems raising and supervising their children, and so on. Such phenomena have then been defined as problems that the welfare state must address. Technological advances like video recorders, computer games, and the Internet aid the diffusion of violence, violent subcultures, and political extremism (such as neo-Nazism), which also has to be dealt with.

The welfare state response to problems includes a lot of worry and concern. These are more than the informal responses of parents or neighbors, and they reflect a general attitude of anxiety about the status of citizens. Worrying is part of the preventive thinking that has characterized the social-democratic parties in Scandinavia. If one is not worried or concerned, then there is no reason for prevention. Turning back to the key issue of this analysis, gangs and youth violence, there are many reasons for being concerned and worried. Some types of youth violence are rather new and frightening; others are old but have increased in number; still others have not increased, but the threshold for worrying and concern has decreased. People are also worried that the situation might get worse. The kinds of action giving rise to worry and concern are varied and large in number; they include such offenses as drive-by shootings, murders, assaults, children robbing children, use of knives and other weapons in fights, mobilization of large networks for a fight, revenge directed toward groups, sexual offenses (sometimes committed by a group), victim intimidation, assaults on public servants, and unlawful entry into schoolyards and school buildings to commit violence. A large percentage of these types of violence happens in a group or collective context. It must also be noted that these offenses are rare, but incidents are often given broad coverage in the media. As such, they generate worrying and concern out of proportion to their actual occurrence.[3]

Selecting Measures in the Prevention Cafeteria

Social problems, including youth delinquency and violence, are met by a multiplicity of strategies and measures at the city, town, or community levels. The two most important strategies to deal with such complex problems have been to organize a new agency or office with a defined expertise or to extend the scope and capacity of existing agencies. Expansion is often motivated by a deep concern for those affected by the problem and worry over the consequences if nothing is done. The first approach more closely mirrors that of the Americans, who seek to invent a new response to each problem rather than seeking answers within the existing governmental structure. At this time, it is unknown whether such an approach is empirically preferable to the former reliance on existing structures. Common to both approaches is the reliance on the welfare state to provide a foundation of support for the intervention. In this sense, both responses build on the existing institutional structure.

The municipal capacity for preventing and intervening in defined youth problems has expanded considerably during the last twenty to thirty years in Scandinavia. For a long time, the predominant response was to establish a youth house or youth club. However, during the last fifteen to twenty years, the situation has changed. A survey of available services in a medium-sized Scandinavian municipality (a Norwegian town with fifty-seven thousand inhabitants) found more than forty separate and distinct services or intervention measures that have some connection to crime prevention.[4] Most of these services and units are provided by the local municipality, some by the local county, and some by nongovernmental organizations with grants from the municipality and county. Not all Scandinavian municipalities will have all of these services and units, but they may have others.

Most of these services are not intended to prevent gang formation, some not even to prevent crime. But many measures aimed at preventing social marginalization, poverty, social problems, youth delinquency, and violence can also be used as antigang measures, particularly in the Scandinavian context. In this regard, it is important to note the distinction between prevention and intervention programs or measures. The former target individuals prior to involvement in serious offending or gangs, and the latter target individuals who have become involved in such activities. In his list of promising gang programs, J. C. Howell (1998) mentions manhood development, employment training, education and counseling, conflict resolution and peer mediation, equipping peers to help one another, community policing, community mobilization, aggression-replacement training, multisystemic therapy, and, of course, police suppression. Howell's examples of gang programs are not that different from the Scandinavian prevention measures mentioned below. Yet, while the categories exist in both the Scandinavian and American contexts, the Scandinavian approach emphasizes prevention within the range of normal government responses, while the United States emphasizes special programs, often with an emphasis on suppression.

Klein (1995) asserts that youth gangs and gang members are characterized by a *cafeteria style of criminal behavior*. From this perspective, gang members are seen as versatile in their criminal behavior; they do a little bit of this and a little bit of that. The Scandinavian preventive strategies have the same characteristics, not on the offending side but on the prevention side, and represent a *cafeteria style of prevention*. That is, Scandinavian countries provide a wide range of services and approaches from which to choose.

In addition to the aforementioned measures and services, the Scandinavian menu contains many dishes with acronyms and some with profit-oriented sponsors. Many of these dishes were originally American, but some were also developed in Europe and in the Scandinavian countries themselves. There are "individual" dishes, such as aggression-replacement training programs like ART and NEW START, "family" dishes, such as Marte Meo,[5] parent management training (PMT) and multisystemic therapy (MST), and "school" dishes, including a great number of programs addressing bullying and behavioral problems. In addition, one finds foreign spice to give an international flavor to the local and traditional dishes, such as community mobilization models like the future workshop, search conference, and participatory learning and action (PLA).

In the Norwegian prevention cafeteria, there are many Danish dishes. The most famous Danish dish in Norway is the social services, schools, and police (SSP) model, a method for coordinating the crime-preventive efforts of the social services, the schools, and the police. The model is used in nearly all Danish municipalities. This is a rather traditional and "rational" model for co-operation and closely resembles a Swedish coordination model.[6] The Danes also have a tradition of developing problem-solving models or projects on the local level with fanciful names, such as the Cockpit, the Spearhead (*spydspidsen*), and the Social Hunting Corps (*det sociale jægekorps*), to address youths at risk.

Sweden has developed the night walkers/night owls—parents patrolling the town center late at night—which is meant to compensate for decades of reductions in social control and adult supervision. This model has spread to the rest of Scandinavia, and every weekend (except during the cold winter months), groups of parents patrol the streets of an estimated one thousand Scandinavian communities. There is also the Värmland *policemodell*, a Swedish adaptation of the San Diego model with an intense focus on problem-oriented police work. It has recently been diffused to Norwegian police districts. There are also a lot of models of coordination and local mobilization from the field of crime prevention.

The Norwegians have contributed the Olweus program, a school-based program to reduce bullying and violence. T. Bjørgo (1997) has developed the EXIT program to get youths out of extreme and violent groups, which has been diffused to Sweden and a lot of German *Bundesstaten*. In addition, Norwegian models like VOKT, MOT, LEV VEL, and SAFT try to cope with violence, drug abuse, or racism.

A Positive Contribution

Each of the programs mentioned above represents a detailed guide for how to solve or reduce complex behavioral problems and youth delinquency. Many of the programs have a scientific and theory-based foundation. However, only a few of the American-based programs have been proved effective by an evaluation that fulfils vital scientific requirements (Sherman et al. 1998). Similarly, an examination of twenty-five programs employed in Norway concluded that an evaluation was either completely absent or insufficient for the majority of them (Norwegian Expert Group 2000). Nevertheless, independent of the scientific status of the program evaluations, such programs offer the municipalities guidance and expert knowledge on problems where the single municipality may have limited competence and experience.

A recent study of crime-preventive work in ten Norwegian municipalities shows that local municipalities and schools are very pragmatic in their selection of measures and programs (Carlsson 2002). Many measures and programs are founded in different theoretical traditions. There can be a lot of disagreement and conflict among the founding fathers and mothers of the programs. Such conflicts can also occur within the municipalities among advocates for different theoretical movements, but a more pragmatic attitude is more common. Different theory-based programs are regarded as complementary, not as competing. One school can, for example, choose one antibullying program that stresses tight supervision and adult interference in conflicts, while the neighboring school may choose a program that stresses mediation between the involved youths. Furthermore, one school may choose one program one year and a competing program the next. Consequently, it is difficult to characterize the Scandinavian way of preventing complex behavioral problems and youth delinquency other than to say that it is characterized by a multitude of measures and programs.

AN INVENTORY OF MEASURES AND PROGRAMS FOR INTERVENTION IN GANGS AND TROUBLESOME YOUTH GROUPS

The field of intervention is characterized by numerous measures and programs. Some of them, as mentioned above, are general delinquency-prevention programs that can also be used for gang-intervention purposes. However, the intervention diet is not as comprehensive as the prevention diet. The field of intervention is characterized by controversies and differences over the causes underlying the establishment of such groups or gangs. In addition, there have been deep controversies about how to define gangs, and different definitions have had consequences for the actions taken.

The Connection between Concept and Action

The influence of definitions on the response to problems is particularly well understood in the American context, where such definitions often determine the intervention undertaken (Curry and Thomas 1992; Fearn et al. 2002; Spergel and Curry 1993). There are two pitfalls in the response process: denial and moral panic (Curry and Decker 2003; Bjørgo and Carlsson 1999). The concept used may lead to one of these pits. The risk of denial is that a gang or troublesome youth group can develop its violence and strengthen its structure to extreme levels before it is officially recognized. The only strategy left when the problem is officially recognized will often then be hard and suppressive police measures.

The opposite pitfall to denial is moral panic. Using the label *gang* or *bande* to emphasize an antigang response when gangs do not constitute a problem might lead to such a panic (McCorkle and Miethe 2000). If such labeling is followed by increased surveillance, police patrol, and incarceration, this may increase the group's solidarity and cohesion and virtually turn it into a gang. If the gang or bande is named and presented in the media, this can make the participants feel important, give them prestige and honor, and thereby meet one important need that the youths cannot satisfy in legitimate arenas. It gives them an identity, the essence of labeling theory.

Denmark and Norway (and Sweden) share the same language. There are only minor differences between them. However, one important difference is between the words *gang* (*gjeng*), which is used in Norway (and Sweden), and *bande*, which is used in Denmark. We assert that the Norwegian word *gang* has associations that might lead to a belittling or denial of the problem. The Danish word *bande* can push people in the moral panic direction. Thus, definitions are important and have consequences for intervention and prevention efforts.

The Norwegian Gang Concept

This concept can give two different associations. For some—especially for well-educated police officers, youth workers, or field workers having read criminology—the word *gang* calls forth the picture of the well-organized American gang with hundreds of members, which has existed for decades. As some American commentators (Klein et al. 2001) have argued, these portrayals of American gangs are, at best, exaggerations, if not completely incorrect. The definition of gangs has been applied so strictly in many European contexts that the result is a denial of their existence.

Moreover, in its everyday Norwegian use, *gang* refers to a cohesive group or a group of friends. Three years ago, Norwegian Prime Minister Bondevik referred to his cabinet as "a nice gang." Sometimes people talk of criminal gangs, but these are often synonymous with petty criminal groups. When the media reports on a "gang fight," it often just means that more than three or four people were fighting. Even if one introduces a strict gang definition, such as *a gang is a group engaged in criminal activity with a common identity (name, symbols) and that has been in operation for at least half a year or so* (Decker and Van Winkle 1996; Bjørgo and Carlsson 1999), the definition will be suppressed by the everyday associations that the concept produces.[7] The word *gang* gives associations that may lead to the denial or belittling of a serious gang problem. When a gang, per this definition, does arise and is labeled as such, this will often be met with a shake of the head and a comment like, "We have always had gangs like this." Thus, the strict definition used by some professionals may lead to denial, and the common use of the word may lead to a belittling of real gang problems.

The Danish Bande Concept

In Denmark, the situation is different. The word *gade-bande* ("street gang") is fairly new in Denmark. In a 1998 report, the Danish national commissioner of police defined *gade-bande* as "a group of children and youth who commit crime or engage in other kinds of troublesome or aggressive behavior in the streets, and who are considered a group by those around them and themselves." This definition emphasizes criminal acts and aggressive behavior and group conduct, but it does not include the duration criterion. The duration criterion is important in American gang research (Klein et al. 2001, 249), as many youth groups coalesce only to disband quickly. Plus, the longer duration is often followed by a more fixed structure. The definition above includes the identity dimension—that the youths are considered a group by themselves and by those around them. Of these two, the last criterion has been the most used in Denmark—that the aggressive youths are considered a group by those around them. Since much violence and troublesome behavior is carried out by more than three people, who thereby look like a group to both victims and spectators, most petty criminal groups fit the *bande* definition.

The police commissioner's definition includes most violent youth groups, both permanent and transitory, in the *gang* concept. This may be a useful definition for a variety of purposes, but it is no gang definition. The problem with some words is that they are immune to official definitions. A *gade-bande* is not only a group of youths who are loose in the streets, but the concept itself is also "loose in the streets" and gives practitioners in the municipalities, local politicians, and the general public a lot of associations, images, and sentiments. The problem with the word *bande* in Denmark is that it has mostly been used for organized and planned crime, especially that related to biker gangs like the Hells Angels and Bandidos.

When the national commissioner of police applied his definition of street *bandes*, he actually found one in nearly every Danish town, especially those with immigrant kids hanging around in the town center or in a mall. When this label is used on petty-criminal groups, on ad hoc-groups who have been engaged in a fight, or on a group of adolescents making problems on the bus or train, there is considerable risk of making them out to be more serious, organized, and evil than they really are. Moreover, the labeling of local groups may virtually turn them into gangs, especially if this labeling is followed up by heavy media coverage and public stigmatization.[8]

There is, of course, a chance that this concept in its everyday use over the years will be reified and come to have the same meaning as the Norwegian word *gang*. However, currently, the use of the concept probably has pushed the public in the moral-panic direction. We have noted how important the issue of *gadebander* has been on the national political agenda in Denmark. It was a major issue in the last election campaign there,[9] due in part to the looseness of the definition and its uncritical use with all kinds of troublesome groups, especially those with an immigrant background. We believe that this focus may contribute to xenophobia, as it stigmatizes whole categories of youths with an immigrant background and contributes to social exclusion, strengthening the forces that give rise to gangs. The moral panic that results may expand this into a huge and nearly insoluble problem, where police suppression may become the most important strategy.

The Network Concept

The *gang* concept has been criticized by the Swedish criminologist Jerzy Sarnecki (2001). He contends that the disadvantages of using the *gang* concept are far greater than the advantages. The main problem is the labeling function when used on a specific group or network. In addition, the *gang* concept may obscure offenders' links and ties to offenders other than their more immediate friends. In real life, young people have many bonds and ties to other people, and these connections exist in numerous ways. The *network* concept represents a tool to see how individuals, groups, and even organizations are interconnected. One can use the network methodology to study gangs, but one cannot use the gang methodology to study networks, Sarnecki contends. And *network* is a neutral concept used on personal, organizational, and technological ties, which will probably not be stigmatizing or labeling.

"Wild Youth"

The use of the *bande* concept has also been heavily criticized by several social scientists in Denmark on the same grounds as mentioned above (Balvig 1999; Andersen et al. 2001; Lihme 2002). In two communities in Denmark with troublesome youth groups and a rather high-percentage immigrant population (Nørrebro in Copenhagen and the eastern part of Aalborg), the concept of *wild youth* has been used. It is indeed a "wild" concept, difficult to define and intentionally imprecise (Qvotrup Jensen 2002). In Copenhagen, these wild youth are characterized as criminal, violent, drug abusing, "shit-difficult" (*røvbesværlige*), distorted (*skæv*), outcast, marginalized, exceptional, and unteachable (Vilde Laereprocesser 2001). The concept points much more to behavior and personal characteristics than the *gang* and *bande* concepts, which refer more to the characteristics of groups, such as structure, cohesion, and identity. An important objective behind the *wild-youth* concept is avoiding stigmatization, condemnation, and labeling.

The *wild-youth* concept, as used by some professionals and researchers in Denmark, reflects a focus on social marginalization, where the youths' wildness is conceptualized as compensation for an inferior position in a highly competitive society. The group is not the point of departure for action, and the concomitant strategy will not be to dismantle the group; rather, it will be to try to do something with youths' disadvantaged position and to find legitimate ways to build up positive self-concepts. The strategy is not gang motivated because the professionals do not see any gangs or the gang is irrelevant to their understanding. When the *wild-youth* concept is used on young people who participate in a group with gang characteristics as defined by the Eurogang network, the strategies put into action are interesting from a gang-intervention perspective.

Intervention—Including Early Intervention and Late Prevention

The presentation of intervention strategies from Denmark and Norway is built on a modest empirical foundation. This is because, quite simply, there are very few studies of interventions for gangs and violent youth groups in Scandinavia, and the few evaluations that exist are primarily descriptive. As such, this section is mainly based on evaluations and descriptions from Copenhagen, an ongoing study of interventions in Kristiansand, Norway, and material from four suburbs in Oslo and two small industrial towns, also in Norway.

A common feature of the target groups of the interventions presented in this section is that they are troublesome and their violence exceeds the level of "ordinary" youth violence. Not all of the groups mentioned fit the usual gang definitions. Some of them do not have a clear identity, and some are not stable enough to be classified as gangs. Some groups are part of a huge network of delinquent youths that operates over a wider geographical area. Within such a network, there may be clusters that resemble gangs, but the groups are more transitory than American gangs. This may be the case in Copenhagen, where the descriptions and evaluations provide a picture of loose groups of wild youth. On the other hand, many of the groups mentioned in this section do fit the most common gang definition (Decker and Van Winkle 1996), including the target group for the Furuset project in Oslo, an immigrant youth gang.

We also mention interventions for neo-Nazi groups. Some may contend that they are part of a national and international network and that the gang perspective is misleading. On the other hand, being a part of the wider network stimulates in them a more persistent local gang structure. The neo-Nazi gangs often start out as ordinary delinquent youth groups. Such delinquent groups most normally dissolve by themselves or turn in prosocial directions when the boys get older (Emler and Reicher 1995). Their contacts to a wider network support the establishment of a more persistent local gang with a clear identity. Racist or neo-Nazi gangs represent one important type of Scandinavian gang made up of youths from the white majority population.

Suppression and Social Control Strategies

The police in the three Scandinavian countries, of course, expend a lot of energy to intervene in gangs or violent youth groups. Some of the major cities have special units addressing gangs and organized crime. Suppression strategies include law-enforcement and criminal-justice interventions like surveillance, quick investigation, arrest, imprisonment, and generally being "tough" on all kinds of criminal acts, even minor offenses. Formal or informal leaders in criminal groups or gangs get special attention from the police. In some Scandinavian cities, the police strategy has been inspired by New York's zero-tolerance model.

Some police districts in Denmark report that suppression has led motorcycle gangs to withdraw from some communities (PLS Ramboll 2003). There is no information about whether the gangs were displaced to other districts. Reports from two Copenhagen communities (Ishoj and Inner Norrebro) indicate that when used on troublesome youths with minority backgrounds, such a strategy has been less successful (Bonke and Caroe 2001, 87; Olsen and Hansen 2001). In Norrebro in Copenhagen, the police used this strategy on several occasions in the 1990s. The police met the wild youths with armored vehicles and officers with helmets and visors, and they cracked down on even minor offenses. Many Norrebro youths with an immigrant background felt harassed and discriminated against and considered this strategy a declaration of war. This, in turn, increased violence and vandalism in the area and improved the violent groups' recruitment, cohesion, and support. This outcome was remarkably similar to the American experience, where external threats have strengthened many street gangs. The Norrebro police later realized that such police methods could not solve or even lessen the problem. The police are currently more careful in using forthright suppressive means and cooperate more closely with the local city administration to find longer-term solutions to the problem.

In Norway, close supervision of informal leaders or core members, surveillance, and quick prosecution have been successful against small and marginalized groups of racist or neo-Nazi youths in many cases. Quick investigation, prosecution, and imprisonment have been important means for dismantling racist and neo-Nazi gangs or groups. Single individuals often act as the glue in a racist or neo-Nazi gang or network; therefore, it is important to neutralize these leaders before the groups become better organized and their persistence depends less on single individuals (Bjørgo and Carlsson 1999). Yet, as we shall discuss later, police suppression has been supplemented by both opportunity provision and other positive strategies directed toward both core and more peripheral participants in violent groups. Such a combination may be very effective in dismantling a violent group or even a youth gang.

In each of the three Scandinavian countries, there has been a reluctance to put youths under the age of eighteen into prisons. A key argument is that prisons function as schools for delinquent behavior. On the other hand, there has been widespread placement of delinquent youths in treatment institutions. In Norway, skepticism toward such treatment institutions has grown during the last years. The effects have been considered meager or even negative, and the institutions have been expensive to run. This has been a major argument for the comprehensive use of multisystemic therapy in Norway since 1999. In Denmark, the conservative government has gone in the opposite direction. In 2001, the Danish parliament passed a new clause in its penal code authorizing two-year sentences to treatment institutions for violent, delinquent youths under eighteen.

There is an ongoing, highly political discussion in each of the three Scandinavian countries about the use of penal institutions. The conservative parties and especially the strong populist right-wing parties in both Norway and Denmark are in favor of using more and stronger punishment in reaction to crime. The social democrats and the left-wing socialist parties, on the other hand, are more in favor of treatment and other nonpunitive measures. As Nils Christie (2004, 53) asserts, it has not been easy to combine welfare thinking and defense of the weak with punishment, especially in small countries where it is difficult to avoid seeing each other as fellow human beings.

Other Methods for Strengthening Social Control

Overt and Direct Social Control by Schools and Youth Clubs

Most large and medium-sized Scandinavian cities[10] are characterized by good public communication and easy travel between cities. The widespread availability of mobile phones among youths also enhances their capacity to mobilize for a fight. I. L. Lien and T. Haaland (1998) and Y. Carlsson (2002) describe how violent groups operate across the whole Oslo area, finding youth clubs and public youth discotheques (and often private parties) in which to posture their manhood and claim respect, often through the exercise of violence. Also, junior high and high schools have been visited by violent groups coming to take vengeance for some offense, with subsequent fighting in the schoolyards and even in the classrooms. The response to such actions has, in many cases, been to increase the control measures and the risk of being caught. Carlsson (2002) describes how two high schools in the southeast part of Oslo increased the use of more direct means of control, including direct supervision. Such means are common in the United States but have been rare in Scandinavia until now. Youth clubs are scenes for testing limits, posturing masculinity, and claiming respect. A common response of officials is to expel youths who behave improperly. In Aalborg, Denmark, a new youth club was started for "those that were expelled from the other youth clubs." The club was closed due to burglaries at the club (Qvotrup Jensen 2002).

Civilian Security Patrols at Night (Night Owls)

In a large number of Scandinavian cities and towns, adults walk the streets to exercise informal social control on Friday and Saturday evenings. In groups of three to five, they walk around those areas of the city or town where youth delinquency is most likely to occur. Their primary objective is simply to be visible,[11] to be there. They do not enter into conflicts, but they usually have a mobile phone connection to both the police and the child-care system that can be used if violent conflicts occur or if they find youths who are dangerously drunk or drugged. This kind of security patrolling is a broad preventive measure, but it has also been used as a gang-intervention measure.

In the Oslo suburb of Nordstrand, ten to fifteen adults in their yellow waistcoats entered a neo-Nazi territory every Friday and Saturday for a period of some months in 1996 and 1997. They did not provoke the youths directly. At the same time, police supervised the area so that they could intervene if violent attacks on the civilian "night owls" should occur. The result was that the neo-Nazis found this situation so intolerable that they moved to a territory in a neighboring suburb three miles away. In this moving process, most fringe members from Nordstrand did not follow, reducing the size of the problem.

In the city of Kristiansand in Norway, the preventive police and the municipal crime coordinator have managed to mobilize parents with Kosovo-Albanian and Somalian backgrounds as night owls. Youths of such origins have played a major role in the multiethnic Valla gang. One purpose of mobilizing adults from these ethnic groups is to let them see for themselves what goes on in the center of the city late at night. Parents with immigrant backgrounds are often unaware of what their sons[12] are doing late at night, while they normally exercise very tight control over their daughters. The information gained by these adults may, in turn, lead them to place more restrictions on their boys. Another purpose of mobilizing adults from distinctive ethnic groups is that the presence of adult Kosovo-Albanians and Somalians is believed to lessen overt aggressive behavior among youngsters of such origins. There are also "fathers groups" in Denmark that similarly attempt to mobilize fathers with minority backgrounds to be present and visible in the public spaces of the city where minority youth groups usually operate. These father groups not only exercise social control but also represent a bridge between wild youths with minority backgrounds and Danish society.

Methods that Combine Social Control with Social Opportunity Measures

Several measures and programs contain important elements of both social control and opportunity provision. As such, these methods represent a merger of the traditional Scandinavian dependence on social institutions with the American tendency to create a new program in the face of a problem. Among these are the "worrying conversation," youth contracts, multisystemic therapy, Exit parent groups, and other complementary methods.

The Worrying Conversation

Preventive police units play a major role in preventing delinquency in Scandinavia. In Norway, they have shifted their focus over the past few years from vaccinating all children against delinquency (through visits in kindergartens and schools) to concentrating on youths at risk of developing a criminal career. The preventive police in Oslo-South have developed a systematic early-intervention method, the worrying conversation, which today is used in most police districts in Norway.

When the local preventive police are informed that a young person (below eighteen years of age) has committed a criminal act or is flirting with delinquent groups or gangs, both the young person and his or her parents are summoned to a worrying conversation at the local police station. The police do not need proof of illegal actions to call such a meeting. The intention of the meeting is to inform the parents and the child of the reasons for police concern. During the structured conversation, the preventive police officer presents information about the child's problematic acts or group affiliation—particularly gang affiliation—and the potential consequences. Thereafter, the officer discusses with the youth and parents possible reasons behind committing such acts or associating with delinquent groups or gangs. With these causes as a point of departure, the officer discusses potential measures to prevent further delinquent acts and to withdraw from such groups. If desirable or necessary, the police may help bring in personnel and resources from the other public child and youth services. Such services normally collaborate closely with preventive policing strategies. If necessary, a worrying conversation is supplemented by follow-up conversations. An important condition for using this method effectively is a commitment to problem solving, where the police have detailed knowledge about the local youth scene and can combine information about the current situation from local schools, youth clubs, street workers, and youth contacts with the police's own information and intelligence channels.

The worrying conversation is a method that can be used for both prevention and intervention purposes. Originally, it was developed as a gang-intervention method in an Oslo suburb. The purpose was to mobilize both parents and the relevant municipal institutions when young people were flirting with a neo-Nazi gang. Later on, the method expanded to cover all kinds of problematic behavior, serve as an early-warning method, and to mobilize both parental and municipal efforts.

Youth Contracts

The youth contract, a Danish method now adopted in Norway, is an alternative to incarceration for youths between fifteen and eighteen years old (Danish Ministry of Justice 2001[13]). The contract is used for juveniles who have committed minor criminal offenses such as theft or vandalism but have not developed a more permanent pattern of criminality. The contract is an agreement between the young offender and his or her parents on the one hand and the police and municipal child-care authorities on the other. In the contract, the young offender commits himself or herself to carrying out specific activities. In return, the police abstain from further prosecution. The contract contains measures that may contribute to a changing of behavior and that may support a more positive development for the young person involved. If the conditions in the contract are broken by the youth, the police will consider a more traditional prosecution of the offense. Youth contracts are not applied to more grave criminal acts like robbery and severe violence, acts that are more common in a gang context. For those having committed such crimes, there is an alternative method called *interdisciplinary consultation* in Denmark. Parental participation is important in this method, too. Motivating the young person to continue his or her education or to get a job plays a vital role.

Multisystemic Therapy

Multisystemic therapy (MST) is a U.S.-based program targeting youths between thirteen and eighteen with severe behavioral problems. The MST program is similar to the aforementioned methods in its insistence on involving the "multiple systems" in coping with a young person's antisocial behavior. It is a method where considerable resources (including an MST therapist who is available around the clock) are used for a limited period of four to six months to give parents the skills and resources to manage their role as parents of a delinquent and violent youth. MST is not specifically a gang-intervention program, but according to Howell (1998), it appears to be a promising treatment and rehabilitation program for gang members and has been documented by several evaluation studies in the United States. Today, there are MST teams in every Norwegian county. In both Oslo and Kristiansand, the program has included members of criminal youth gangs as clients. An essential question is whether the program will show good results with parents with immigrant or refugee backgrounds who are poorly integrated into the Norwegian society, who hardly speak Norwegian, and who may suffer from grave psychiatric problems due to war experience and torture.

Exit Parent Groups

The Exit projects carried out in Norway and Sweden (and Germany) represent a more targeted intervention method for violent groups and gangs (Bjørgo 1997). The Exit projects in Norway have concentrated on building groups of parents with children in neo-Nazi groups. The parent groups are modeled after self-help groups known in other parts of the social and health sector. The parents in the group share information about what their children do, give each other mutual support, discuss ways to avoid being manipulated by their children and how to restore their parental control. One important task for such groups is to encourage the parents not to turn their backs on their extremist offspring, even if they hold disgusting attitudes or commit violence. Parents who turn their back on their children ultimately push them deeper into the extremist scene, whose members they see as their new family. A great majority of the parents with children in neo-Nazi gangs in the city of Kristiansand participated in such mutual-assist groups in Kristiansand from 1997 to 2001. Forty-nine out of sixty youths with parents in such groups were out of the scene by December 2001. This result was, of course, not solely caused by parents' mobilization, but the groups were definitely an important support for many of the parents.

Complementary Methods

The methods mentioned above have several similarities. The most obvious are parental involvement, assisting parents in exercising control over their children, and supporting them so that they do not give up their parental role or ostracize the child from the family. Another similarity between these methods is that they combine the social control aspect with opportunity provision through the mobilization of resources from other parts of the welfare system, including leisure activities, education, and job provision. These are prototypical Scandinavian responses and stand in contrast to American interventions, which are strongly based on the use of arrest, prosecution, and incarceration. Ultimately, the differences between the two approaches focus on the degree to which the former approach seeks to keep youths integrated in the institutions of support (family, school, and community) and the latter seeks to separate them from those institutions. The worrying conversation and the youth contract have the same target group, youths who are about to embark on a criminal career. These methods may also be used as an early-intervention method when youths are about to join criminal groups or gangs, and the worrying conversation was actually designed for this purpose.

Relationship Building and Opportunity Provision

A common feature of these projects has been the building of relationships and trust with youths in violent groups, gangs, or scenes. In Oslo-Furuset, this is done through three professional social workers. In Copenhagen Norrebro, former criminal youths with an immigrant background are used as social or street workers. They have quit the criminal career, are streetwise, and have credibility among the wild youth and their families (Lihme 2002). In the Swedish Exit project, most of the work is done by nonprofessional workers with similar backgrounds and experiences as their "clients" (Swedish Council for Crime Prevention 2001). In Kristiansand, both professional and voluntary workers from the Norwegian Protestant church play major roles as relationship builders (Haaland and Carlsson 2002). Individuals with other personal characteristics than those mentioned above may also build such relations.

In a period where programs with detailed recipes are flooding the Scandinavian prevention and intervention markets, it is important to note that in a lot of interventions, the most important ingredient is probably the building of personal relationships and trust, which become the springboard for using opportunity-provision measures.

IS THERE A SCANDINAVIAN GANG-INTERVENTION STRATEGY?

This presentation of Scandinavian methods of intervening in violent groups, gangs, and networks has provided a very general picture of intervention strategies. The most important reason for this is that youth gangs (or troublesome and street-oriented youth groups) are not numerous in Scandinavia. The body of gang research is limited, and the body of research on intervention in gangs or similar troublesome youth groups is even more limited. The research done is very descriptive, and there are very few outcome evaluations. In addition, there is considerable disagreement on the use of the gang concept. For some, social marginalization and maladjustment, not the gang or violent group, have been the research focus. This has also been the case for many practitioners for whom the point of departure for action has not been the local gang but the problems of social marginalization and social exclusion.

Even though this chapter covers just a few interventions into gangs and troublesome youth groups in Scandinavia, the examples mentioned should be fairly representative of such activity. The examples cover interventions with violent youth groups in Scandinavia's largest city (Copenhagen, with 1.5 million inhabitants), in the third largest city (Oslo, with 800,000 inhabitants), and in a medium-sized city (Kristiansand, with 75,000 inhabitants). Some examples from industrial towns with eight to ten thousand inhabitants have also been mentioned. The interventions presented have been directed toward both white racist or neo-Nazi gangs and gangs or troublesome groups mainly comprising youths with immigrant backgrounds. The focus has been on local community interventions because this is the primary mode of intervention. This means that more national strategies—for example, police intervention in gangs and their related national and international networks—are missing in this inventory. Instead, the local aspects of the Scandinavian welfare state, the municipalities, address violent groups and gangs.

The wealth of the Scandinavian states, their large public sectors, and the great freedom of local municipalities to find their own solutions to problems has resulted in a very rich diet in the field of crime prevention. The core of that diet, the main dish, is still based in established public institutions such as schools, the child-care system, social services, youth clubs, sport facilities, and, more traditionally, the police. Yet, these institutions have been supplemented with a number of appetizers and desserts in the form of problem-solving measures and programs, many of which are also used in gang intervention. Some of these appetizers and desserts are theory-based programs that have originated not only in the Scandinavian countries but also in other corners of the world. Some are brought into Scandinavia by the thousands of professionals with master's or doctoral degrees from "program-producing countries" like the United States, Canada, Australia, the Netherlands, and the United Kingdom. Indeed, some programs are actively promoted internationally by university centers, worldwide nongovernmental organizations, and consulting companies that sell program software. We are seeing a huge international cafeteria of programs directly or indirectly connected to crime prevention. The Scandinavian countries are included in this market.

The Scandinavian countries no longer have a stable social democratic rule. In Denmark and Norway especially, there have been steady shifts between social democratic and liberal/conservative governments. One government will often introduce crime-prevention measures and programs that symbolize a shift in crime-prevention policy. When one measure or program has been established and carried out in hundreds of municipalities, it is difficult for the next government with a different political complexion to withdraw reforms, measures, or programs. This creates a lot of unnecessary political noise. It is easier to launch a new reform, program, or measure than it is to remove those in operation. The result is an increase in the number of dishes in the national diet. While many reforms are broad and national, the local municipalities

choose many measures and programs. There are nearly one thousand municipalities in the three Scandinavian countries with the freedom to compose a
major part of their own diet for addressing delinquency and youth violence.
Thus, it is not possible to speak of a uniform way of handling the question of
violent groups and gangs in Scandinavia other than to say that this challenge
is met by a multitude of measures and programs.

The Scandinavian intervention diet represents a mixture of both suppression and social-intervention strategies. Police suppression plays an important
role everywhere, but there are local differences in the "sharpness" of this suppression. The Scandinavian welfare states, on both the state and municipal
levels, have several social-intervention measures and programs at their dis-
posal, especially for gang or group members below the age of eighteen. Suppression is balanced by several measures and programs that may be
characterized as social intervention and opportunity provision. Suppression
and opportunity-provision measures are used in combination to dissolve
gangs. Especially when gangs contain few members and are in an emergent
stage, Norwegian experiences (Bjørgo and Carlsson 1999) show that it is possible to dissipate the gang through this combination of suppression and opportunity provision. When the gangs become larger and have adult members,
this strategy will probably be less successful. These young adults are outside
the reach of their parents and most of the problem-solving municipal apparatus.

The experience in the United States has many parallels but some important
differences. In Scandinavia, the state is expected to provide a basic level of
health, employment, and social services, which form the basis of a "social
safety net" shared by all citizens. Thus, historically, "special programs" have
not been viewed as necessary as the safety net should take care of most needs.
In the United States, the safety net is much smaller and has many holes. Thus,
there is a need for special programs to take the place of what the state is expected to provide in many Scandinavian contexts. However, the recent trend
has been to introduce special programs to respond to the emerging challenges
of gangs, increasing youth crime, and in some cases, the intersection of these
problems with immigration issues.

We have also emphasized that many of the implemented programs and measures in both the Scandinavian and U.S. contexts have not been evaluated.
When programs are used in combination, it becomes difficult, even impossible,

to document the effect of a single ingredient. There are several examples in which interventions have been successful through either a decrease in youth violence or through the dissolution of local gangs. However, it is difficult to find the active ingredient that can explain the outcome. This is the case with comprehensive local gang-intervention programs (Carlsson 1995) and comprehensive programs that deal with delinquency in general (Ringman 1997). This can be formulated as the Scandinavian Prevention Paradox: the more we do, the less we know. On the other hand, one cannot conclude that such a diverse strategy is an irrational strategy. Youth delinquency in general, and violent gangs or youth groups in particular, are complex problems, and complex problems must be met with complex solutions. There is no single dish with all the necessary preventive ingredients to be effective.

The challenge for the research community is to develop knowledge about the effects of different combinations of measures and programs, not just the effect of a single program. The challenge for the local municipalities, including professional workers, bureaucrats, and politicians, is to make "rational" choices in a situation characterized by ambiguity, complex causal connections, and a rich menu of both prevention and intervention measures and programs. The challenge is to choose a nourishing and balanced diet. Ultimately, it appears that with regard to the cafeteria of prevention, the Scandinavian and American experiences have more in common than one might expect at first glance.

NOTES
The authors want to thank the Norwegian Ministry of Children and Family Affairs and the Center for International Studies (University of Missouri, St. Louis) for their support of the work reported in this chapter.

1. *Bande* is a term that loosely translates the word *gang* in the European context. There is no direct equivalent for the American term *gang* in many European languages (Klein et al. 2001). In Denmark, they use the word *bande*. In Norway and Sweden, the word *gang* (*gjeng/gäng*) is used much more widely.

2. Scandinavia has a population of 20 million people and comprises Sweden (9 million), Denmark (5.4 million) and Norway (4.5 million). The Nordic countries also cover Finland and Iceland.

3. The Scandinavian countries have a yearly murder rate between ten and fifteen murders for each million inhabitants, compared with the U.S. rate of seventy per million. While only a few of these murders happen in a group context, such murders get

a lot of public attention in the media. If immigrants are involved, such occurrences usually trigger a public debate on immigration (including national immigration policies) and crime.

4. This town, Drammen, has for some years had problems with criminal youth groups, especially those with an ethnic minority background. In economic terms, the town is not especially rich, but it is fairly affluent compared to the Norwegian average. Services and measures with some crime-prevention relevance comprise a culture house for youth, a motor center for youth, rock workshops, leisure administration, supporting sports organizations and other nongovernmental organizations, a health center for youth, a media workshop, an Internet cafe, community houses, community police, a community consultant, an outreach worker unit, social teachers in every school, social workers in some schools, a children's spokesman in municipal planning, pupil-council contact teachers, a conflict resolution council, an introduction school for new refugees, health services for refugees, a home for orphan refugees under eighteen, a unit for drug prevention, a twenty-four-hour watch service for adults with social problems, an alternative junior high school for pupils having problems within ordinary high schools, a debt and mortgage counselor, a day-care center for drug addicts, culture therapy for young people with psychiatric problems, a day center for people suffering from psychiatric diseases, a mobile psychiatric staff, twenty-four-hour child care (at the police station), life assistants for youth at risk, relief people for parents with demanding children, a leisure consultant for children and youths with physical, mental, and social handicaps, a crime-prevention coordinator, adventure holidays for demanding children, a support team for children with mental handicaps (ADHD, Tourette's syndrome, Asperger's syndrome, etc.), a multisystemic-treatment team, a "multisystemic light" team, alternative vocational school for youths having problems within the ordinary vo-tech schools, follow-up service for school dropouts (between sixteen and nineteen), coordination groups for children with medical or social problems, a crisis center for mistreated and battered women (and children), a support center for incest victims, an aggression-replacement training unit, youth contracts as an alternative to prison, and sport activities for youth at risk.

5. A Dutch method to study the interplay between parent and child using video and to giving positive instruction based on that video material.

6. There is a widespread myth in Scandinavia that the Swedes sometimes "overorganize" their complex welfare system. They have a cooperation model for nearly all kinds of problems or challenges; the word *samverkan* ("cooperation") best describes it. But in the field of crime prevention, the Danes have probably been more systematic.

7. In the Norwegian town of Drammen, four researchers participated in a one-day workshop to survey and discuss the problem of criminal gangs in this relatively modest

town (57,000 inhabitants) in 2000. The aforementioned gang definition was presented. Yet, during the workshop, the common meaning of the word immediately suppressed this definition. The result of this survey was the identification of ten gangs. A closer examination showed that these were petty-criminal youth groups.

8. In 2002, the national commissioner of the police in Denmark sponsored a new report on gangs in Denmark. This time, a much stricter gang definition was used, and the research group only found a few gangs that met the criteria. This report was hardly mentioned in the Danish mass media.

9. In 1999, it was a major issue in the prime minister's (Poul Nyrup-Rasmussen) speech to the Danish national assembly when he presented the government's program and the state budget for the next year. In Norway and Sweden, this speech would solely be a presentation of economic policy, care for the elderly, health service, improvements in schools, and so on.

10. Copenhagen has about 1.5 million people in the urban area, Stockholm has between 1 and 1.5 million, Oslo has 0.75 million, and Gothenburg has 0.5 million. The urban areas are often divided into many municipalities.

11. In 360 Norwegian communities they wear yellow waistcoats given by an insurance company.

12. While there are some daughters, the overwhelming majority of youth involved are males.

13. Jusitisministeriet, Det kriminalpræventive Råd and Socialministeriet, Copenhagen 2001

REFERENCES

Andersen, M., R. Morck, S. Christensen, and L. Minke. 2001. Rodet ungdom—unge roedder. *Social Kritik* 77: 18–47.

Balvig, F. 1999. *Risikoungdom.* Copenhagen: Det Kriminalpraeventive raad [Danish Crime Prevention Council].

Bjørgo, T. 1997. *Racist and right-wing violence in Scandinavia: Patterns, perpetrators, and responses.* Oslo: Tano Aschehougs

Bjørgo, T., and Y. Carlsson. 1999. *Vold, rasisme og ungdomsgjenger: Forebygging og bekjempelse.* Oslo: Tano.

Blanc, C. S. 1995. *Urban Children in distress: Global predicaments and innovative strategies.* Florence, Italy: UNICEF.

Bonke, J., and C. Caroe. 2001. *En forstaerket indsats over for kriminalitetstruede born og unge. En evaluering.* Copenhagen: Socialforskningsinstituttet 01:9.

Brunsson, N. 1989. *The organization of hypocrisy: Talk, decisions and actions in organizations.* Chichester, United Kingdom: John Wiley and Sons.

Carlsson, Y. 1995. *Aksjonsplan Brumunddal—ga den resultater?* Oslo: NIBR.

———. 2002. *Utviklingsprogrammet for styrking av oppvekstmiljøet. Rapport fra en følge-forsker.* Oslo: NIBR, available at www.nibr.no/static/pdf/notater/2002-125.pdf (accessed May 19, 2005).

Christie, N. 2004. *En passende mengde kriminalitet.* Oslo: Universitetsforlaget.

Curry, G. D., and R. W. Thomas. 1992. Community organization and gang policy response. *Journal of Quantitative Criminology Physics* 8: 357–74.

Curry, G. D., and S. H. Decker. 2003. *Confronting gangs: Crime and community.* Los Angeles, CA: Roxbury.

Danish Ministry of Justice. 2001. *Ungdomskontrakter—et inspirasjonshefte om anvendelse af sankstionsformen over for 15–17 årige lovovertredere.* Copenhagen: Justisministeriet, Socialministeriet og Det kriminalpraeventive raad.

Decker, S. H., and B. Van Winkle. 1996. *Life in the gang: Family, friends, and violence.* Cambridge: Cambridge University Press.

Emler, N., and S. Reicher. 1995. *The social psychology of delinquency and adolescence.* Oxford: Blackwell.

Fearn, N., S. H. Decker, and G. D. Curry. 2002. Public policy responses to gangs: Evaluating the outcomes. In *Modern gang reader,* ed. J. Miller, C. Maxson, and M. Klein, 2nd ed., 330–43. Los Angeles: Roxbury.

Haaland, T., and Y. Carlsson. 2002. *Kirkens ungdomsprosjekt—en virksomhetsbeskrivelse.* Oslo: NIBR, available at www.nibr.no/static/pdf/notater/2002-198.pdf (accessed May 2004).

Halvorsen, K. 2001. *Sosiale problemer: En sosiologisk innføring.* Bergen, Norway: Fagbokforlaget.

Howell, J. C. 1998. Promising programs for youth gang violence prevention and intervention. In *Serious and violent juvenile offenders: Risk factors and successful interventions,* ed. R. Loeber and D. P. Farrington, 284–312. Thousand Oaks, CA: Sage Publications.

Huff, C. R. 1989. Youth gangs and public policy. *Crime and Delinquency* 35 (4): 524–37.

Klein, M. W. 1995. *The American street gang.* New York: Oxford.

Klein, M. W., H.-J. Kerner, C. L. Maxson, and E. G. M. Weitekamp. 2001. *The Eurogang paradox: Street gangs and youth groups in the U.S. and Europe.* Dordrecht, Netherlands: Kluwer Academic Publishing.

Lien, I. L., and T. Haaland. 1998. *Vold og gjengatferd. En pilotstudie.* Oslo: NIBR og Ungdom Mot Vold.

Lihme, B. 2002. *Det kulørte akvarium. Artikler om unge, kriminalitet og bander.* Copenhagen: Hans Reitzels Forlag.

McCorkle, R. C., and T. D. Miethe. 2000. *Panic: The social construction of the street gang problem.* Upper Saddle River, NJ: Prentice Hall.

Olsen, C. B., and H. Hansen. 2001. *Kriminalprævention og integration på Indre Nørrebro.* Copenhagen: CASA.

Norwegian Expert Group. 2000. *Vurdering av program og tiltak for å redusere problematferd og utvikle sosial kompetanse. Innstilling fra faggruppe oppnevnt av Kirke-, utdannings- og forskningsdepartementet, juni 2000.* Oslo: (E-postbestilling: publikasjonsbestilling@ft.dep.no. Publikasjonsnummer: F 4100/2).

PLS Ramboll. 2003. Grupperelateret kriminalitet i Danmark. Del 2. Forebyggelse og bekjempelse, available at www.ramboll-management.dk/dan/sites/cases/uddannelse_integration_social/analyse_grupperelateret_kriminalitet_danmark.htm (accessed May 19, 2005).

Qvotrup Jensen, S. 2002. *De Vilde Unge i Aalborg Ost.* Aalborg: Aalborg Universitetsforlag.

Ringman, K. 1997. *Brottsförebyggande aatgärder i en förort—teori och praktik.* Stockholm: Kriminologiska Institutionen, Stockholms Universitet.

Sarnecki, J. 2001. *Delinquent networks: Youth co-offending in Stockholm.* Cambridge: Cambridge University Press.

Sherman L. W., D. Gottfredson, D. Mackenzie, J. Eck, P. Reuter, and S. Bushway. 1998. *Preventing crime: What works, what doesn't, what's promising. A report to the United States Congress prepared for the National Institute of Justice.* College Park, MD: Department of Criminology and Criminal Justice, University of Maryland.

Spergel, I., and G. D. Curry. 1993. The National Youth Gang Survey: A research and development process. In *Gang intervention handbook,* ed. A. Goldstein and C. R. Huff, 359–400. Champaign-Urbana, IL: Research Press.

Swedish Council for Crime Prevention. 2001. *Exit for avhoppare. En uppföljning och utvärdering av verksamheten aren 1998–2001.* Stockholm: Brottsforebyggande raadet.

Vilde Laereprocesser. 2001. Arbeidsgrunnlag for vilde laereprocesser, available at www.vildelaereprocesser.dk/arbgrundlag/arbgrundlagramme.php3 (accessed May 2004).

12

European Street Gangs and Troublesome Youth Groups: Findings from the Eurogang Research Program

Frank M. Weerman and Scott H. Decker

In this concluding chapter, we look at the preceding contributions as a whole and try to analyze what they reveal about the characteristics and background of European street gangs and troublesome youth groups. What are the results of bringing together the findings of current research on European gangs and troublesome youth groups? We analyze similarities and differences between the contributions and draw conclusions if possible. We selected the following specific themes as deserving special attention, as they received important coverage in the chapters of this book:

1. The issue of definition
2. Gang structure and characteristics
3. Individual member characteristics and risk factors
4. Neighborhoods
5. Immigration and ethnicity
6. The impact of groups and gangs on individual delinquent behavior

After addressing these issues, we describe the contribution that this book has made to the Eurogang program as a whole, especially in demonstrating the viability of the different research instruments that have been developed. To conclude this chapter, we address some possible directions for future Euro-gang research.

THE ISSUE OF DEFINITION

The issue of defining gangs is crucial to understanding what a gang is, what it means to be a gang member, and the activities that gang members engage in. There has been considerable debate about this issue in the United States in the past (see, e.g., Ball and Curry 1995; Esbensen and Peterson Lynskey 2001). The Eurogang program has developed a specific definition to gain consensus on these problems. Under this definition, a gang is "any durable, street-oriented youth group whose involvement in illegal activity is part of their group identity."

This definition has been put to the test by the authors of this volume. Many chapters use the Eurogang definition as the foundation for their studies, and despite linguistic, cultural, and institutional differences across study sites, the definition proved useful. The utility of the definition cuts across both qualitative and quantitative approaches and across different methods of research. For example, Frank van Gemert and Mark Fleisher (chapter 1) and Inger-Liese Lien (chapter 2) use the definition with the traditional ethnographic strategies of observation and interviewing, while Frank Weerman (chapter 6) and van Gemert (chapter 7) use the definition in formal questionnaires with selected respondents. Alexander Salagaev, Alexander Shashkin, Irina Sherbakova, and Elias Touriyanskiy (chapter 8) also use the definition with a mixed research strategy that uses both questionnaires and observation. These approaches have certain commonalities in their view of what a gang is and what gang membership means to individuals, but the different chapters also highlight contrasts and nuances in the gang or group concept in the European situation.

Van Gemert and Fleisher refer to a Dutch debate about the appropriateness of using terms like *gang* or *jeugdbende* for groups of Moroccan boys in Amsterdam. They argue that the many existing stereotypes about gangs obscure a good understanding of the phenomenon and that even American gangs often do not fit these stereotypes (a paradox that was described exhaustively in M. Klein et al. 2001). In chapter 1, they use the Eurogang definition to describe and analyze the nature of a specific group of Moroccan boys in Amsterdam. They conclude that the definition clearly applies to this group, which appeared to be durable and street oriented and whose involvement in (sometimes serious) illegal activity was part of its group identity. However, the group had no name, no specific symbols, and no territory, as would be characteristic of the stereotypical view of gangs. Further, the group members had relatively loose relations with each other, and there were no group rules, although members knew what to expect from each other. Van Gemert and Fleisher show that the Eurogang definition provides a better understanding of these groups than traditional stereotypes about American gangs do.

Lien's extensive ethnographic work in Oslo shows that many of the key structural features of the A- and B-gangs in Oslo make them similar to gangs in many American cities. However, certain features are also unique to the Oslo gangs, for example, the important role of kinship, particularly among Pakistani boys, in linking members to a gang. Lien describes a series of overlapping and intersecting connections among gang members that intersect with kinship, ethnicity, the gang, and connections to the welfare system. She emphasizes that kinship and family ties often trump gang ties when loyalties are tested, contrasting with the oft-told American myth that the gang functions as a surrogate family (Decker and Van Winkle 1996). Lien addresses a number of different metaphors of the gang concept and concludes that many existing conceptualizations of gangs are too restrictive. For example, the container metaphor (which describes status as inside or outside a certain type of gang) denies the many connections and ties outside the gang. As an alternative, she suggests that we use a network metaphor for gangs and combine it with the image of a tube or railway system.

The gangs reported by the Dutch schoolchildren surveyed by Weerman in chapter 6 provide a contrast to the gangs described by Lien. Weerman uses the funneling approach developed by the Eurogang working group. This approach begins by asking questions about group associations and memberships, working toward involvement in crime and, ultimately, involvement in a gang. This method, Weerman reports, worked quite well. He found that 6 percent of the school youths he surveyed belonged to a gang as defined by the Eurogang definition, a figure not inconsistent with that offered by school- and youth-based surveys done in the United States in Seattle, Rochester, and Denver. Few of the gangs in the Dutch sample had a special name for their gang, but those that did most often chose names that reflected the neighborhood in which they lived, were inspired by the American gang phenomenon, or adhered to names that otherwise expressed danger and toughness. About half of the respondents that were categorized as gang youths using the funneling procedure said they belonged to a *jeugdbende*, the Dutch word for *gang*. At the same time, a large minority denied that their group could be identified as such. More interestingly, a substantial percentage of youths in groups that were not defined as gangs in the procedure claimed that they did belong to a gang, even if they did not report any delinquent activity on the part of their fellow group members. Weerman concludes that self-identification as a gang member is very subjective in the Dutch situation and depends on the individual youth's image of what a gang is, while the funneling method results in a more reliable measure for gang research in the Netherlands.

Van Gemert's work in Amsterdam employed the Eurogang Expert Survey, and he used it in a way that resembled the funneling procedure described in chapter 6. First, he determined how many youth groups the police had reported, then selected as gangs those groups that were reported as durable, street-oriented youth groups whose illegal activities were seen as okay or accepted by the group. Turf (street orientation for Weerman) was not considered to be an important part of gang identity by the experts surveyed in Amsterdam, and the groups did not resemble the popular stereotypes of American gangs. Van Gemert found that a large number of gangs had names that reflected their location within the city, but these names often were given to them by the police instead of coming from the youths themselves.

The gangs reported on in Russia come from the cities of Kazan in the Tartarstan Republic and Moscow. Chapter 8 is based on both the Expert and School surveys and finds consistency between the two approaches to studying gangs. For the city of Kazan, the prevalence of gang membership (as defined through the funneling procedure) was the same as found in the Netherlands, but for Moscow it was two times higher. Clearly different from the Netherlands, gangs in Russia seem to be more turf oriented, more like black and Hispanic gangs in American cities. The chapter further underscores clear differences between gangs and other youth groups, an important distinction for both understanding and responding to gangs. Unlike the diminished role of self-identification in the Netherlands, the Russian research found that gang members had high levels of self-identification. In addition, Salagaev et al. were able to offer the basis for what may evolve into a more formal typology of Russian gangs. Their typology combines three sets of characteristics (attributive, functional, and structural) with three types of youth communities (territorial, neighborhood, and gangs) to depict the sorts of activities that groups engage in. The Russian gangs appear to be more developed than their counterparts in the Netherlands or Norway, reflecting involvement in crime and the role of turf.

GANG STRUCTURE AND CHARACTERISTICS

Gangs vary in a number of dimensions. Cheryl Maxson and Malcolm Klein (1995) have observed five different types of gang structures: traditional (or classical), neotraditional (or neoclassical), compressed, collective, and specialty. They argue that six key features distinguish these types: the presence of subgroups, size, age range, duration, territoriality, and versatility. Scott Decker (2001) has found that gangs vary along the dimensions of structure, organization, and behavior and that structure and organization have a distinct effect on the behavior of gangs. A number of the chapters in this book shed considerable light on the structure of gangs, providing our first glimpses of the nature of this key variable in the European context. The results show that while the European gangs studied for this volume share many characteristics with their American counterparts, there are also important differences.

The ethnographic work of van Gemert and Fleisher in Amsterdam-West illustrates the intersection of ethnicity and immigration patterns with behavior and structure. They report on a Moroccan street gang known as the Windmill Square group, named for its hangout location, which originated in the late 1990s. It has had a core membership group of ten individuals, with total membership at any time of around twenty-five individuals and an average age of nearly eighteen. The group does not use identifiable symbols to identify members and does not use gang argot. However, there are generalized symbols of membership mostly linked to rap music. The group does not have conflicts with other youth groups and lacks a sense of territoriality. In this sense, the Windmill Square group is radically different not only from American gangs but also from gangs reported in Norway, Germany, Scotland, and Italy. There are no identifiable leaders in the group and no rules to govern members. Cliques seem to be as important as the group and can change in membership from activity to activity and day to day.

This Dutch gang stands in contrast to the A- and B-gangs reported on by Lien in chapter 2. These gangs have been in existence for fifteen years and include older members who are often in their twenties. As such, they have somewhat more structure, and leaders and rules can be observed. That said, the role of smaller cliques in these Oslo gangs is quite important. The A-gang is territorial, while the B-gang is not, an interesting contrast between these gangs and one that bears watching over the longer term.

The comparative work of Frank Weerman and Finn-Aage Esbensen in chapter 10 provides an interesting contrast to our understanding of gang structure and characteristics. Their work shows that American gangs tend to be larger by a factor of two and much more organized. The organization measures on which American gangs demonstrate more formality include symbols, initiation rites, leaders, rules, and meetings. Both Dutch and American gangs report the presence of subgroups and girls in their gangs, an area of similarity. Perhaps more importantly, levels of gang involvement in delinquency were quite comparable. The differences may reflect the length of time gangs have been in existence. The higher level of organization in American gangs may be the result of their longer period of development.

The Scottish gangs described by Bradshaw in chapter 9 demonstrate considerable similarity with American gangs. This is particularly true with regard to the level of involvement in delinquency, with which gang membership is strongly associated, as well as regarding the proportion of youths surveyed who report being gang members. In addition, Scottish gangs tend, in the main, to have symbols such as a name and are described as being "fiercely territorial." This territoriality appears to reflect the demographic and geographic characteristics of Edinburgh.

The research on Russian gangs reported on in this volume (chapter 8) provides a comparative view of gangs. Salagaev et al. note that the "Kazan type" has emerged as a particular type of gang. This gang type is homogeneous with regard to gender and recruitment patterns and engages in considerable revenue-generating and violent activity. Indeed, this type of gang is described as being quite entrepreneurial. In addition, Kazan-type gangs have a strong cultural component, and the transmission of countercultural and criminal values is seen as a major gang activity. These gangs can be distinguished from traditional neighborhood groups of youngsters by their more formal structures, which include roles, leaders, common purposes, meetings, and turf.

INDIVIDUAL MEMBER CHARACTERISTICS AND RISK FACTORS

Gangs and groups comprise individual members with certain characteristics (demographics like gender and ethnicity, social backgrounds, individual traits, attitudes, and behavior). The classic question of why people belong to or join certain types of youth groups overlaps partly with the explanation of delinquent behavior in general. In some periods, especially the 1950s and 1960s, it almost seemed that the issues were synonymous: some of the most important theoretical developments of that era focused on gang delinquency (Cohen 1955; Cloward and Ohlin 1960). Nowadays, explanations of gang membership and youth group problems still draw from general etiological theories, although the study of both fields is more separated now. In order to make progress on these matters, we must investigate differences between gang members and nonmembers. Not only are demographic factors important in this respect but so are socioeconomic, attitudinal, and behavioral risk factors.

The qualitative chapters in this book offer some general information about demographics and other characteristics of the youth groups and gangs that were studied. Van Gemert and Fleisher report that the twenty-four Moroccan boys of the Windmill Square group generally come from big families with low incomes, some with an absent father or mother and some with recognized "problem families." They are unsuccessful in their work or at school and lack discipline. They all have a history of police contact for all kinds of offenses. They are described as "ill prepared for a role in society." The members of the Pakistani gangs that Lien describes are also boys who have had an impressive numbers of charges brought against them. Interestingly, however, there is no background of problematic family situations. On the contrary, the fact that the Pakistani members have such broad family networks and belong to tightly knit families has become a risk factor of its own. Kinship connections often lead to recruitment into the gangs, as Lien shows, and kinship shapes the behavior of the gang members. Lien further suggests that gang members straddle two worlds and may be described as "part-time conformists," that is, individuals who put on the appearance of conformity with regard to traditional religious attendance and observations but combine such conformity with Western-influenced activities, including going to nightclubs, drinking, and participating in crime. These young Pakistani immigrants resemble the Mexican American gang members of the Los Angeles barrios described by Diego Vigil (1988). Vigil coined the term *double marginalization* to describe these gang members as marginalized not only by the majority Anglo community but by their own ethnic community as well. Lien's descriptions of A- and B-gang members seem consistent with this view.

The members of the old-fashioned Genoa gang described by Uberto Gatti et al. are also males and clearly come from a very marginalized group of poor southern Italian migrants. The interviewed youths "share the experiences of failure at school, family breakdown and law breaking." Their criminal activity started early in their lives, their families have disintegrated, and there have clearly been major problems, although interviewees were reluctant to reveal detailed information. An interesting characteristic of some members is that they have been institutionalized in group homes and imprisoned. The violent Russians of German descent (*Aussiedlers*) described by Elmar Weitekamp, Kerstin Reich, and Hans-Jürgen Kerner are clearly not socially integrated into mainstream German society. Their remaining in their own ethnic group is partly forced and partly voluntary. The overwhelming majority of Aussiedlers had belonged to a youth group or clique when in Russia. These groups functioned as social spaces where youths were relatively free from state authorities. The interviewed imprisoned Aussiedlers had relatively older peers as friends than other Aussiedlers, suggesting that orientation toward older peers is a risk factor for this group of youths. These youths also have a "high tendency to commit violent acts," which was present already in their country of origin.

Taken as a whole, the five chapters in which qualitative methods were used sketch an image of gang members as marginalized individuals who grew up in adverse social circumstances. Two of these chapters report major problems in the areas of family, education, and work, and all authors reveal that gang members have been criminally active for a long time. It is also clear that group members are predominantly male.

The groups studied in the qualitative studies are a selection of some of the most interesting and troublesome gangs in the population. It is possible that the individual characteristics of those who join other troublesome youth groups are less exceptional. More generalizable information about the individual characteristics of gang members can be found in some of the quantitative contributions (chapter 8 and especially chapters 9 and 10).

A particular insight from these chapters is that the gender distribution reported using the survey method is very different from that reported in the qualitative chapters. Salagaev et al. report that the girls in their sample report about the same involvement in gangs as boys, which was true in Kazan as well as in Moscow. Bradshaw reports that substantial percentages of girls belong to gangs, although the exact distribution depends on the degree of gang organization. He found that in groups with no name for themselves and no special signs or symbols, girls and boys were almost equally represented (in fact, girls were slightly overrepresented). Girls were less represented than boys in other types of gangs but were still very present: more than one-third of all respondents who belong to the most organized gangs were girls. The work of Weerman and Esbensen reflects these results. They report that for both the United States and the Netherlands, males are somewhat overrepresented but not much. In both countries, the estimated mean number of males in respondents' gangs was about twice the mean number of females in these groups, but girls were a substantial portion of all gang youths. In short, quantitative studies based on surveys result in much higher prevalence rates among girls than qualitative studies. These results also depart from those for gender distribution among gang members based on the Expert Survey in Amsterdam (chapter 7). The substantial representation of girls in gangs is consistent with American gang research based on surveys. This can be traced to the fact that surveys cover a broad array of gangs and troublesome youth groups, while ethnographic studies and expert surveys are always biased in one way or another toward the more serious and most visually prominent groups. We can learn from this that the involvement of girls in troublesome youth groups and gangs is substantial, not very different from that of boys, and probably often overlooked.

Chapters 9 (Bradshaw) and 10 (Weerman and Esbensen) report detailed information about risk factors for gang membership other than gender. In the study among Scottish youth, children from single-parent families and the lower classes, especially those with unemployed parents, were overrepresented among the gang members. All attitudinal variables showed significant differences between gang and nongang youths. Those in a gang had lower supervision from parents, were punished more often, and had more conflicts with parents. They were less attached to school, were more impulsive and risk seeking, had less conventional moral beliefs, and were more exposed to negative peer influences. The results from the U.S. and Dutch surveys provided similar results. Here, youths from single-parent homes were also overrepresented in troublesome youth groups and gangs, although the differences were not very large, especially not in the Dutch sample. The results with regard to attitudinal variables mirrored those from Scotland. Compared to nongang youths, those who belonged to troublesome youth groups and gangs were less attached to parents, less monitored, less committed to school, and adhered less to conventional moral standards. They had more delinquent friends and experienced more peer pressure. These risk factors were present among the U.S. as well as the Dutch gang youths, and in most cases, the differences even had very similar magnitudes in both samples. These studies confirm the American results on risk factors (see the reviews in chapter 9 and 10) and suggest that these risk factors might be quite universal, or at least might be generalizable to the European situation.

NEIGHBORHOODS

One of the classic themes in the literature about troublesome youth groups and gangs is the importance of neighborhoods. First of all, these groups are often connected to the deteriorating neighborhoods or ghettos of big inner cities. Marginalization and the lack of social capital of entire communities is often seen as an important cause of gang formation. Further, neighborhoods are often a defining unit of different gangs or youth groups. Nearly eighty years ago, Frederic Thrasher (1927) described the different gangs of early twentieth-century Chicago and drew a "gang map" of the city, illustrating that each part of the city had its own youth groups and street gangs. Further, a well-known component of gang life is turf, a place where members meet and that they consider their own. The classic type of street gang is very territorial and gets involved with other gangs in conflicts and fights if its turf is violated.

The neighborhood of the Moroccan Windmill Square group has a relatively high percentage of ethnic minorities but is still heterogeneous. Although it is not a rich area, the neighborhood is not deteriorated: there are many public services, and it is clean and green (certainly not a ghetto or no-go area). The youth group hangs out in certain undefined places on the street or in shopping areas. Their activities are not confined to their own neighborhood; they can cause trouble in the city center and have created incidents during the summer in a coastal city near Amsterdam. The group never gets into conflict with other gangs over territory and does not fight over turf. Van Gemert and Fleisher highlight the interaction between this group and their neighborhood. Certain escalation processes lead to conflicts with citizens and especially shopkeepers.

The Pakistani gangs in Oslo described by Lien are clearly not territorial. In fact, these gangs are not restricted or connected to a particular neighborhood at all; gang members often meet each other in restaurants or clubs. The members from B-gang come from various suburbs and move in cars from town to town. As a result, the gangs are not territorial. However, the different gangs can be seen as rivals, and there have been severe fights and incidents between the A- and B-gangs. In other words, the gangs seem to compete to gain status instead of dominance over a particular area or neighborhood.

The southern Italian group studied by Gatti et al. hangs out on the street or in a bar, but its members do not identify with a specific place, and there are no indications that they are territorial. However, they stay within their neighborhood, which is clearly a deprived and poor area. It consists of low-cost housing, with sometimes big, uniform blocks of flats, which are allocated to low-income families. There are many migrants from South Italy and some non-EU immigrants. Gatti et al. describe the families from this neighborhood as cut off from the rest of the city and mention the bad reputation of the neighborhood among other citizens. Like the Moroccan gang described in chapter 1, this gang intimidates the neighborhood residents. In addition, some groups of younger kids from the neighborhood cause nuisance because they vandalize property. Although there is a bad relationship between gang members and citizens, the neighborhood plays an important role in maintaining the behavior of the gang members, according to Gatti et al., who see the culture of the gang as the result of "a spatial and cultural isolation and a tendency to remain within the confines of the neighborhood."

Aussiedlers from the groups described in chapter 4 also live in very deprived neighborhoods. Russians of German descent are often housed in bad conditions, in crowded temporary units. Youths are forced to hang out in the hallways or outside the buildings because in their homes they have no place of their own to go.

The Expert Survey conducted in Amsterdam (chapter 7) showed youth groups and gangs in all of the surveyed parts of the city (police districts), which differed in population distribution and mean income. The exact figures are somewhat uncertain because there were differences between districts in response rate and experts' willingness to cooperate. Nevertheless, there were clearly surprisingly few differences in the number of gangs and groups between districts. In most districts, there were about fifteen groups and about seven to eight gangs reported. Fewer groups and gangs appeared in two of the districts, Old West and the city center, but the delinquent behavior of their members was relatively serious. The lower numbers for Old West can be traced to the fact that this neighborhood had very low response rates, but the response rate for the city center was 100 percent. It is unclear if the center really contained fewer troublesome youth groups on the street or if such groups were less visible or recognized in this part of the city, which is always busy for the police and in which there are always groups of people on the street.

In short, several chapters show that neighborhood circumstances are also important for European troublesome youth groups and gangs but not in exactly the same way as for American groups. The context of the Italian gang and the Aussiedler violent groups is a poor and deprived neighborhood with unfavorable housing conditions, but the two studies from the Netherlands (the ethnography of the Moroccan group and the Expert Survey) show that the emergence of gangs and troublesome youth groups is not necessarily restricted to deteriorated areas in the city. The neighborhood clearly played a role in bringing youths with the same background together in these groups and in confining them to their own areas and culture. The low tendency of gangs and groups to see the neighborhood as a place to identify with clearly departs from the classical picture of American street gangs. None of the studies reports on territoriality and fights over turf. Gangs may be rivals without having a territory (like the Oslo A- and B-gangs), and they may be bound to a particular area without having to defend a territory (like the gang of southern Italians).

IMMIGRATION AND ETHNICITY

The role of immigration and ethnicity has been crucial to the understanding of gangs. Indeed, the study of gangs in the United States has largely been a study of immigration and ethnicity. Thrasher's (1927) study notes the important role that immigrants, particularly those of European origin, played in the creation and expansion of gangs in Chicago. Ironically, evidence is now coming to light that American gangs have an influence on the emerging gangs in Europe. In this sense, the role of immigration has come full circle, whereby European immigrants played a central role in the formation and membership of American gangs in the twentieth century, and American gangs are now influencing the symbols, style, and activities of European gangs in the twenty-first century.

The role of immigration in the formation of gangs, gang behavior, and gang identity can be seen very clearly in several of the chapters. Perhaps the most direct assessment of this role comes in chapter 4, the intriguing chapter prepared by Weitekamp et al., which examines the repatriation of Russians of German descent, Germans who migrated to Russia during the post–World War II separation of Germany into East and West. This repatriation was fraught with irony, as the former German citizens had lost most of their language, customs, and relationships with Germany. Indeed, in many ways, these Germans were more Russian than German, and their transition has been similar to that faced by many immigrant groups new to a country or culture. Weitekamp et al. report that these repatriated Germans engage in a large number of fights with other Germans and ethnic groups. And their ethnic origins are important to group formation, with most gang members belonging to a group with members of their country of origin. There appears to be a considerable level of animosity between native Germans and Aussiedlers, often attributable to the language, culture, and common stereotypical images of Aussiedlers. The majority of groups, including gangs, formed by these repatriated individuals comprise a single ethnic group, an observation that was even truer for those who were incarcerated. The social, economic, and cultural deprivation faced by Aussiedlers who returned to their "native" country is compounded by these affiliational patterns. These individuals also fit the pattern of double marginality identified by Vigil (1988) for Mexican Americans in southern California. Aussiedlers are neither fully German nor Russian and, as such, find cultural and economic integration into mainstream German society quite difficult, which closely parallels the experience of other ethnic groups in America (Vigil 2003).

The experience of young Moroccan boys in Amsterdam-West offers a contrast to the German Aussiedlers. Moroccan families were recruited to Windmill Square in the 1980s to fill labor shortages in Dutch factories. The gang boys that van Gemert and Fleisher report on are the children of the first generation of immigrants, adults who were raised in Morocco according to Moroccan norms and values. The majority of gangs form along ethnic lines, with Moroccan boys dominating the membership of these gangs. There are also reports of informal community and business opposition to these groups of boys within their own communities. The Moroccan boys have adopted American gangster rap music, with some adaptation to their own style. It is clear that there are elements of culture conflict at work in the lives of these gang members; however, it is interesting to note the role of global youth culture in the midst of the Moroccan-Dutch conflict.

The gang reported on by Lien in chapter 2 is largely Pakistani in ethnicity, a factor that plays an important role in understanding its members' integration into—and exclusion from—Norwegian society. We already have noted the appropriateness of the concept of double marginality with regard to these youth. Interestingly, Pakistani caste differences that would be exclusive in their home country are ignored in their country of emigration, Norway. However, the importance of kinship relations from Pakistani culture does remain for these youths in Oslo. Kin networks can promote fighting and conflict between individuals, as members of the same kinship group will fight to defend other kinsmen. Lien notes the extent to which this can blur the lines between gang and family conflicts, an important observation, particularly for first-generation immigrant youths already marginalized by economic and cultural factors. This marginalization also can help to explain the straddling of Pakistani and Norwegian cultural and behavioral categories that Lien reports in the behavior of "part-time conformists."

Gatti et al. (chapter 3) report on the impact of ethnicity in the formation and activities of Italian gangs. There are immigrants from different regions of Italy, as well as from several non-EU nations in North Africa and western Asia. Gatti reports that these new immigrants are met with distrust and viewed as outsiders. The gangs of Begati in the north of Italy have defined territories, although this seldom leads to conflict. The role of family honor and culture are important aspects of the gangs that Gatti et al. discuss.

THE IMPACT OF GROUPS AND GANGS
ON INDIVIDUAL DELINQUENT BEHAVIOR

An important reason for public concern about gangs is that they are seen as major facilitators of crime. American research has shown that gang members are disproportionately arrested (see Howell 1994) and that they are significantly more delinquent than nongang youths (i.e., Esbensen and Huizinga 1993). Further, American research has shown that gang membership makes a unique contribution to delinquent behavior beyond the influence of delinquent peers (Battin et al. 1998) and that delinquency levels increase after youths have entered a gang (e.g., Thornberry et al. 1993; Gordon et al. 2004). It will be interesting to see if this crime-enhancing effect of gang membership is also observed in the European youth groups described in this book.

All of the chapters in this volume have reported that members of European troublesome youth groups and street gangs are relatively often involved in violent acts and other offenses. The Moroccan Windmill Square group described in chapter 1 is criminally active in a wide range of offenses. The members of the Oslo Pakistani gangs are very familiar to the police, having been charged in the past with a large number of felonies (ranging from property crimes and drug offenses to violent offenses, robberies, and also some murders). The Genoese old-fashioned gang and the Aussiedler are particularly known for their fighting activities and their violence. The historical overview in chapter 8 by Salagaev et al. makes clear that Russian gangs in the past have sometimes been very violent and criminal. The Expert Survey in Amsterdam showed that many youth groups were involved in nuisance and light offenses but also that the groups defined as gangs were rated by experts as relatively delinquent. Groups and gangs clearly differed in the kind of criminal activities they were involved in, and there were also differences between districts. Groups in the city center were rated as the most serious in delinquency, and groups in which members committed more serious forms of property crime were found especially in three districts of Amsterdam (East, Southeast, and Old West).

The survey studies from chapters 9 and 10 offer information about the prevalence and seriousness of delinquent behaviors among gang youths in comparison to nongang youths. Weerman and Esbensen show that youths in gangs or troublesome youth groups are quite delinquent and are often involved in illegal activities. Interestingly, the magnitude of the differences is the same in both the U.S. and Dutch sample, suggesting that gangs and troublesome youth groups in both countries have the same crime-enhancing influences. Bradshaw shows that gang members among Edinburgh youths are also relatively delinquent. The mean delinquency scores of gang youths are higher than those of nongang youths, and these differences increased with more restricted definitions of gang membership, with respondents in gangs with names and signs having the highest mean scores (cf. Esbensen and Lynskey 2001). Bradshaw also shows that youths in gangs were more delinquent than youths who had delinquent friends but who were not in a gang. For all measures of delinquency, nongang youths without delinquent peers had the lowest mean scores, gang members had the highest, and nongang youths with delinquent peers had mean scores somewhere in the middle. Strictly taken, this does not disentangle the effects of gang membership and delinquent peer influence, but it is in line with American research showing an independent effect of gang membership above and beyond the exposure to delinquent friends (Battin et al. 1998).

Circumstances in which the gang or group process is a facilitator of delinquent behavior are described in some of the qualitative studies. The gang is important first because it provides potential co-offenders. Criminal activities are often perpetrated by a small number of group members—two, three or four. The gang brings the offenders together, but only some members commit the offenses. The moral attitudes within these gangs also facilitate delinquency. Many authors believe that violence or criminal behavior in the studied groups is "normal" in many cases. Van Gemert and Fleisher give an example of an instance in which the group as a whole stole lots of things. Violence in this group is further facilitated by the fact that loyalty in fights is expected from other members and that they back up each other no matter what the reason is for the fight. The normalization of violence is further illustrated in chapters 3 and 4. Gatti et al. show that the use of violence to solve conflicts and to retaliate is normal in the culture of the gang of southern Italian immigrants in Genoa.

Violence is also seen as a normal and honorable activity and is perceived as fun in the Aussiedler groups. Fights are opportunities to demonstrate power and strength to other young males in these groups. Like the members from the Windmill Square group, the Aussiedlers are expected to back each other up. Weitekamp et al. write that they are "obliged to unconditional solidarity" and to "defend the honor and reputation of the group." Honor and reputation are also important for the Pakistani gang members described by Lien in chapter 2. A man must be able to defend himself and others in the Pakistani gangs, especially his relatives. This is important because brothers and cousins who are not members of the gang sometimes become the targets of a rival gang. Another aspect of honor in these gangs is that it functions as a justification for illegal behavior. According to Lien, members of the A- and B-gangs see themselves as helping their families when they make money in illegal ways and as helping their community in that they can be asked to use threats and violence to rectify injustices.

Chapter 5 about the role of crime acts in constituting gang mentality highlights the importance of being part of a group of like-minded people to deal with the emotions involved in committing crimes. This chapter offers an in-depth analysis of the emotional structure of the criminal acts of violence and robbery: it illustrates the force and threat needed for robberies, the pride or "competence pleasure" that results from successful offenses, the blocking of empathy needed to be violent, and the fear and shame that can be the result from criminal acts. It also describes an important psychological process in which the gang facilitates delinquent behavior. Lien posits that offenders need to see themselves in a positive way and want recognition, like everybody else. During crime acts, however, they need to inflict harm and pain, blocking their empathy; this can result in shame and fear. The gang acts as a stage where offenders get positive reactions for these acts: they can feel superior because they succeeded, they can be generous with the money they garnered from their crimes, and they can get status and recognition. In other words: the offender can be a "good guy" in the context of a gang while he or she is a "bad guy" otherwise.

The processes described in these chapters add to other social-psychological mechanisms that occur in many peer groups in adolescence, like peer pressure through ridicule and diffusion of responsibility (see Warr 2002). They show that troublesome groups and gangs have an important role in facilitating violence, criminal behavior, and illegal behavior, and they underline the special meaning of these groups for the youths who belong to them.

THE VALUE OF THIS BOOK FOR THE EUROGANG RESEARCH PROGRAM
In addition to the substantive contributions that these chapters have made, they also demonstrate the utility of the Eurogang Research Program. As described in the introduction by Malcolm Klein, the Eurogang program has evolved since its initial meeting in 1996 in Schmitten, Germany. What began as an international seminar to explore the possibility that American-style gangs were emerging or active in Europe has now become a mature research platform helping to define the research agenda on street gangs, youth groups, and intervention programs across a host of European nations. That program comprises five related components: a definition of gangs, an ethnography protocol, a survey instrument for use with school or other institutional populations, an expert survey, and a policy-assessment tool. This volume has made many substantive contributions to our understanding of street gangs and troublesome youth groups in Europe. The utility of each of these components has been demonstrated by each of the thirteen chapters of this book.

Perhaps the most important and likely enduring component of the Eurogang Research Program will be the utility of the definition of a street gang. This was not a definition arrived at easily or without controversy. Indeed, much of the debate during the first two full meetings of the working group was given over to the discussion of what constitutes a gang. In many ways, those discussions paralleled those that took place in the United States in the 1960s and again in the 1990s, as American scholars grappled with issues similar to those of their European counterparts. Some of the components of the Eurogang definition of a street gang seem straightforward, particularly the group character of a street gang. The role of the street, however, proved to be a bit more difficult. *Street oriented* means something slightly different in the European context than in the American setting, and there is variation in the meaning of the term across Europe. However, as with most valid definitions, the similarities outweighed the differences. The debate over the involvement in illegal activity—taken to be a key component of the definition by most of the American scholars assembled—was another matter. Concern was expressed over the creation of moral panic and possible stigmatization of ethnic minorities, the very groups struggling for economic and political acceptance in much of Europe. Despite those concerns, at the end of the day, consensus was reached that such involvement was critical to separating street gangs from youth organizations that were primarily involved in sports or community activities. Including criminal involvement as a key component of group identity was one way that the Eurogang working group sought to assign importance to the role of identity among group members. Despite the differences in setting, the definition has been proved to work well. Street gangs from six European countries (the Netherlands, Germany, Russia, Scotland, Italy, Norway) and Scandinavia in general are represented in this book. This research was served well by the robust definition developed by the Eurogang working group. Each of the chapters used the Eurogang definition as the foundation for its study, and despite linguistic, cultural, and institutional differences across study sites, the definition proved useful. The resulting clarity brought to the study of a social issue by using a commonly agreed-on operational definition with documented validity and reliability is quite important. In this regard, the study of gangs in Europe proceeds on a much stronger foundation than is the case in the United States.

The contributions of the group can be seen in other areas as well. In their work, Lien, van Gemert, Fleisher, Gatti, and Salagaev et al. all used various aspects of the ethnography protocol developed and refined by the working group. This protocol is necessarily flexible and suitable for guiding research, formulating conclusions, and framing questions in a variety of cultural and institutional contexts. As much can be said for the other instruments. The work of van Gemert in the Netherlands documents that the Expert Survey is a useful and flexible tool for assessing the views and knowledge of experts regarding the nature and extent of the gang problem in a particular political jurisdiction. Similarly, Weerman and Esbensen document that the Youth, or School, Survey is a powerful tool, suitable for use in a number of different sorts of countries, cultures, and settings. This conclusion is supported by the work done in Russia (Moscow and Kazan), another example of the sort of comparative cross-cultural work that is possible using the Eurogang research instruments as a foundation for such research. Finally, the chapter by Yngve Carlsson and Scott Decker documents the significance of the cultural and institutional setting for understanding policy and programmatic interventions. The Eurogang policy instrument served as a basis for this comparative research, helping to focus attention on the problem of definition, the use of existing resources, and differences in intervention based on the existing institutional and cultural resources available in a country.

As a whole, the chapters in this book provide a wealth of new information on the emerging phenomena of street gangs and troublesome youth groups in Europe. Together they give a clear picture of the current state of research, and many of the chapters show the first results of the new methods and common instruments developed by the Eurogang program. Each of the chapters describes characteristics of European street gangs and troublesome youth groups, and many authors explicitly compare these characteristics to those of American gangs.

It is important to note that just as is the case in the United States, street gangs and troublesome youth groups in Europe are not a monolith. One of the most important lessons learned from American gang research is that gangs vary considerably with regard to the background and demographic, social, and economic characteristics of gang members, as well as with regard to the organizational and structural characteristics of the gang. One of the strengths of this volume has been its emphasis on the differences in gangs. While some gangs have existed for quite a while and have developed structures and leaders, many others (probably most in Europe) are shorter lived and more loosely organized. Many gangs in

Europe are not territorial and differ from American turf-based gangs; some European gangs do fight to defend their own territory. There are many groups that have no names for themselves and do not see themselves as gangs; others do self-identify as gangs and have dangerous names based on locality or inspired by the American gang culture. Thus, it is not correct to speak of "European gangs" as if all gangs in Europe were the same or shared a number of common features that distinguish them from their American counterparts. Similarly, it is not appropriate to speak of Dutch gangs, or Norwegian gangs, or Italian gangs as if all gangs in any of those countries (or a number of others, for that matter) were all the same or shared a large number of features in common.

However, when we do make a comparison between the youth groups studied in European countries and street gangs in the United States, we do see some general differences. It is clear that European street gangs and troublesome youth groups are often more loosely organized and less territorial than their American counterparts and that many of these groups do not need clear symbols, colors, and names. The meaning of the word *gang* itself, or its counterparts in the different languages, seems to be less clear and more ambiguous to young people in most European countries than it is to youths in the United States.

An important contextual factor for the gangs that this book has studied is that European countries have many youths who are second-generation ethnic minorities, and their number has increased in the last decades. Three factors have contributed to this trend: (1) the need for working migrants in the expanding Western European economies (and subsequent family formation and reunion), (2) a substantial influx of refugees and asylum seekers in many European countries due to global instability, and (3) population changes after the fall of the Berlin Wall and the end of Communism in Central and Eastern European countries. All three of these factors can be clearly recognized in many of the chapters of this book. It is obvious that this book has demonstrated in particular the important role of immigration and ethnicity for European gangs and troublesome youth groups.

FUTURE RESEARCH DIRECTIONS

Despite the valuable contributions to this book and the impressive progress being made within the Eurogang program, there is still much to do. First of all, the scope of our research could benefit from expansion to other youth groups, other samples, and other countries. The qualitative material presented in this book is rich and informative, but it is limited to a couple of the most visible youth groups and street gangs. It would be interesting to see if the observed patterns are present in other youth groups as well, especially in less remarkable or eye-catching street gangs. The quantitative studies in this book do have this wider scope, but of course they can never reach the depth of ethnographic research. Another limitation of the quantitative surveys is that they are yet limited to a few countries and samples. It would be interesting to have some indications about the prevalence of gang membership in representative samples and in more countries of Europe. It would be especially interesting to get information about gangs and troublesome youth groups in the quickly changing countries of central and eastern Europe. It is our hope that the five research instruments developed by Eurogang will be widely picked up and used in many countries—that would make it possible to work toward standardized comparisons of the gang situation in different countries.

This book demonstrates the strengths of multimethod research strategies: the qualitative chapters offered us in-depth insights about the characteristics, culture, and context of particular street gangs and groups, while the quantitative material described broad and generalizable information that enables comparisons among different countries. In a sense, both strategies are complementary, but with some extra effort, they may benefit from each other's findings. It would be interesting to use the Expert and School surveys to investigate how common phenomena found in the ethnographic research—for example, the importance of kinship relations, the "grip of the group," the emphasis on honor and respect—really are. In general, quantitative methods can be used to test if assumptions based on case studies of gangs may be generalized. On the other hand, we need qualitative research on certain issues raised by the findings of the Expert and School surveys. For example, it would be very important to use ethnographic methods to elaborate on the finding that girls are much more involved in street gangs than many people think. In the United States, female involvement in gangs has been studied quite intensively already (see, e.g., Miller 2001; Fleisher 1998), but there is a big gap in our knowledge about girl gang involvement in Europe. Further, qualitative research methods could add greatly to our understanding about what gang involvement means for individual behavior and thus supply a better understanding of the relationship between gang membership and the heightened levels of delinquency found in quantitative studies. Lien's chapter about the meaning of crime offers an example of this.

It would be even more interesting to combine qualitative and quantitative methods in the same areas and on the same gangs. Such a strategy would result in a more complete picture of the prevalence of troublesome youth groups and gangs among a certain population because each of the different methods covers a different set of groups with different degrees of seriousness. It would also give an indication of the blind spots and biases of each method; in other words, it would provide a cross-validation of the results of each instrument. Of course, such an endeavor is not easy to organize, but it would be interesting to pursue. In fact, multimethod (and multisite) research has always been an ultimate goal of the Eurogang Research Program.

Complementing our expanding empirical research, it would be desirable to work on theoretical ideas about gangs and troublesome youth groups. For example, it is important to think about why some youths join gangs while others do not, and to understand better how problematic youth groups are formed and under which circumstances. The research presented in this book suggests that the same risk factors are valid for Dutch youths as for U.S. youths, which would imply that general theories about delinquent behavior could be useful. But we have to keep in mind that gang membership is not exactly the same thing as general delinquency or deviance. Only a portion of all young lawbreakers join groups of likeminded contemporaries, and there are also youths who become delinquent only after they join these groups. Therefore, we also need to elaborate on the reasons or circumstances that attract youths to street gangs and troublesome youth groups and on the processes that cause increased levels of delinquency among those who join a gang.

The need for theory is even more urgent if we want to understand comparative findings about gangs in different countries. As said, the results of this book show that there are similarities but also many differences between gangs, and our theoretical tools to analyze these differences remain very limited. Europe, which consists of a vast number of very culturally and socioeconomically different countries, is especially equipped to make progress on these comparative issues. It would be interesting to discuss and analyze the specific situations of different countries and their possible influence on the prevalence and characteristics of youth groups and gangs in these countries.

A crucial element in these efforts would be to incorporate the impact of immigration and ethnic background on the gang situation. As we said earlier, this theme is especially visible in European gangs. Consequently, this implies that there are many chances for developing new ideas about this issue in Eurogang research.

To conclude, there is an interesting road ahead with many possible directions for future research. There are many empirical and theoretical questions left to answer, and in many of them, the European context offers special opportunities. With the development of several Eurogang instruments that have proven their value throughout this book, we expect an interesting future for research on European street gangs and troublesome youth groups.

REFERENCES

Ball, Richard A., and G. David Curry. 1995. The logic of definition in criminology: Purposes and methods for defining "gangs." *Criminology* 33: 225–45.

Battin, Sara R., Karl G. Hill, and Robert D. Abbott. 1998. The contribution of gang membership beyond delinquent friends. *Criminology* 36: 93–115.

Cloward, Richard A., and Lloyd E. Ohlin. 1960. *Delinquency and opportunity: A theory of delinquent gangs*. New York: Free Press.

Cohen, Albert K. 1955. *Delinquent boys*. New York: Free Press.

Decker, Scott. 2001. The impact of organizational features on gang activities and relationships. In *The Eurogang Paradox: Street gangs and youth groups in the U.S. and Europe*, ed. M. W. Klein, H.-J. Kerner, C. L. Maxson, and E. G. M. Weitekamp. Dordrecht, Netherlands: Kluwer.

Decker, Scott H., and Barrik Van Winkle. 1996. *Life in the gang: Family, friends, and violence*. Cambridge: Cambridge University Press.

Esbensen, F.-A., and David Huizinga. 1993. Gangs, drugs, and delinquency in a survey of urban youth. *Criminology* 31: 565–89.

Esbensen, F.-A., and Dana Peterson Lynskey. 2001. Youth gang members in a school survey. In *The Eurogang Paradox: Street gangs and youth groups in the U.S. and Europe*, ed. M. W. Klein, H.-J. Kerner, C. L. Maxson, and E. G. M. Weitekamp. Dordrecht, Netherlands: Kluwer.

Fleisher, Mark. 1998. *Dead end kids*. Madison: University of Wisconsin Press.

Gordon, Rachel A., Benjamin B. Lahey, Eriko Kawai, Rolf Loeber, Magda Stouthamer-Loeber, and David P. Farrington. 2004. Antisocial behavior and youth gang membership: Selection and socialization. *Criminology* 42: 55–87.

Howell, James C. 1994. Recent gang research: Program and policy implications. *Crime and Delinquency* 40: 495–515.

Klein, Malcolm W., Hans-Jürgen Kerner, Cheryl L. Maxson, and Elmar G. M. Weite-kamp, eds. 2001. *The eurogang paradox: Street gangs and youth groups in the U.S. and Europe.* Dordrecht, Netherlands: Kluwer.

Maxson, Cheryl L., and Malcolm W. Klein. 1995. Investigating gang structures. *Journal of Gang Research* 3: 33–40.

Miller, Jody. 2001. *One of the guys: Girls, gangs, and gender.* New York: Oxford University Press.

Thornberry, Terence P., Marvin D. Krohn, Alan J. Lizotte, and Deborah Chard-Wierschem. 1993. The role of juvenile gangs in facilitating delinquent behavior. *Journal of Research in Crime and Delinquency* 30: 55–87.

Thrasher, Frederic M. 1927. *The gang: A study of 1,313 gangs in Chicago.* Chicago: University of Chicago Press.

Vigil, Diego. 1988. *Barrio gangs.* Austin: University of Texas Press.

———. 2003. *A rainbow of gangs: Street cultures in the mega-city.* Austin: University of Texas Press.

Warr, Mark. 2002. *Companions in crime: The social aspects of criminal conduct.* Cambridge: Cambridge University Press.

Index

Aalborg, Denmark, 270, 274
Africa, 133, 219, 260. *See also* North
  Africa(n)
African American, 148, 196, 223, *232*,
  233. *See also* black
afsos, 45
A-gang, 36–37, 38, *39*, 40, 41, 42, 45–46,
  106, 115–19, 292. *See also* B-gang
age: and hierarchical order, 84; as part of
  gang definition, 148, 153, 174–75; of
  majority, 60, 67; of members, 18, 86,
  87–88, *88*, *135*, 135–36, *154*, 154–57,
  155, *158*, 166, *175*, 237, *241*, 281, 291;
  range, 33, 135, 176, 203, 214n1, 291;
  of sample, 132, *133*, *179*, 231, *232*,
  238, *239*; span, 32, 36; stratification,
  171, *175*; structure of group, 88; and
  substance use, 87–88
Ageeva, L. V., 169
Akers, R. L., 200, 210

Alasia, F., 53
Albania, 56. *See also* Kosovo-Albanian
alcohol, 22, 23, 44, 67, 87–89, 97,
  163–64, 167, 184–86, *185*, 187–88,
  197, 252, 293
Algerian, 53, *161*, *162*
America. *See* United States
American: gangs, 5, 11–12, 78, 86, 142,
  143, 148, 165, 170, 173, 182, 188n2,
  193, 195–98, 211, 213, 288, 289, 290,
  291, 292, 298, 303, 305, 306;
  stereotypes, 15, 28, 148, 165, 289,
  290; studies, 195, 196, 199, 200, 202,
  205, 295, 296, 300, 302, 304, 305
amphetamines, 61
Amsterdam, 13, 15–16, 223, 260, 288,
  290, 295, 296, 297, 301; -West, 11, 12,
  13, 15, 16, 19, 21, 23, 291, 299
Andersen, M., 270
Anderson, E., 42, 43, 78, 105–106

networks of, 149; youth groups in,
148, 163, 174–75, *175*, 183, 292
neo-Nazi, 262, 274; gangs/groups, 43,
271–72, 273, 276, 277, 278, 280;
youths, 272
Netherlands, the, 28, 134, 164, 167, 280,
290, 291, 295, 298, 304, 305; crime in,
24; gangs in, 131, 132, 141;
Moroccans in, 11, 14, 16, 23, 24, 25,
163
Netherlands Institute for the Study of
Crime and Law Enforcement (NSCR)
School Project, 131, 228
network model, 34, 35, 48–49
network structure, 34, 36, 38, 39–40
neutralization, techniques of, 114–115.
See also justification
New English and Welsh Drug Abuse
Monitoring (NEW-ADAM) program,
195, 205
NEW START, 265
New York City, New York, US, 77, 182,
188n2, 222, 226, 272
newspaper, 15–16, 23, 25, 37, 48, 54,
74–75, 115, 147. *See also* media;
radio; television
Niddrie housing estates, 202
Niederhoffer, A., 174
nightclub. *See* discotheque
Nisbett, R., 118
Nordstrand, Norway, 274
normlessness, state of, 24
norms, 23, 24, 45, 78, 107, 111–12; of
gangs, 32, 84, 173, 213; German, 96;
Moroccan, 299; prison, 171, 173
Nørrebro, 270, 272, 278–79
North Africa(n), 16, 24, 56, 75, 300. *See
also* Africa

North America, 193, 195
Norway, 40, 45, 115, 118, 300; drug trade
in, 37; gangs in, 291, 304
Norwegian Expert Group, 266
Norwegian Protestant church, 279
nuisance, 17, 22, 23, 24, 27, 147, 157,
163, 167, 297, 301

observational study technique, 2, 6, 193
Occupati Project, The, 73
Office of the Public Prosecutor of
Tatarstan Republic, 177
Ohlin, L. E., 293
O'Kane, J. M., 112
Old West (Amsterdam), *151*, *152*, 153,
155, *156*, *158*, *160*, *161*, *162*, 163, 164,
166, 167, 297–98, 301
Oleynik, A. N., 170
Olsen, C. B., 272
Oltmer, J., 81
Olweus program, 265
Omaha, Nebraska, US, 227, 228
Omelchenko, E. L., 176
operationalization of the gang concept,
130–31, 135, 136, 174, 231, 245–46
opportunity-structure theory, 3
organization(al): gang, 33, 200, 223, 230,
291, 292, 305; characteristics, 130,
223, 305; structure/framework, 33,
42, 43, 225
organized crime, 51, 84, 170, 173, 259,
272
original gangster, 165
Orlando, Florida, US, 228, 227
Osgood, D. W., 196, 205, 227
Oslo, Norway, 36, 40, 43, 46, 47, 271,
274, 275, 276, 277, 278, 279, 284n11;
gangs in, 36–39, 41–42, 106, 112–13,

Scottish: gangs, 213, 292; youth, 195, 214, 295
Seattle, Washington, US, 198, 202, 211, 224, 225, 234, 289
Seattle Social Development Project, 195, 196, 198, 211
secrecy, 122; code of, 75, 76
self-control, 112–13, 207, 217, 234–35, 250–51; theory, 200–01, 231, 234–35, 236, *237*, 243
self-definition. *See* self-identification
self-esteem, 111, 118, 224
self-fulfilling prophecy, 27
self-identification, 32, 100, 170, 180–84, *183*, 186, 199, 230, 245, 290, 306
self-image, 115, 140, 148
self-nomination. *See* self-identification
sexual: abuse, 67; offenses, 163, 263; relationships, 99; violence, 70, 85
shame/shameful(ness), 60, 62, 63–64, 68, 69, 76, 77, 78, 105, 109, 110, 111, 113–15, 116, 117, 119, 303
Shaskin, A., 170
Shaw, C. R., 166
Sherman, L. W., 266
Shesler, A. V., 169
shopkeepers, 13, 17–18, 19, 21, 27, 43, 147, 149, 296
shoplifting, 21, 22, 231, *241*, 242
Short, J. F. , 129
Sibiryakov, S. L., 169
siblings, 20, 37, 40, 41, 42, 66, 67, 68, 98, 113, 116, 302
Sicily, Italy, 56, 59, 63
signs, 200, 205, 295, 301; hand, 165. *See also* symbols
Sijtsma, J., 11, 12
Silbereisen, R. K., 95

Simmel, G., 35
sister(s). *See* siblings
size, gang, 32, 33, 134, 153, 154–55, *156*, 176, 203, 214n1, *241*, 291
skæv, 270
skinheads, 52, 171, 178, 187, 194
Skirbekk, S., 116
Smith, C., 197, 224, 226
Smith, D., 199, 214n2
Smith, D. S., 214n2
social-learning theory, 200, 207, *237*, 251 253
social: capital, 78–79, 296; class, 42, 52, 87, 99, 173, 174, 200, 203, *204*, 226, 295; control, 11, 16, 44, 157, 227, 253–55, 265, 272–78; control theory, 231, 236, *237*, 243–44; disorganization, 226; integration programs, 54; security, 16, 47, 261, 262; selection, 213; services, 52, 60, 67, 260, 262, 265, 280, 281; services, schools, and police model (SSP), 265; worker(s), 21, 34, 36, 45, 46–47, 48, 52, 54, 60, 65–73, 278, 283n5
Social Hunting Corps, the (*det sociale jægekorps*), 265
Social Services Department of the Juvenile Court, Italy, 72
sociology, 110
Somalian, 157, 275
South America, 260
sovereign manifestation of life, 113
Spain, 14
Spearhead, the (*spydspidsen*), 265
specialization, criminal, 21, 22
Sperber, D., 110
Spergel, I., 2, 267

About the Contributors

Francesca Angelini graduated in law from the University of Genoa, where she is now working on her Ph.D. in psychological sciences and techniques. She is also doing a research doctorate in clinical criminology at the Free University of Lugano (LUDES) in Switzerland. Her research interests are youth gangs and the history of criminological thought.

Paul Bradshaw is a Senior researcher with the Centre for Social Research. He is a graduate of both the universities of Glasgow and Edinburgh with degrees in sociology and criminology. After graduating, he spent almost three years as a research associate with the Edinburgh Study of Youth Transitions and Crime at the University of Edinburgh before moving to his current post. His principal interests, youth gangs apart, are in the areas of youth justice, persistent youth offenders, and the links between substance use and juvenile delinquency.

Yngve Carlsson is a senior researcher at the Norwegian Institute for Urban and Regional Research, which is an interdisciplinary applied social science center in Oslo. During the last ten years, he has also been involved in a number of projects, both as a researcher and consultant, in communities experiencing problems with racist youth groups, groups with immigrant youth, and conflicts between these types of groups. He received his Mag.art in sociology from the University of Oslo. His main research interests are community development, municipal problem solving, and cooperation between nongovernmental organizations and the municipal administration. He has written several research reports and coauthored two books (in Norwegian/Scandinavian) on this topic.

Scott H. Decker is Curator's Professor of Criminology and Criminal Justice and a fellow at the Center for International Studies at the University of Missouri, St. Louis. He received his B.A. in social justice from DePauw University and his M.A. and Ph.D. in criminology from Florida State University. His main research interests are in the areas of gangs, juvenile justice, criminal justice policy, and the offender's perspective. He is a research partner for the Project Safe Neighborhoods Project in the Eastern District of Missouri and the Southern District of Illinois, and he is completing an evaluation of the Juvenile Accountability Incentive Block Grant and SafeFutures programs in St. Louis. His most recent books include *Life in the Gang* (1996), *Confronting Gangs* (1998), *Policing Gangs and Youth Violence* (2002), and *Responding to Gangs* (2002).

Finn-Aage Esbensen is the E. Desmond Lee Professor of Youth Crime and Violence in the Department of Criminology and Criminal Justice at the University of Missouri, St. Louis. He received his B.A. in German and sociology and his M.A. in sociology from Tufts University, and his Ph.D. in sociology from the University of Colorado, Boulder. He has been involved in several longitudinal studies examining the causes and correlates of delinquency and has served as the principal investigator on two longitudinal school-based prevention programs. His publications include a criminology textbook and recent journal articles on gangs and juvenile delinquency.

Mark S. Fleisher is the Dr. Semi J. and Ruth W. Begun Professor in the Mandel School of Applied Social Sciences at Case Western Reserve University, and the director of the Begun Center for Violence Research. He received his Ph.D. in cultural anthropology and anthropological linguistics at Washington State University. His research interests include youth violence, youth gangs, gang intervention, street culture, prisons, and social networks. His publications include articles and book chapters on corrections and on youth gangs, as well as four books: *Warehousing Violence* (1988); two awarding-winning books, *Beggars and Thieves: Lives of Urban Street Criminals* (1995) and *Dead End Kids: Gang Girls and the Boys They Know* (1998); and the coedited volume *Crime and Employment: Issues in Crime Reduction for Corrections* (2003).

Uberto Gatti, MD, is a professor of criminology, and the director of postgraduate courses in clinical criminology at the University of Genoa in Italy. He is also the president of the Italian Society of Criminology (2002–2005). He has organized and conducted numerous research projects for the National Council for Research (CNR), for the Italian Ministry of Justice, and for the National Center for Prevention and Social Defense (Milan). His main research interests are in the areas of gangs, juvenile justice, immigration, violence, and the relationship between social capital and crime.

Hans-Jürgen Kerner is a professor of criminology and director of the Institute of Criminology at the University of Tübingen. He graduated in law (*Rechtsreferendar*) after studying in Munich, Berlin, and Tübingen. He received his second law degree (*Rechtsassessor*) at Stuttgart. He received his doctoral degree (Dr. jur., on the topic of problems of crime statistics) and his further qualification degree (Dr. habil., in the fields of criminology, juvenile law, penal procedure, and corrections) in Tübingen. His areas of interest include juvenile delinquency, group delinquency, gangs and crime, the effects of sanctions and treatment measures, organized crime, crime, and criminal justice statistics. He is one of the coeditors of *The Eurogang Paradox* (2001).

Malcolm W. Klein is emeritus professor of sociology at the University of Southern California, Los Angeles. He received his B.A. in psychology from Reed College and his M.A. and Ph.D. in social psychology from Boston University. His research has dealt with all kind of issues regarding social psychology, delinquency, and crime. His most recent research studies, supported by grants from the federal Centers for Disease Control and the U.S. Department of Health, involve the nature and control of street-gang violence, gang involvement in illegal-drug distribution systems, gang migration, and gang resistance. Selected publications are *The American Street Gang* (1995), *Cross-National Research in Self-reported Crime and Delinquency* (1989), and

Western Systems of Juvenile Justice (1971). He is one of the coeditors of *The Eurogang Paradox* (2001).

Inger-Liese Lien is a senior researcher at the Norwegian Center for Violence and Traumatic Stress Studies. She received her Ph.D. in social anthropology from the University of Oslo on the topic of morality and emotion in Pakistani Punjab. Since 1997, she has researched crime and gangs within the ethnic communities of Oslo. She has written extensively on subjects related to the migration and integration of Pakistani immigrants into the Norwegian welfare state. Among her publications are several books in Norwegian about gangs, violence, and immigration and a chapter on the dynamics of honor in violence.

Gilberto Marengo works as an educator in communities for minors in Genoa (Italy). He graduated in philosophy from the University of Genoa.

Natalia Melchiorre works as a family mediator and educator in communities for minors in Genoa (Italy). She graduated in educational sciences from the University of Genoa.

Kerstin Reich is a research associate at the Institute of Criminology at the University of Tübingen working on research dealing with the processes of integration, social rejection, and deviant and criminal behavior of young male ethnic Germans from Russia. She received her Dr. rer. Soc. from the University of Tübingen. Her main research interests are troublesome youth groups and migration, as well as developmental psychology. Among her publications is a chapter about violence among so-called Russian Germans in the edited book *Criminology at the Millennium* (2000).

Alexander Salagaev is an associate professor in the Department of Public Administration and Sociology at Kazan State Technological University, Kazan, Russia. He received his Ph.D. in sociology from Kazan State University. He has been studying juvenile gangs in the Volga region of Russia for almost twenty years. His research interests include social deviance, youth crime, gangs, and group juvenile delinquency. He is the author of several books in Russian, including *Youth Criminality and Delinquent Communities in American Sociolog-*

ical Theories (1997) and *Drug Abuse in the Tatarstan Republic: Strategies of Social Reaction* (2005).

Marcello Sasso works in the urban-security sector of the municipality of Genoa. He graduated in political science, with a specialization in clinical criminology, from the University of Genoa and trained in forensic sciences at the University of Padua. His research interests are youth deviance and urban deprivation.

Alexander Shashkin is a senior researcher at the Sector for Studies in Social Deviance, Institute of Sociology, Russian Academy of Sciences, Moscow, Russia. He received his Ph.D. in sociology from Kazan State Technological University. His research interests include the social problems of youth, juvenile delinquent gangs, gender and violence in youth cultures, and the victimization of young people. Several of his scientific publications are included in Russian and English peer-reviewed paper collections.

Irina Sherbakova is a research assistant at the Institute of Sociology, Russian Academy of Sciences, Moscow, Russia. She received her M.A. and Ph.D. in sociology from Moscow State University. Her dissertation study and research interests focus on the cultural and political identity of young people.

Elias Touriyanskiy is a senior researcher at the Centre for Analytic Studies and Dvelopment, Kazan, Russia. He received his M.A. and Ph.D. in public administration from Kazan State Technological University. He is currently researching social control of youth crime and delinquency in the Russian context.

Frank van Gemert is an assistant professor at the Free University in Amsterdam. He received his Ph.D. in anthropology from the University of Amsterdam. His research interests include juvenile delinquency, drug dealing, prostitution, and homicide. His publications are mostly based on ethnographic data, often gathered through participant observation.

Frank M. Weerman is a senior researcher at the Netherlands Institute for the Study of Crime and Law Enforcement (NSCR) in Leiden. He graduated in sociology (specializing in criminology) from the University of Groningen and obtained a Ph.D. for his thesis on social bonds and delinquency from the same university. His research interests include juvenile delinquency and criminological theory, and he is involved in a longitudinal study focused on schools, peers, and social network formation (the NSCR School Study). His publications include a book on co-offending and articles on juvenile delinquency, the role of delinquent peers, and criminal groups.

Elmar G. M. Weitekamp is a professor of criminology, victimology and restorative justice in the Department of Criminal Law and Criminology, Faculty of Law, University of Leuven, Belgium. He received an M.A. and Ph.D. in criminology from the University of Pennsylvania, Philadelphia. His research interests are internationally oriented, and current research projects include the study of the processes of integration of former Russians in Germany, a cohort study in Wuhan, People's Republic of China, the emergence of gangs in Europe, the processes of privatization in juvenile welfare and justice, the evaluation of victim-offender mediation programs in Germany, and hate crimes. He is one of the coeditors of *The Eurogang Paradox* (2001).

DATE DUE